IF YOU WANT TO RAISE MONEY FOR A BUSINESS you want to know where to look for investors and how to look good to them.

IF YOU WANT TO INVEST IN A BUSINESS you want to know what to look for and what to look out for.

That's why, whether you're an entrepreneur or an investor, you'll want to keep looking into—

THE *VENTURE* MAGAZINE COMPLETE GUIDE TO VENTURE CAPITAL

CLINTON RICHARDSON is a partner in the corporate department of a major law firm in Atlanta, Georgia. He has represented entrepreneurs and investors in numerous venture financings. He has also assisted entrepreneurs, investors and underwriters in public offerings, private placements, leveraged buyouts, borrowings, licensings, franchisings and other transactions. He is the author of many business law articles, and is a founder and director of the Atlanta Venture Forum, a trade association for risk capital investors.

VENTURE is one of America's leading business magazines, with more than 330,000 subscribers and over 1,000,000 readers. It provides news and feature stories focused on entrepreneurs who create or market innovative products and services, and the professional and informal investors who provide them with capital. *VENTURE*'s chairman, publisher and editor-in-chief is ARTHUR LIPPER III, a well-known investment banker and venture capitalist.

The *Venture* Magazine Complete Guide to Venture Capital

Clinton Richardson

With an Introduction by
Arthur Lipper III

A PLUME BOOK
NEW AMERICAN LIBRARY
NEW YORK AND SCARBOROUGH, ONTARIO

NAL BOOKS ARE AVAILABLE AT QUANTITY DISCOUNTS WHEN USED TO PROMOTE PRODUCTS OR SERVICES. FOR INFORMATION PLEASE WRITE TO PREMIUM MARKETING DIVISION, NEW AMERICAN LIBRARY, 1633 BROADWAY, NEW YORK, NEW YORK 10019.

PUBLISHER'S NOTE

This publication is designed to provide accurate and authoritative information in regard to the subject matter covered. It is sold with the understanding that the publisher is not engaged in rendering legal, accounting, or other professional service. If legal advice or other expert assistance is required, the services of a competent professional person should be sought. *From a declaration of principles jointly adopted by a committee of the American Bar Association and a committee of publishers.*

PLUME TRADEMARK REG. U. S. PAT. OFF. AND FOREIGN COUNTRIES
REG. TRADEMARK—MARCA REGISTRADA
HECHO EN HARRISONBURG, VA., U. S.A.

SIGNET, SIGNET CLASSIC, MENTOR, ONYX, PLUME, MERIDIAN and NAL BOOKS are published *in the United States* by NAL PENGUIN INC., 1633 Broadway, New York, New York, 10019, *in Canada* by The New American Library of Canada Limited, 81 Mack Avenue, Scarborough, Ontario M1L 1M8

Library of Congress Cataloging-in-Publication Data

Richardson, Clinton.
The Venture magazine complete guide to venture capital.

1. Venture capital. I. Venture (New York, N.Y. : 1979)
II. Title. III. Title: Complete guide to venture capital.
HG4751.R52 1987 332'.0415 87-5721
ISBN 0-452-25918-5

First Printing, August, 1987

1 2 3 4 5 6 7 8 9

PRINTED IN THE UNITED STATES OF AMERICA

To my entrepreneurial father
F. William Richardson
(1922–1983)

CONTENTS

ARTICLES FROM *Venture*

FOREWORD

The starting of new businesses is vital to our country, because it is our new businesses that provide most of the new jobs in our country. It is also these younger enterprises that supply the bulk of product innovation and therefore are the basis of progress upon which larger corporations depend (and from which they prosper disproportionately to their willingness to venture and their developmental contribution). This aspect of our American economy means the entrepreneur as well as the entrepreneurial investor—one who provides start-up capital to companies when more conservative financing sources are unavailable—are two of the country's greatest natural resources.

For the entrepreneur to better understand how to treat the entrepreneurial investor in a private company, and for the mutual benefit of both, he must try to understand the probable mind-set of the investor. First, it must be understood that the investment will most likely be made for at least two very different, if not conflicting, reasons. Clearly, one reason is to earn a greater return than can reasonably be expected to be available from more liquid investment opportunities. The second reason is to help the entrepreneur. It is my experience and observation that investors are more likely to be successful in the second objective than the first. This is not, however, the appropriate time or place to inventory all the things that can go wrong in business and frequently result in the business projections on which the investor relied not being achieved.

What Clinton Richardson has done in this book, which provides a great service to both private company investors and entrepreneurs, is to describe all the concepts of venture investing that affect the relationship between the investor and the entrepreneur in terms that make it more likely that the relationship between them will be—and will remain—a constructive one. The entrepreneur should know, better than most others, what the investor expects. With the editorial assistance of Steve Cohen, *Venture*'s manager of special projects, Mr. Richardson has provided the most comprehensive inventory of venture capital concepts I have seen. This should help ensure that the entrepreneur knows what to expect from an investor and knows how to communicate with the investor before and after the deal.

My prescription for a healthy and mutually supportive relationship between investors and entrepreneurs is full, intelligent, and timely information transfer and honest, open communication. Entrepreneurs can and should ask their investors to help the enterprise after funding. But to do so effectively, the entrepreneur must be aware of the questions to ask and the evolution of the investor's perspective. The investor's expectations can go through a metamorphosis from eagerly awaiting the payout of extraordinary profits to fear of embarrassment and loss of capital. The investor should never be permitted to feel that he was used preclosing and discarded thereafter. This book covers every important aspect of the venture capital process and thus provides the entrepreneur with the information he can use to establish and maintain supportive communication with investors.

Most professional venture capitalists are agents, just as portfolio managers of mutual funds are agents. They are rewarded by their superiors if they do well, and so they want to do the best they can. But, as agents, in some cases they fear embarrassment and career-damaging ramifications of poor investments as much, if not more than, loss of capital. (Syndications between venture capital partnerships are, in part, a reflection of this fear.) Thus, to be successful in raising venture capital, the entrepreneur must provide something that is as important as a winning product or company—and that is *comfort*. The job of the capital-seeking entrepreneur really is to identify the capital-investing bodies that are most likely to be comfortable with his project and himself. If the entrepreneur is successful in making the prospective investor comfortable with himself as a person and his projections for the project, then he is halfway to getting the funding. Why only halfway? Because seldom is it the case that the person the entrepreneur is dealing with is the sole decision maker for the investment; others in the organization will have to be persuaded, so they need to be made comfortable as well.

This need for the entrepreneur to provide comfort before, during, and after the investment is made places a premium on information. This book should make the entrepreneur comfortable with the entire venture capital process and in turn allow him to be more successful in providing comfort to those who are in a position to have an impact on the entrepreneur's vision.

Venture magazine is in business to provide "profit education." This means we help entrepreneurs, entrepreneurial business owners, and private company investors alike to make more, or lose less, money. *The Venture Magazine Complete Guide to Venture Capital* fits perfectly within that mission, and we are pleased to bring it to you. In other words, I'm comfortable with it as a constructive contribution in communications, and believe me, that is not faint praise.

ARTHUR LIPPER III

ACKNOWLEDGMENTS

The Venture Magazine Complete Guide to Venture Capital did not happen overnight or without the help of many people. It started, as do many things, with a simple idea. The idea was that entrepreneurs and investors could benefit from a source book on venture capital that was direct, comprehensible, and dealt with how deals are structured as well as how investors are found.

The book's inspiration was my father. His enthusiasm for entrepreneurship and for business help books inspired me to begin this book. He was the quintessential entrepreneur, working long hours making businesses from ideas and loving it. Like most entrepreneurs, he saw life as a challenge to be embraced and enjoyed.

My wife and children also deserve special mention. They sacrificed many family hours and activities while I drafted and redrafted the manuscript. Their enthusiasm and encouragement were as important to completing this book as was my inability to see the folly of expecting a lawyer to write a succinct, "plain English" volume about anything.

The next acknowledgment belongs to Steven M. Cohen, special projects editor at *Venture*. His enthusiasm and expertise helped mold this book into the readable version you have in front of you. Not only was he expert in his editing skills, but his experience, and that of the other editors of *Venture*, added greatly to the content of the book. Most enjoyably, Steve saw the need for this book immediately and threw himself enthusiastically into the project.

Finally, thanks to my partners and associates at Arnall Golden & Gregory and especially to James E. Dorsey, Robert P. Finch, T. Clark Fitzgerald, Cleburne E. Gregory III, and Peggy A. West who patiently reviewed portions of the manuscript and offered helpful comments. Thanks also to Robert G. Schwartz, president of Strategic Business Development Corporation, and John J. Huntz, president of the Atlanta Venture Forum, for their support and advice. Michael D. Easterly, senior vice-president and managing director of the Investment Banking Division of Thomson McKinnon Securities Inc., Thomas R. Barry, president of North Riverside Capital Corporation, and John J. Rathbone, president of Rathbone-United Holding Company also deserve special thanks for their help in refining specific entries in the manuscript, as does Emily A. Kelley for cheerfully completing the manuscript and enduring its many revisions.

—Clinton Richardson

INTRODUCTION

The Venture Magazine Complete Guide to Venture Capital contains 189 entries arranged in alphabetical order. Each entry describes a word or phrase commonly used by investors and entrepreneurs to describe an important venture capital concept. Together, the entries explain what entrepreneurs need to know about venture capital to deal successfully with investors.

The book is comprehensive. It describes the types of investors who invest in new companies, the methods companies use to attract investors, and the ways entrepreneurs evaluate funding proposals. It also describes tactics for negotiating better deals with investors and methods for protecting company secrets and attracting key employees.

The Venture Magazine Complete Guide to Venture Capital is different from other books about venture capital. It is not written by a venture capitalist, who may be biased toward protecting investors, or by an entrepreneur, whose experience may be limited to a few financings. Rather, it is the result of a cooperative effort between an attorney who has represented both investors and entrepreneurs in numerous venture capital financings and the editors of *Venture*, a recognized leader in the field of "profit education."

The Venture Magazine Complete Guide to Venture Capital has a unique format. Its design allows readers to get directly to the information they want. For example, if a reader wants to know how venture capitalists price their investments, he can find out by simply turning to the entry entitled "Pricing." If an investor offers funding but wants preferred stock and registration rights, the reader can quickly turn to the entries for those terms and learn the reasons behind the investor's request and the consequences the request may have to the company. In each case, the reader will also be directed to other entries in the book that treat related subjects.

The book's design also reflects the way most entrepreneurs learn about venture capital. They learn about it by becoming familiar with the language of venture investors while they search for money. In this way they pick up some of the concepts that govern how investors work and structure deals. If they are lucky, they learn enough to protect themselves when they find funding. If they are not, they may pay too dearly for their funding, if they find it at all.

Most entrepreneurs are not lucky when it comes to raising venture capital. They simply have too many things to do and too few resources to do them with to take the time to really learn about venture capital. As a result, many good ideas don't get funded. And even the entrepreneur who obtains funding usually finds himself dealing on uneven terms with an investor whose business it is to know the finer points of venture capital investing.

The Venture Magazine Complete Guide to Venture Capital is designed to help entrepreneurs improve their odds when dealing with investors. It does so by answering the questions most frequently asked by entrepreneurs as they search for investors and, later, negotiate for favorable financing terms. And it does so in a format that allows readers to find the answers they need quickly.

Use the book as a tool during your fund-raising efforts. Don't read it from cover to cover and put it away. Instead, keep it handy and use it like an encyclopedia or reference book. Don't feel that you have to read the book from beginning to end. Start with an entry that interests you and proceed as you like through the others.

Good luck in your search for capital. We hope you find this book helpful.

A Word of Caution

Don't use this book as your only source of information about venture capital. It does not answer every question, and its answers do not apply to every situation. Many of the answers in the book reflect personal judgments about what is "standard" or "fair" in the "usual" situation. Those answers may not always apply to your particular funding.

Try to stay current with changes that affect the venture capital process by reading periodicals and getting good professional advice. Much of what directs venture capital and the structures investors use to fund companies is related to the provisions of the Internal Revenue Code, the securities laws, and the methods accountants use to report company operations. These change regularly.

For example, the 1986 Tax Reform Act phased out preferential long-term capital gains rates, restricted the ability to preserve net operating loss carry-forwards, and reduced the top individual tax rates below top corporate tax rates for the first time in history. These and other tax changes will no doubt affect the popularity of some of the deal structuring devices discussed in this book. (See Appendix A—A Few Words About Tax Reform for a more complete discussion of the effects of recent tax reform on venture capital.) The safe harbor securities laws described in the *Reg D* entry are relatively recent (1982) and subject to constant review and re-evaluation by the Securities and Exchange Commission. The Financial Accounting Standards Board (FASB) can also affect venture capital by changing the way accountants report company operations. A good example of how big an impact these changes can have is described in the *Junior Common Stock* entry on page 112. There, a single FASB change removed junior common stock from a prominent venture financing tool to a device which is now infrequently used.

Also, remember that the venture process differs with each entrepreneur, each idea, and each investor. It is an intense activity —one that can cloud the judgment of even the shrewdest of businessmen. To protect your interests, get independent counsel and learn as much as possible about the process. Read other books about venture capital and talk with entrepreneurs, investors, and others who know the process.

Conventions

I have used masculine pronouns throughout this book. This is not to imply, however, that all investors are men or that only men make good entrepreneurs. This is certainly not the case. The male pronouns are used to make the book easier to read.

Also, the book makes repeated references to product businesses but none to service businesses. Some of the best entrepreneurial opportunities are in service industries, but again, for convenience and ease of reading, I have referred to products whenever I could have referred to products and services. The principles discussed in this book, however, apply to service businesses as well as they do to manufacturing companies.

A

Adventure Capitalists are entrepreneurs who invest money in other entrepreneurs. Like other venture capital investors, they invest to make money. Unlike traditional venture capital funds, however, they invest their own money instead of money others have placed in their care. Usually, the money they invest is money they made by selling a company they started and made grow.

Adventure capitalists fund new enterprises for a combination of reasons. They know that a wise investment can be very profitable. They believe their experiences as entrepreneurs help them to identify attractive deals. Also, venture investing gives them something they cannot get from other investments: the chance to relive the excitement they experienced in getting their own businesses started.

For many adventure capitalists, this last reason is the telling motivation. The exhilaration they experienced when starting their business may be waning. They may operate a public company that is long past its start-up stage or run a division of a large company that acquired their business. Many have retired from daily management activities. For each, there is something about making a new business succeed that draws them into adventure investing.

Like other investors, adventure capitalists expect to receive and study a business plan before they proceed. They usually also require a seat on a company's board of directors and reports from management on the company's progress. Their active participation is important to them. They expect to be consulted by management and to have their advice heeded.

Adventure capitalists do not see as many deals as venture capital firms do. And, while most investigate companies before investing, few do so as thoroughly as a sophisticated venture capital firm would. This, coupled with the fact that they do not have to consult with others before making an investment, often means a faster response on a deal.

The smaller deal flow and the "part time" nature of their investment activity mean that entrepreneurs can sometimes get funding from an adventure capitalist when they could not obtain it from a venture capital firm. This is particularly true in smaller financings. Many venture capitalists, with their high administrative costs and large deal flows, will only invest in deals above, for example, $100,000 or more. Adventure capitalists are not so constrained.

This lack of sophistication in venture investing, however, can cause problems for a company. If the company is delayed in meeting a milestone, the adventure capitalist may feel misled and become difficult to work with—for example, he may refuse to provide follow-on investments he has agreed to make. This may happen even though the company's problems are not severe.

This reluctance to fund subsequent stages can be catastrophic because it forces management to divert its attention to raising money when other aspects of the company's business need managing. And fund-raising can be very difficult with an unwilling investor in a company. His refusal to fund often frightens away other investors. Also, he may have contractual rights that *prevent* others from investing.

Even binding contracts that require an investor to provide follow-on funding may not be enough to prevent disaster. The expense and effort required to enforce those contracts against an unwilling investor may be too great for a company to afford. The result can be an impoverished company forced to begin the search for money anew while dealing with a struggling business and a dissatisfied adventure capitalist.

To protect against this, entrepreneurs should investigate an adventure capitalist's reputation and ability to fund before they accept his money. If he offers to fund the company's needs in stages, management should ascertain how he intends to meet his funding commitments. If he must borrow or liquidate other promising investments to fund the company in later stages, he may become difficult to deal with when the money becomes due

—even if the company meets or surpasses its benchmarks. Also, management should be sure its financing agreements allow the company to secure other funding or buy out an investor who refuses to complete his funding requirements. *See: Angels, Deal Flow, Due Diligence, Ethics, Venture Capitalists.*

Angels are people who provide funding for very young companies to help get them started. The term comes from Broadway, where show backers have traditionally been referred to as "angels." In venture capital, the term refers to an entrepreneur's first investors who put their money in before there is a product or a viable business.

Angels are most often friends, relatives, or business acquaintances who, because of their belief in an entrepreneur's abilities or in the value of his idea, are willing to invest significant sums of money in the entrepreneur long before his business is established. Most invest only a few times during their lifetime and are unsophisticated about investing in small companies. Many invest once, lose their money, and never do it again.

More often than not, an angel's investment is poorly documented and not particularly well thought out. Because they lack familiarity with the types of problems young companies face and the difficulty of getting money out of a young company, angels often invest without obtaining an adequate method for cashing out. Entrepreneurs who value the friendship and commitment of their angels, however, will take pains to discuss how the angel can get his investment out so that both the entrepreneur and the investor share realistic expectations. *See: Adventure Capitalists, Cashing Out (or In), Seed Capital, Venture Capitalists.*

FINDING YOUR ANGEL

Angels do walk the earth—at least in one New Hampshire neighborhood. Stephen Albano found one when he waved to Bob McCray, who was out for a spring walk through their neighborhood. Albano, thinking about starting his own company, wanted to toss around ideas with his tennis buddy. Six months after that front-lawn conversation, McCray grubstaked Albano with $30,000. "I like to get money around," muses McCray. "I like to help."

McCray is an angel, one of a host of private investors who so often put up the first $20,000 to $200,000 to get a business off the ground. "I'd hazard a guess that at least 10,000 businesses get angel money each year," says William Wetzel, the University of New Hampshire business professor who authored the pioneer study in the field. Angels may, in fact, double the amount of money invested by venture capital firms, says Kirk Neiswander, director of entrepreneurial programs at Case Western Reserve University in Cleveland. "Let's say the venture capital community has put a couple of billion dollars into companies in the last few years," he estimates. "Private money at least equals that, if it's not two or three times greater," he speculates, based on his own research in northeastern Ohio.

The traditional networks for finding private money operate through accountants, lawyers, and business acquaintances. William E. Conway, for example, a major owner of Best Sand Corp., a miner and maker of industrial sands in Chardon, Ohio, has invested through friends, consultants, and even through a seminar held by Neiswander at Case Western. His investment in Clamco, a Cleveland industrial packing company, came through his lawyer. Conway put a total of $40,000 into the firm in return for a 5% stake in Clamco and a subordinated debenture, payable over eight years. "The debenture promised current income," he notes, "and it helped the founder get a sizable capital infusion without giving away too big a stake in his company."

Venture capital clubs and some business seminars try to formalize this networking. At the start-up clinics run five times a year by the MIT Enterprise Forum in Cambridge, Mass., and Seattle, Wash., one to three entrepreneurs each session get to present their business plans to a panel chosen to fit their companies. Later, the audience grills them again. "It's a board of directors meeting in public," says Paul E. Johnson, national director of the MIT Enterprise Forum. At the least, the entrepreneur comes away with an improved business plan and some fresh contacts. Or such is the theory.

A few new ventures find their angels the old-fashioned way: by praying for them. Allen Michels began Convergent Technologies Inc. with $16.22 in 1979. William D. Rollnick had been one of Michels's best customers when Michels ran the microcomputer systems division at Intel Corp. Rollnick had also just sold one of his computer rental companies. "I bought cheap and sold it for more than I paid," says Rollnick, "just like my daddy always told me."

"I asked him if he'd like to spend it," says Michels. "To my astonishment he said yes." In 40 minutes they cut the deal for a $2 million investment from Rollnick and two of his friends; Michels gave up 64% of Convergent.

—From an article by William Bryant Logan
in the March 1986 issue of *Venture*

Antidilution Provisions are agreements that insure a company's early investors that later investors will not obtain more equity per dollar than they did. Many investors insist on some sort of antidilution protection as a condition to their investing, particularly if they are the company's first major investor. Antidilution protections can appear as provisions of a financing agreement, in the terms of a warrant or option, in a shareholders' agreement, or in any other agreement between investors and a company.

One common antidilution provision provides that the percentage of a company owned by an investor will not be reduced until some future event occurs. The event could be the passage of time, the funding of an additional $500,000, or some other occurrence. Any stock issued by the company before the future event occurs would entitle the protected investor to receive more shares, either for free or for some agreed-upon price.

Another typical antidilution provision requires a company to give an investor "free" stock if it sells any to a later investor at a lower price. For example, an investor who purchased one hundred thousand shares for $2 a share would be given more shares at no charge if the company later sold stock to another investor for $1 per share. If the earlier investor receives enough free shares to reduce his average cost per share to the price paid by the new investor (one hundred thousand shares in this example), his antidilution rights are called a "ratchet."

Another antidilution provision allows an investor to purchase additional stock if later share prices are lower or if more than a certain number of shares is sold. Preemptive rights, and provisions that entitle investors to obtain a percentage of outstanding stock in the future instead of a fixed number of shares, are also antidilutive.

There are many other variations of antidilution provisions. Any agreement that tends to insure an investor his relative price advantage or percentage ownership is an antidilution provision.

All antidilution provisions dilute the interests of the shareholders who are not protected by them. This usually includes management. As a result, these provisions should be considered carefully before they are completed. To protect management, all antidilution provisions should stipulate an expiration date after which they no longer apply. *Under no circumstances* should antidilution provisions be allowed to survive a public offering of the company's stock or the sale or merger of the company, since they can hamper management's ability to raise funds in the public market or close a favorable merger or sale of the company. Also, whenever possible, investor antidilution rights should exclude the issuance by management of a number of shares for use in an incentive stock option plan or other employee incentive plan to help the company attract and keep personnel. *See: Dilution (Percentage), Equity Penalties, Financing Agreements, First Refusal Rights, Incentive Stock Options (ISOs), Preemptive Rights, Ratchets.*

Audits are methodical reviews by a disinterested third party of a company's accounts or, more generally, its financial situation. They are usually conducted by independent accounting firms.

Few venture capitalists expect a new company to have audited financial statements. Audits are expensive, and most investors believe a new company's money is better spent in other areas. This is not to say, however, that investors do not expect a company's books to be complete and accurate. They do. Venture capitalists usually examine a company's books and records thoroughly before they invest. Most of them also interview the company's accounting firm and check "behind" the company's books by calling suppliers and creditors.

When a company anticipates conducting a public offering, it is wise for it to have audits conducted or, at least, to have independent certified public accountants verify the company's yearly inventories. This is because companies are usually required to disclose three years of audited financial statements in their initial public offerings. Sometimes only two years are required for limited offerings and, of course, a company that has been in existence for less than three years can only provide financial statements for the period it has been in business.

The audits required by initial public offerings can sometimes be performed just beforehand, but this can delay the offering and result in unexpected changes to the offering documents when the independent accountants apply their procedures to and make the company's statements comply with the requirements of the Securities and Exchange Commission.

When a company plans to go public, the safer, and often cheaper, course of action is to engage an independent accountant to conduct audits on a regular basis. Most accountants will take this opportunity to get to know the company better and suggest reporting mechanisms for management that can help management run the company more efficiently. Also, they will prepare statements that comply with the requirements of the Securities and Exchange Commission so that the company can move more quickly to consummate a public offering. At the same time, they can help management organize other records, such as reports on industry segments, to fit the disclosure requirements of initial public offerings. While audits may seem expensive for a young company, having an independent CPA oversee and review the company's books may reduce the time and cost of having the audit done at a later date. *See: CPAs (Certified Public Accountants), Due Diligence, Going Public, IPOs (Initial Public Offerings), Reports and Records.*

B

Bargain Stock is corporate equity that is acquired at low cost, usually in the early history of a company. Sometimes called "cheap stock" or "founders' stock," bargain stock almost always includes the original stock issued to the company's founders. *See: Cheap Stock, Sweat Equity.*

BDCs (Business Development Corporations) are companies organized under special state statutes for the purpose of providing funds to small businesses in their state. Most can provide debt and equity financing.

Business development corporations borrow the money they provide to businesses. Because of this, they tend to finance companies in ways that will generate enough cash to permit them to make their interest and principal payments to their lenders. In other words, BDCs usually lend money instead of making pure equity investments. This way the portfolio companies support the BDC's obligation to repay its lenders by making regular payments of principal and interest to the BDC. Even when a BDC acquires stock in a company it is usually through a warrant or option to purchase stock that accompanies a loan.

Because BDCs need to make regular debt service payments to their lenders, they (unlike other venture investors) tend to be more interested in a company's ability to support and repay debt in the short term than in the company's prospects for rapid and, eventually, profitable growth. As a result, BDCs are often precluded from investing in early stage companies or companies that lack the ability to show a profit in the near term. *See: CDCs (Community Development Corporations), Debt Service, SBICs (Small Business Investment Companies), Venture Capitalists.*

Beads and Trinkets is negotiating jargon. It refers to a small concession made by one party in return for a Manhattan-sized concession from the other party.

While conceding "beads and trinkets" in the heat of negotiations may seem insignificant at the time, the negotiator should ask himself why the other party seeks the concession. What seems like a trinket to one party may be quite valuable to the other.

Benchmarks are performance goals against which a company's success is measured. Often, they are used by investors to help determine whether a company will receive additional funding or whether management will receive "extra" stock. Sometimes management will agree to issue more stock to its investors if the company does not meet its benchmarks, thus compensating the investor for the delay of his return.

Whatever purpose benchmarks serve in a financing arrangement, failure to arrive at one on schedule almost always punishes management in some way. As a result, management should be certain to negotiate conservative benchmarks. Whenever possible, they should be at a level that management, as well as the investor, thinks is achievable realistically. In that way, failure to achieve the benchmark is a true signal that something is wrong with the company or its plans.

For example, a benchmark could be stated as "the sale of at least five hundred product units during a month before one year after the funding date." Failure to sell five hundred product units in a month before that time would indicate to management and investors that the forecast was too optimistic, or that the sales department is not fully staffed.

As a rule, the financial projections contained in business plans make poor benchmarks because they are usually prepared long before unforeseen, but inevitable, problems arise. Since many business plans are prepared to attract investors, they tend to be optimistic in their assumptions. In fact, venture capitalists discount most company projections when they price a deal and do not really expect a company to meet all of the goals stated in their financial projections.

Nonetheless, business plan projections almost always provide a starting place for determining benchmarks. Some investors even try to impose benchmarks that are the same as the performance estimates contained in a company's projections. When this happens and the projections are not met, the unfortunate entrepreneur may find his investor released from future funding obligations, entitled to more company shares, or vested with greater control over company operations. To avoid these consequences, attempts to use business plan projections as benchmarks should be resisted vigorously, and conservative benchmarks should be used whenever possible. *See: Projections, Stage Financing.*

Blue Sky Laws refer to state statutes that prescribe the methods by which stocks and other securities may be sold or offered for sale within the state. As with the federal securities laws, these statutes generally prohibit companies and shareholders from selling (or offering to sell) stocks and securities unless the sale is registered with the state's securities commission or fits into one of the exemptions from registration provided by the state's blue sky statute.

In most states, these exemptions parallel or complement many of the federal exemptions. Nevertheless, management should be certain, before offering or selling any securities, that the offer and sale will comply with the securities laws of the state in which the company is incorporated and in the states of residence (or formation) of each person to whom the shares are offered or sold. Failure to comply with the requirements of applicable blue sky laws can subject a company and its principals to substantial liability. *See: Legend Stock, Private Placements, Reg D, Restricted Securities, Safe Harbors, SEC (Securities and Exchange Commission), 33 Act.*

Board of Directors is the governing body of a corporation. It is elected by the shareholders and, in turn, elects the company's officers. The board of directors sets the direction of the company and oversees the activities of its officers. Investors often require a seat on a company's board of directors as a condition to funding.

The configuration of boards of directors varies greatly from company to company. Boards can consist of as few as one individual or as many persons as the company's bylaws permit the shareholders to elect. Many entrepreneurial companies have small boards consisting of the company's president or the president and one or two key shareholders. Others contain many members and include general business advisers, industry experts, and others with skills to lend to the company. The size and configuration of a company's board of directors usually depend in large part upon the founder's method of operation and the concessions he has had to make to raise money.

Company boards also differ in the degree to which they become involved in the management of a company. Some consult regularly with the company's officers and set specific directions for its operations. Others may meet regularly but function more as sounding boards for management, becoming involved only at the request of management and then usually only to approve a specific action. As with the size and configuration of a board, the method of its operation usually reflects the personalities of the individuals involved. If the company has a strong chief executive officer and profitable operations, the board may be relatively quiet. However, if the board members have a significant stake in the company's success, they may stay very active with the company even when it is doing well.

What's the best configuration for a growing company's board of directors? The answer depends in part upon the talents of the company's officers and its success in attracting outside board members who can add significantly to the company's prospects. As a general rule, however, smaller boards are easier to work with than larger ones and also tend to be more actively involved in the companies they represent. Too many members on a board can create inertia, making it difficult to call a board meeting and difficult for the board to arrive at a consensus when it does meet. As a result, entrepreneurs should try to keep their boards small, inviting only those people to serve as directors who have the interest and the time needed to devote to the company's affairs. Members should only be added to the board if they are required to complete a substantial funding or important contract, or if they can add significantly to the strength of the company. *See: Board Committees, Bylaws, Charter, Control, Cumulative Voting, Stock Committee.*

Board Committees are groups of board members assigned a particular corporate responsibility to oversee. In many companies, significant responsibilities, such as review and approval of executive compensation, are delegated to committees. Usually, the authority to establish committees is contained in the company's bylaws and the laws of the state in which the company is incorporated. Committees make boards and companies more efficient by giving management smaller groups of directors to work with on particular types of questions and by reducing the number of full-member board meetings that must be called.

The most common committees are audit committees, compensation committees, and stock committees. Audit committees set up and oversee auditing and accounting standards for a company and, thereby, establish the mechanisms by which management and the board monitor the operations of the company. The compensation and stock committees are often combined into one committee that establishes salaries for company employees and recommends the issuance of stock options to selected employees. Often the power of this committee includes the actual issuance of options within guidelines established by the board of directors.

The establishment of a stock committee without ensuring that the committee is properly constituted can create problems for a growing company. If the committee consists of one person, as is often the case, the company can find itself in trouble when it prepares to go public or merge with another company. This is because granting one person the power to issue options makes it too easy to inadvertently grant them to employees and others. And often, these unintended stock grants do not come to light until deals have been made to go public or merge.

In start-up situations, companies often find themselves short of cash and in desperate need to hire or keep qualified people. Without adequate cash, it can be difficult for a company to retain the people it needs. To bridge this gap, many companies issue shares or options to new and senior employees. The stock and options attract key people by giving them the opportunity to participate in the company's growth.

The problem with one-person stock committees, however, is that without the reservation of stock-granting power to a larger group, even casual conversations with employees about the desire to issue more stock or options can turn into legally binding obligations on the company. Given the intense pressures new companies and their employees face, the discussing of "more stock and more options" becomes commonplace. If the company president participates in these discussions and is the only person on the stock committee, they can easily lead to binding agreements to issue company stock.

To reduce this risk of inadvertent stock issuances, companies should avoid single-member stock committees so that stock and option grants require the approval of two or more persons before they become binding on the company. It is also helpful for the company's bylaws or board minutes to require options to be in writing and signed by all committee members. If company employees know this is the case, casual conversations are less likely to lead to misunderstandings or unintended stock grants. *See: Going Public, Incentive Stock Options (ISOs), Stock Committee, Vesting Schedules.*

Boilerplate is a lawyer's word referring to "standard" terms and conditions that accompany most financing agreements but that are rarely negotiated when the major terms of a deal are discussed.

They are not, however, as standard or innocuous as many people believe (or would lead others to believe). In fact, boilerplate often consumes more than half of a financing agreement and contains important promises and representations made by the company and its principals. These promises and representations should be reviewed carefully, even if the tendency is to skip them because "they are just boilerplate."

One standard provision that appears in many financing agreements is the "accurate business plan" boilerplate. Its purpose is to assure the investor that management has not made any misrepresentations in its business plan. It usually appears in the representations and warranty section of the financing agreement and is a warranty of both the company and its management. It is a legitimate provision that can have very different effects depending on whose boilerplate is used. The provision sometimes appears as a representation that:

> the business plan of the company is accurate and complete and does not contain any untrue statement or omit to state any fact which is necessary in order to make the statements contained therein not misleading.

A literal reading of this particular boilerplate can make company management a guarantor of the facts, assumptions, and conclusions contained in the business plan. If any of those facts, assumptions, and conclusions turn out to be untrue, the company and its management could wind up liable to the investor for damages. Since much of a business plan is based on "soft" information instead of hard, verifiable facts, and since much of it is judgmental and prospective, business plans almost always turn out to be untrue in some respect. And when they do, management making this representation may find itself surprised by the liability it has assumed.

A better boilerplate provision about the company's business plan, at least from management's perspective, would read:

> to their knowledge, the business plan does not contain any untrue statement of a material fact or omit to state a material fact that is necessary in order to make the statements contained therein not misleading in light of the circumstances under which they are made. To their knowledge, the financial projections contained in the business plan were prepared accurately based on the assumptions described therein.

This boilerplate gives the investor what he needs with less exposure to the company and its key officers. It talks in terms of knowledge instead of absolute facts and acknowledges that the projections are merely estimates based on disclosed assumptions. These differences can be important as a company's progress varies from its projected plans. For management, they can mean the difference between business as usual and defending a lawsuit brought by an investor.

Every lawyer has his own version of "standard" boilerplate. Some are more exacting than others. All boilerplate terms are negotiable, notwithstanding any claims by their authors that they are "standard" or "required as is" in all of their deals. Management should never sign an agreement until it is comfortable with the boilerplate it contains. *See: Financing Agreements, Investment Reps, Reps and Warranties, We Always Do It This Way, We Never Exercise Our Rights under This Section.*

Bricks and Mortar refers to a company's physical plant and facilities. Sometimes the phrase is used in a more general sense to refer to a company's tangible assets, such as land, buildings, machinery, and equipment. *See: Collateral, Nonrecourse Debt, Personal Guarantees.*

Bridge Loans are short-term financing agreements that fund a company's operations until it can arrange a more comprehensive longer-term financing. The need for a bridge loan arises when a company runs out of cash before it can obtain more capital investment through long-term debt or equity.

Bridge loans are risky. Whether a company's original investors or an outside lender provides the bridge loan, its short-term nature creates pressure to complete the long-term financing package quickly. A default under a bridge loan usually gives the lender substantial rights to company assets or personal assets of management. Management's eagerness to liquidate a bridge loan can cause it to make concessions it would not otherwise agree to when negotiating the longer-term financing that will "take out" the bridge loan.

When accepting bridge financing, management should be careful to understand the consequences if the long-term financing does not come through on time. It helps to negotiate as long a term as possible on a bridge loan and to borrow enough money to carry the company through the loan's term. If the bridge financing is with an outside investor, management should explore the possibility of converting it into longer-term financing if the need arises, even if the terms of extending the bridge are less favorable than the anticipated terms of the "take-out" financing. Bridge loans should be documented and follow a clear written understanding of the main business terms of the company's total financing package. *See: Financing Agreements, Investment Memorandums, Letters of Intent, Leverage, Negotiation.*

Brokers are people who help companies find investors and who help investors find attractive companies in which to invest.

Many entrepreneurs hire brokers to reduce the amount of time they will have to spend raising money. For a busy entrepreneur, time spent raising money almost always takes time away from running the business.

In some cases, brokers can provide companies with valuable introductions that lead to financing. Some brokers can explain alternative sources of funding and help structure viable financing packages. Few, however, can remove management entirely from the funding process. Usually, the most they can do is provide management with introductions and a chance to "pitch" the company. Potential investors invariably want to deal directly with management. As a result, almost all entrepreneurs stay involved in the fund-raising process and continue to look for investors on their own, even when they hire a broker.

Entrepreneurs should be careful when dealing with a broker. They should make their agreements explicit and put them in writing. The agreements should define what the broker's responsibilities are, when he is entitled to a commission (usually when an investor he introduced to the company funds the company's needs), how much the commission will be, and when his assignment expires. To the extent possible, entrepreneurs should investigate the broker's reputation by talking with his present and former clients. They should also have explicit written understandings about the limits on the broker's authority to commit the company to any funding proposal.

Most brokers will work on a contingency fee or other prearranged fee basis. Whatever arrangements are made, however, management should understand that the broker's fee will usually come out of management's pocket. Many investors will insist that money they put into a company go toward developing the company's product, not toward paying a broker.

Other professionals who can provide introductions and advice about finding money and structuring financing packages include bankers, accountants, lawyers, and—probably the best source—other entrepreneurs. *See: Consultants, CPAs (Certified Public Accountants), Due Diligence, Lawyers, Packages.*

Business Plan is a concise document, usually written by a firm's management, that describes the company, its products, business methods, financial condition, and needs for funding. Business plans are written to clarify company purposes, to plan new directions, and to raise capital from private investors. Often, business plans are written exclusively to raise money.

A good business plan should be concise, complete, and easy to understand. It should introduce a company and its objectives in a positive way that makes investors want to learn more about it. The content of the plan should show that management knows what it is doing. It should show that the company's management has the experience and talent necessary to make the company succeed.

Most venture capitalists insist on seeing a company's business plan before they will even consider an investment. The document's content gives them a basis upon which to evaluate their interest in a company. If the plan interests them, they will investigate further. If it does not, they will reject the company as a potential investment. Most venture capitalists see too many deals to spend time with companies whose business plans fail to excite them.

It is important, therefore, to prepare a business plan carefully and to make it easy to understand. Enough time should be allocated to writing and rewriting the plan so that it articulates clearly the excitement the company presents. At the same time, it must be well organized and carefully researched. Its discussion of the company and its industry should be based on thorough analysis. It should be thoughtful and realistic. After reviewing it, an investor should be excited about the company's prospects and impressed with management's preparation and candor.

There are many sources of help available to entrepreneurs who are preparing their first business plan. For example, accounting firms will often help prepare financial statements and projections. Some have professionals who will review a business plan and provide constructive criticism. Consultants can be used to conduct market research, assist at arriving at reasonable assumptions for projections, or help prepare parts of the plan. Other businessmen and lawyers will sometimes critique a business plan if asked.

For more information about business plans, entrepreneurs can check with accountants, lawyers, and other entrepreneurs. Many accounting firms have detailed brochures on how to prepare business plans that are available for the asking. Local bookstores and libraries also have valuable materials on business plans. A number of these sources are listed in the *Venture Books* entry.
See: Brokers, Business Plan Format, Deal Flow, Downside, Due Diligence, Summary, Three Questions.

THE WRITING OF THE BUSINESS PLAN

Everyone talks about the importance of the business plan and they are correct to do so. Whether the plan is read by potential investors, friendly business associates or magazine editors, it represents the first opportunity to make an impression upon them. It will take lots of fancy footwork to overcome the bad impression created by a poor one. Therefore, when all else is said and done, your plan's key points should be abundantly clear. [Clear means easy to read, easy to understand, complete and accurate.] The authors of books on plan writing are right to point out all the details one should remember when constructing a plan, and the importance of a well-rehearsed presentation to accompany it.

However, no book on plan writing I have read focuses on one particular benefit that I have learned from several attempts at writing business plans: to write a clear plan, one must have a clear idea of the business being planned. And it is the process of writing that clarifies.

Long ago, in journalism school, I learned two axioms that kept occurring to me as I wrote the business plan for this publication: If You Can't Explain It, You Don't Understand It; and, Muddy Writing Reflects Muddy Thinking. As I wrote the plan for VCCM *[Venture's Capital Club Monthly]*, all the areas that I thought I could "fudge" became so apparent that the plan started to become farcical. At that point, I knew the only way the plan would get funded was for me to stop writing a plan and start planning a business. After that realization, the hard work really began, as I had no choice but to answer the questions I knew others would ask. Sure enough, readers asked questions about exactly what I knew was weak in the plan.

The process of writing itself benefits the business plan. Through the process of writing, the business becomes defined, its weaknesses become evident and demand to be rectified. As the plan goes through subsequent drafts, the thoughts of new readers can be included, so that the plan becomes consensual. By following the outline in many of the "How To" books, the gaps in your own thinking should emerge. As you gather the information necessary to respond to the suggested outline, your plan becomes denser, containing more of the stuff it is supposed to contain and you become more confident of the quality of the business.

Sales and financial projections were the hardest part for me. I resisted making projections in which I had no confidence, and yet I knew the plan was supposed to contain them. I resolved this dilemma three ways: (1) I did a lot of research to find "comparable" information; (2) I assigned probabilities to the projections, thus indicating those numbers where I had great certainty and those where I did not; and (3) I went ahead and made projections based on nothing but "feel," and when the time came, I admitted to "making the numbers up" where no data were available. I asked the readers to suggest sources of data I may have overlooked. When no one could suggest a source, they were more understanding of the necessity to "plug" a number in.

My point is to appreciate the writing of the plan as a necessary thinking exercise, totally separate from the necessary fund-raising exercise. While you may hate to write at all, in this case it is unavoidable and you had better plunge in. Show your work around, don't be defensive about the criticism, re-draft to include good suggestions and anticipate the questions others will ask and include the answers.

One last thing: once you've written it, start updating it.

—From an editorial by Steven M. Cohen,
editor and publisher, *Venture's Capital Club Monthly*,
which appeared in the July 1985 issue of *VCCM*

Business Plan Format should allow a business plan to reflect management's thorough understanding of its company, its products, and its market. The organization of the plan should be apparent so that investors can find what they want quickly, without getting distracted by material that does not interest them. There are many formats an entrepreneur can follow when writing a business plan. The key is for the resulting plan to present the company's opportunity well. Here is an example of one acceptable format and the type of information investors expect each section in the plan to provide:

Sample Business Plan Format

Table of Contents

1. Summary
2. Company and industry
3. Products (or services)
4. The market
5. Marketing
6. Management
7. Development plan
8. Overall schedule
9. Risks
10. Financial statements and projections
11. Appendix

Contents

1. *Summary.* Investors expect a short summary of the important aspects of the company's proposal at the beginning of the plan. The summary should highlight the company's opportunity in a way that leaves no doubt in the reader's mind what the company has and what it needs to succeed. If the summary is confusing or poorly presented, the venture capitalist will probably read no further.

The summary should contain brief statements about:

- the company's name, address, and telephone number
- who the investor should contact and how that person can be reached
- the company's product and what distinguishes it from others in the market
- a description of the company and its management team
- why the company's market is attractive
- a summary of the company's financial projections
- how much money the company needs and when it will need it
- how the company will use the money
- how the investor will get his money back

It pays to write the summary first and to revise it several times. Have friends and business associates review this portion of the plan, and ask them: Did it hold their interest? Did they understand what the company is making and why its product is unique? Did they remember how much outside capital management needs and how management intends to use it? Revise the summary if any of these points are missing or unclear.

2. *Company and industry.* This is the background section of the business plan. It should contain a concise history of the company, when it was formed, how management decided on its product, and what operations have been conducted. A brief description of the product and who its customers will be should also appear here.

This section should give management's analysis of the company's industry and the opportunity it provides to the company and its product. The company's competition in the market should be described. What are competitors doing and how will the company's strategy be different and better? If there are economic, technological, or social trends that management believes will affect the company and its market, they should be mentioned here.

It is important for this section to be well researched. Venture investors will conduct a thorough review of the industry and of management's analysis of it. If the company's analysis appears shallow or unsophisticated, they will not invest.

Most investors will have their own view of the company's industry. They will not, however, know the industry from management's point of view or why management thinks the industry holds an opportunity for their company. If this section does not express the company's opportunity clearly, management should not be surprised if no one invests.

3. *Products (or services).* This section should contain a detailed description of the company's product. The description should emphasize what distinguishes its product from others in the marketplace. Diagrams and pictures can be used if they will help investors understand the product and what makes it distinctive.

The plan should be candid about the product's shortcomings as well as its strengths. Is it ready for market? Can it be easily copied? Will competitors bring out the next generation of the company's product soon? A venture capitalist will not expect the product to be perfect. If management pretends that it is, it will only make him suspicious. In being candid, however, it is also important to describe the product enthusiastically.

This section should describe whatever protection the product has from competition. If patented, the nature and importance of the patent should be explained. This may involve explaining why a particular patent claim is important to the distinctive features of the product, or why it would be difficult, costly, or time-consuming to engineer around the patent claim. If the protection of the product depends upon trade secrets or copyright protection, that should be explained.

Finally, if management knows what the company's next product will be, it should be mentioned here. Few products dominate a market for long. Venture capitalists realize this and like to know that management has given some thought to what comes next.

4. *The market.* This is an important and difficult part of the business plan. Here management must describe in detail why

the market for the company's product is such that the company can expect to achieve its sales goals despite the existing competition. It is here that management must explain and justify its choice of marketing strategy.

In describing the market, management should identify the major buyers for the company's product. Are they more interested in price, quality, or features? How does the company's product meet these interests? The results of any research management has conducted with customers should be described. Are customers interested in the product at the company's price? If so, how concrete is their interest? If not, why not, and how does their lack of interest affect the company's plans?

Give the magnitude of the market the company is going after in whatever measurements are appropriate—units, revenues, etc. Who are the players? How much will the market expand, and how much of the market must the company capture to succeed? Describe in detail the factors that are moving the market and the direction in which it is going. Is the company's product positioned to take advantage of the trends?

Avoid overestimating the size and growth rate of the market. Base the company's estimates of market size and projections of market growth on discussions with potential customers, distributors, and competitors. Also, review the available market surveys, but do so critically. Markets change quickly, and the most respected market survey is often considered outdated by insiders.

Finally, evaluate the competition realistically. Evaluate competitors' products and their histories in the marketplace. Consider the market share and reputation for aggressiveness of each of the company's main competitors. Explain why potential customers buy from the company's competitors and why some of them will switch to a new supplier.

5. *Marketing.* This section should contain an analysis of the company's marketing strategy and projections of the unit sales management believes the company can achieve.

The company's marketing strategy should be explained in detail. The company's sales techniques and pricing policies should be described in relation to the distribution channels it will employ. How did management arrive at its pricing? How does that method compare with the pricing practices of the company's competitors?

What part will advertising play in the company's marketing? What type of advertising will be employed, and who will direct the effort? How will the company sell and distribute its product? Will it use a direct sales force, independent agents or distributors? Discuss why management chose the sales and distribution channel it selected. Explain how management will organize the company's sales effort and how that effort will compare with that of its competitors.

6. *Management.* This section should contain résumés of the important members of the company's management team and describe what function each person will perform. The résumés should emphasize relevant experience, training, and education. Business accomplishments that illustrate the ability of management to make the company successful should be highlighted.

If the company's management team has weaknesses, as all do, discuss them candidly and describe what plans management has for overcoming these weaknesses. Also, describe *briefly* the accounting, legal, advertising, banking, and other professional relationships the company has established.

7. *Development plan.* This is the section in which management discusses how it will go about achieving the company's objectives. What is the current status of the company's product? If it requires development work, who will do it? Will the company use an outside design house for some of the work? If company employees will do the work, are they all on board, or does management still have to locate key personnel?

The development plan should describe the company's requirements for space, facilities, equipment, and personnel. Will the company begin manufacturing immediately or contract out manufacturing at first? If the company will do some assembly work or testing, explain why and how. Describe who the company's suppliers will be and how management will control quality, production, and inventory.

8. *Overall schedule.* This schedule should show when management plans to accomplish each of the milestones that are critical to the company's success. A well-considered and realistic schedule demonstrates management's ability to plan the company's growth. It also displays management's ability to identify the critical tasks to be achieved by the company and how they interrelate.

This section should contain a flowchart analysis that shows

the timing of the company's product development and operational activities and when the company plans to meet the important thresholds in its marketing plans. Some of the events management might cover include:

- when the company was incorporated
- when the management team will be completed
- when the company's product prototype will be finished
- when the company will complete product testing
- when the company will begin producing products for sale
- when products will be offered for sale
- when the company will begin receiving orders
- when the company will make its first deliveries
- when the company will begin receiving payments for products shipped

The schedule might also show:

- when the company will need money and in what amounts
- when trade shows or exhibitions are scheduled
- when and what additional people will need to be hired
- when the company will need to add new facilities or significant amounts of equipment.

Be realistic in the schedule. Follow it with a narrative discussion of those events that are most likely to be delayed and how those delays could affect the company's overall schedule. Also, explain what management can do to make up for any schedule slippages that occur.

9. *Risks*. Every venture capitalist knows that new businesses are risky. They may not, however, understand which risks are most dangerous to the company or how management intends to neutralize them. This section enables management to discuss those risks and how it plans to overcome them. By doing this thoroughly, management increases its credibility with investors and demonstrates its foresight. Some risks that might be discussed include:

- risks that relate to the industry
- risks associated with not obtaining financing on schedule
- risks of not meeting the development schedule or the product cost estimates

- risks that competitors may develop new, more competitive products
- risks that key personnel cannot be located or retained

Every major risk of which management is aware should be addressed. *Nothing is gained by omitting important items from the list of risk factors.*

10. *Financial statements and projections.* This section should contain historical financial statements of the company's operations and projections of future operations. The projections should be for a period of three to five years. They should include profit-and-loss forecasts, cash flow projections, and pro forma balance sheets broken out on a monthly basis.

Narrative explanations should accompany the financial projections, highlighting important facts and assumptions contained in the projections as well as conclusions management wants the investor to draw.

11. *Appendix.* The appendix should supplement the business plan and support management's conclusions. Use the appendix to attach full résumés of key management members when those résumés elaborate on relevant experiences. Copies of key contracts or commitments from suppliers and customers that demonstrate the viability of the company's product or concept can be included. If there are any surveys or studies that emphasize the company's good prospects or explain a key concept, photocopies of relevant portions of those surveys can help an investor understand the company better. *See: Brokers, Business Plan, Downside, Due Diligence, Exits, Five Factors, Market Research, Packages, Projections, Summary, Three Questions.*

Buy-Sell Agreements are contracts that entitle one shareholder to force others either to buy his stock or to sell him theirs. These contracts often appear as provisions in a financing or shareholders' agreement.

Many investors insist on buy-sell agreements with the managements of companies they fund. They view these agreements as a way to help them withdraw from a company that does not live up to their expectations. With a buy-sell, investors know they can either get their money out or get management's shares. With management's shares, they can usually replace management or have enough shares to sell control of the company to others.

Buy-sell agreements usually work like this: Two or more shareholders agree that if the company fails to meet certain goals, either may buy all of the other's stock in the company. By the terms of the agreement, whichever shareholder exercises this option must first offer to sell his stock to the other shareholder. The purchase price per share is usually the same for both shareholders (although sometimes the price is slightly lower for management). In this way, either shareholder can force the other out of the company but only by risking being bought out himself.

In practice, buy-sell agreements often work to remove management. This is because they are usually exercised only when the company is not living up to expectations. In these circumstances, it can be hard for management to raise enough money to buy out the investor. Even when management succeeds in raising the money, it often does so only by selling more stock to a new investor than it purchases from the old one. This reduces management's percentage in the company.

When management cannot raise the money it loses its stock and its control of the company. If management has given personal guarantees to secure company borrowings, management not only loses its interest in the company but also remains bound on its guarantees. Because many new company borrowings require guarantees, management should be sure that any buy-sell agreement it signs requires the investor to get management released from any personal guarantees it has made for the company. Otherwise, management may remain liable on its guarantees while the company's ability to repay its loans is determined by how well others (that is, new management) manage the company.

Whenever a buy-sell is required by an investor, management should try to structure the agreement in ways that reduce the investor's ability to exercise the buy-sell and increase the chance that the investor, and not management, will be the party that sells. The best way to keep a buy-sell silent is to make its exercise contingent on the company failing to meet goals that are easily attainable. As long as these goals are met, the investor has no right to force a buy-sell on management. Making the purchase price lower for management can discourage an investor's exercise by forcing him to give management a bargain or pay a premium himself. The lower price makes it easier for management to buy out the investor and stay in control. Giving management the right to use promissory notes for part of the purchase price helps too, by making it easier for management to pay for the investor's shares. So does giving management a long time in which to respond to the investor's offer. It is much easier to raise $500,000 in 120 days than in 30 days. Finally, buy-sells should expire if they are not exercised within a fixed period of time. The shorter the period the better. *See: Co-Sale Agreements, Exits, First Refusal Rights, Liquidity Agreements, Puts, Shareholders' Agreements, Unlocking Provisions.*

BUY-SELL AGREEMENTS

If your company has more than one stockholder, what happens to shares you don't control when one of your partners dies? It's a problem faced by many closely held businesses. Because there is no public market to price the shares, it is often difficult to liquidate those interests in the event of the death, retirement, or termination of a principal.

One solution is to draw up a buy-sell agreement that establishes a fair price for the eventual sale and purchase of the company's stock. For the survivors of the deceased shareholder, there is the assurance of easy liquidation and help in estate-tax planning. Because there is a stipulated worth of the stock, the Internal Revenue Service is unlikely to dispute the reported value of the company. A buy-sell agreement can also provide a business with an uninterrupted transfer of ownership. It may also prevent stock from falling into the hands of outsiders.

Often the biggest obstacle in a buy-sell agreement is a mutually agreeable way of determining the value of the company.

The most common methods include:

- book value, or the cost of a company's fixed assets, less depreciation, plus cash
- book value adjusted for the fair market value of real estate, which may be undervalued on the balance sheet
- appraisal price, the breakup value of all fixed assets plus goodwill
- formula, representing some multiple of a company's sales or earnings
- fixed price, some mutually agreeable figure for the sale of the company

You might consider the economic outlook for your industry, the profit potential of your company, and the earnings or sales multiples that are commonly used in your business. It is generally a good idea to reassess the valuation on a regular basis every two or three years.

There are two basic ways to set up buy-sell agreements. One is a stock redemption that provides for the corporation to purchase shares from the estate following the death of a shareholder. (The deal can also trigger a repurchase in the event of retirement or termination.) The second way is a cross-purchase in which each equity holder buys the stock of the other shareholders upon their deaths.

The most common way to fund a buy-sell agreement is with life insurance. Proceeds from the policy can then serve as funds to purchase the shares of the deceased. In the case of a stock redemption, the corporation is apt to own the policy on the life of the shareholder, serve as beneficiary of the proceeds, and pay the premium. Conversely, in a cross-purchase agreement, individual stockholders take out policies on each other's lives and often pay for the premiums themselves.

—From an article by James Edmunds Wilson
in the January 1986 issue of *Venture*

Bylaws are the operating rules of a corporation. They are adopted by the company's board of directors and govern such things as the election of directors, the size of the board of directors, and the election and function of each of the company's officers. Bylaws can normally be amended by the company's directors and are more easily changed than the company's charter, which can only be amended with shareholder approval. *See: Charter, Directors' Indemnities.*

C

Calls are a company's contractual rights to require a shareholder to surrender shares of company stock in return for payment of an agreed-upon sum of money. Calls are usually contingent upon the happening of some future event, such as the passage of time or the accomplishment of some goal by the company.

Management might exercise a call and redeem an investor's stock if another investor was willing to pay a higher price for shares than the call price. Even without a ready investor, management might call an investor's stock if it believed the market value of the company's stock had risen to more than the call price. In each case, redeeming stock at a call price that is below market value can increase the value of the remaining shareholders' stock.

The cost to the company is the cash required to pay the investor for his shares. In deciding to exercise a call, management must weigh the potential benefit of redeeming shares at below-market prices against the company's need for the cash used to exercise the call and its ability to replace that cash when needed.

Calls are usually optional but can, by express agreement, be made mandatory. A mandatory call, however, is nothing more than a contract to redeem stock. As with a put (which entitles a shareholder to force a company to redeem shares), an obligation to exercise a call should be conditioned on the company's ability to meet the corporate law requirements of the company's state of incorporation. These laws often restrict the types of funds a company can legally use to redeem shares. *See: Cash Flow, Exits, Puts.*

Cash Flow is the money coming into (actually received) and going out of (actually disbursed) a business. The three main sources of cash coming into a company are product sales, stock sales, and borrowing. Operating expenses (for example, payroll), capital expenditures (for example, equipment purchases), and debt service on borrowed money (interest and principal payments) account for most of the cash going out.

Having enough money coming into a company to meet its obligations to pay money out is critical to a company's success. Venture capitalists are very interested in whether a company will have sufficient cash flow and very sophisticated in analyzing a company's need for cash. Most investors will study a company's monthly cash flow projections carefully before making an investment decision.

Inadequate cash flow can cause acute problems for any business. A shortage of cash can create a series of crises that divert management from the crucial business of running the company to the business of searching for "new" money. Cash flow problems quickly become visible to suppliers and competitors and can be used by them to suggest to customers that the company is unstable and, therefore, unreliable. The damage such suggestions can cause, even if unfounded, is considerable.

For a company anticipating rapid growth, the problems can be compounded. Fast growth, even with growing profits, can put extreme pressures on a company's available cash. Growing sales are usually accompanied by demands for cash that grow faster than the growth in cash receipts. This is due, in part, to the fact that more sales create more receivables *before* they create more cash receipts. At the same time, demands for payment from suppliers grow, and other new expenditures must be made to support the growth. Many of these expenditures cannot be delayed. The mistiming of the receipt of funds and their disbursement can become so severe that profitable expansions must be postponed. Because of this possibility, companies should thoroughly analyze and review their anticipated cash flow needs on a regular basis, even when they are not searching for "new" capital. *See: Debentures, Debt Service, Equity, Leverage.*

PINCHING THOSE PENNIES

"Conservation of cash in good times is a practice you learn only after you've been burned a few times," advises Arthur D. Perrone, president of Geneva Business Services, a Costa Mesa, Calif., firm specializing in venture financing and merger and acquisitions. Stanley Rich, president of Venture Resources, a Grantham, N.H., consultancy, thinks startups should follow and react to leading indicators, including the frequency of customer inquiry, the rate of converting client interest into purchase orders, the pattern of prices for competing products, and the history of your own costs. "Anything that's important has to be tracked," says Rich. "If you track it, you'll at least have a warning."

Following is a sample of tactics to reduce costs:

Leasing. Such deals offer tax benefits—instead of equity—to investors for funding capital equipment. Leasebacks can reduce upfront expenses and interest rates for the entrepreneur.

Moonlighting. Stephen S. Smith, CEO of Reference Technology Inc., a Boulder, Colo., laser optical and software maker, slashed costs by persuading several employees to reduce their hours for him by 50% and to fill their time by consulting outside.

Customer financing. Thomas E. Stone's Tesdata Corp., McLean, Va., needed hardware for a new generation of its computer network performance measuring equipment. So his engineers took some computers that were destined for customers and used them, instead, to program improvements for later models.

Subcontractor financing. Stephen M. Hicks, president of United Software Security Inc., Vienna, Va., saved $75,000 last year by getting his manufacturing subcontractor to buy and hold components used for USS's computer security devices. It bills USS only when Hicks orders assembled products.

Many specialists counsel letting your investors, creditors, and suppliers learn of problems early on. "Call them before they call you," urges Henry Barratt, an ex-banker and current chief financial officer for ACS Systems Inc., a Herndon, Va., software maker. "If they're good, they'll try to help you. If they're not, you'll be in the same position you would've if you hadn't talked to them. Eventually, they'll find out anyway."

—From an article by Edmund L. Andrews
in the January 1986 issue of *Venture*

Cashing Out (or In) refers to a shareholder selling his shares of company stock for cash, and thus realizing his return (or his loss). It is a term near and dear to the hearts of investors when it refers to a profitable sale of shares. Cashing out at a loss is even preferable in many cases to holding stock in a declining company, particularly when the stock is "illiquid" because of restrictions on its resale. Cashing out can be accomplished in a variety of ways, including going public, exercising a put, or transferring shares to a new investor. *See: Buy-Sell Agreements, Calls, Convertible Securities, Co-Sale Agreements, Demand Rights, Exits, Going Public, Liquidity Agreements, Piggyback Rights, Puts, Registration Rights.*

CDCs (Community Development Corporations) are governmental or quasi-governmental agencies that lend and invest in companies that locate in their communities. They are often affiliated with a local municipality or economic development agency.

CDCs review investments and conduct due diligence as other investors do. But because of their interest in community development, they often consider factors that do not interest traditional venture capitalists, such as the employment opportunities and tax revenues the proposed business will generate for the community. Businesses that meet a community need can often secure funding from a CDC when other investors might not be interested. And the funding they secure is sometimes at lower rates and for longer terms than other sources will provide. This is because of the special investment criteria CDCs have relating to job and tax generation, which enable them to justify lower returns on investment and longer-term loans. *See: BDCs (Business Development Corporations), Corporate Venture Capital, Due Diligence, ROI (Return on Investment), Venture Capitalists.*

Charter is the document that enfranchises a corporation. It is sometimes called "articles of incorporation" and is usually filed with the secretary of state in the state in which the company incorporates. The charter spells out what activities the corporation may undertake, the number and type of shares of capital stock it is authorized to issue, and the names of the company's founding members. As a general rule, the charter can only be amended by a vote of the shareholders. Often a vote of two-thirds of the shares is required. An example of a simple charter is provided below. *See: Bylaws.*

ARTICLES OF INCORPORATION OF IMAGINARY NEWCO INC.

The undersigned, being a natural person of the age of at least 18 years and acting as sole incorporator to organize a corporation (the "Corporation") under the provisions of the Georgia Business Corporation Code, does hereby adopt and sign the following Articles of Incorporation:

I.
NAME

The name of the Corporation is: Imaginary Newco Inc.

II.
AUTHORITY

The Corporation is organized pursuant to the provisions of the Georgia Business Corporation Code.

III.
DURATION

The period of duration of the Corporation is perpetual.

IV.
PURPOSE

The nature of the business and the purpose to be conducted and promoted are as follows:

> To buy, sell and generally deal in products which are imaginary; and
>
> To engage in any lawful act or activity for which corporations may be incorporated under the Georgia Business Corporation Code, and to exercise all the rights, privileges, immunities, and authority granted to or exercised by business corporations under the laws of the State of Georgia now in effect or that will become effective during the existence of this Corporation.

V.
CAPITALIZATION

The aggregate number of shares of stock which the Corporation shall have authority to issue is Ten Thousand (10,000), all of the par value of $.01 each. All such shares are of one class and are designated as Common Stock.

VI.
MINIMUM CONSIDERATION

The Corporation will not commence business until consideration of at least Five Hundred Dollars ($500.00) has been received by the Corporation for the issuance of shares.

VII.
DENIAL OF PREEMPTIVE RIGHTS

No holder of any shares of any class of the Corporation shall be entitled as a right to subscribe for, purchase, or otherwise acquire (a) any shares of any class of the Corporation which the corporation proposes to issue, (b) any rights or options which the Corporation proposes to grant for the purchase of any shares of any class of the Corporation, or (c) any bonds, securities or obligations of the Corporation which the Corporation proposes to issue or grant which are convertible into or exchangeable for, or which carry any right to subscribe for, purchase, or otherwise acquire any shares of any class of the Corporation.

VIII.
CAPITAL SURPLUS

The Corporation may make distributions to its shareholders out of its capital surplus and purchase its own shares out of its unreserved and unrestricted capital surplus upon such terms and conditions as the Board of Directors shall deem appropriate.

IX.
REGISTERED AGENT AND OFFICE

The address of the initial registered office of the Corporation is: 55 Park Place, Suite 400, Atlanta, Georgia 30335, and the name of the initial registered agent at such address is: Clinton Richardson.

X.
DIRECTORS

The number of directors constituting the initial Board of Directors of Imaginary Newco Inc. shall be one (1), and the name and address of such director is as follows:

Ann McArthur	Imagination Lane Atlanta, Georgia 30335

XI.
INCORPORATOR

The name and address of the incorporator is as follows:

William Francis	55 Park Place Suite 400 Atlanta, Georgia 30335

IN WITNESS WHEREOF, the undersigned executes these Articles of Incorporation this 1st day of January, 1987.

____
William Francis
Incorporator

Cheap Stock is a securities term referring to corporate shares that are priced below the price of an anticipated public offering. A number of states impose restrictions on stock issued to company promoters when the company conducts a public offering. These states generally consider cheap stock to be that issued to company promoters within three years for less than the public offering price. If the state securities commission finds the founders' stock to be cheap stock, it may impose escrow requirements on the founders' stock as a condition to the company conducting its offering in that state. While these escrow requirements can be waived in certain circumstances, the net effect is often to reduce the number of states in which a company conducts its offering and to deprive the residents of states that are excluded of the opportunity to consider investing in a new company's public offering. *See: Bargain Stock, Blue Sky Laws, Going Public.*

Closing is when all of the agreements between investor and entrepreneur are completed and the signing of documents occurs. Immediately thereafter, the investor begins funding the company. The agreements signed at a venture capital financing are usually referred to as financing agreements. Those agreements govern the ongoing relationship between the investor and the entrepreneur.

Closings are usually a time of excitement and high expectations. In most instances, closings follow a long process of negotiation, document preparation and revision, and personal stress. A sense of euphoria accompanies most closings, and often the entrepreneur rushes out after the closing to make long-delayed expenditures for the company. These expenditures, if planned, can help the company grow and lead it to its next round of success. If made impetuously, however, they can lead to wasted expectations and the realization that the expensive fund-raising process must begin again before it should have. *See: Financing Agreements.*

HOW TO CARE FOR AN ENTREPRENEURIAL INVESTOR—AFTER YOU CASH HIS CHECK

Intelligent information transfer and timely communication are my prescriptions for a continuing happy (or at least satisfactory), healthy and nondestructive investor/entrepreneur relationship. What I mean is very simple. The entrepreneur should prepare the investor for realism, frequently spelled the same as disappointment. Remember, the investor will take the entrepreneur's "best case" projections and think of them as the "most likely" case, or even "worst case" projections. The investor likes to think that the entrepreneur has been overly conservative in the projections he has given the investor. The entrepreneur recognizing this must constantly assert realism by discussing fully the problem areas and the areas wherein expectations are likely to be frustrated.

Specifically, the entrepreneur should establish a regularly scheduled series of communication elements with the investor(s). These communication elements should be both written and personal. I am a strong believer that monthly newsletters with charts should be sent to investors. The charts should be the reflections of a living business plan. The charts display previously achieved results, current period results, and projected results as well as new or amended projections.

The entrepreneur should meet with the investor at least quarterly, and probably monthly, for the purpose of keeping the investor within the family and delaying, for as long as possible, the development of the "we v. they" syndrome. Once the we/they thinking has developed and the camps become established, the problems begin. The entrepreneur should do everything possible to have the investor play a role which keeps him feeling that he is on the entrepreneur's team and is in fact making a contribution. If the problems of the company in achieving objectives are fully and fairly understood by the investor and he feels that he is on the team, he will possibly be available for additional funding and certainly not be resentful of the need for it.

The text book "what if" list of things which can go wrong, kept updated, is another good idea. Certainly, the management has such a listing, formally maintained or not. Why then should the investor not also have this list of possible horrors? After all, he is an owner of the company and at, or before, the closing should have been told it was for better or for worse. Should he not have the pleasure of relief when one of the horrors fails to materialize?

Entrepreneurs can ask their investors to help: Help to gain information, help to gain customers, help with public relations and, on occasion, help with personnel matters. The entrepreneur should recognize that in most cases the investor had to have been competent in some areas of activity which are, or can be, useful to the entrepreneur's company to have made the money which he has invested. A knowledge of the investor's strengths should be in the entrepreneur's asset file.

—From an article by Arthur Lipper III,
chairman of *Venture*, author of
Investing in Private Companies and
"Venture Capitalist," which appeared
in the June 1985 issue of
Venture's Capital Club Monthly

Collateral is any asset pledged as security for a loan. If a collateralized loan is not repaid as agreed, the creditor can call upon the collateral to secure repayment. By reducing the lender's risk, collateral makes it easier for a company to borrow and to borrow at a favorable rate. In contrast to bank loans, which are often collateralized, most venture capital investments are made with little or no collateral.

Available collateral should not be ignored. When borrowing from traditional lenders, it can decrease the risk and thereby increase the principal amount lent to the company. It can also reduce the interest rate charged for the loan. By making borrowed funds available to a company, collateral can delay the need for expensive venture capital and the dilution of management's stock ownership that occurs when an equity investment is made. Also, collateral can be used to secure portions of a venture capital investment, which is structured as debt, and thereby make the capital easier to attract. *See: Dilution (Percentage), Equity, Factoring, Inventory Financing, Nonrecourse Debt.*

Commitment is what venture capitalists look for in an entrepreneur. They want to invest only in companies whose management is 100 percent committed to the company's success. They want management's full-time attention.

Starting a new business is an exhausting and all-consuming endeavor. Entrepreneurs often work more than twelve hours a day, day after day, seeing to all the details that make a company succeed. Weekend work is common. In the process, family relationships can suffer. Investors understand this. They want to know that the entrepreneur and his family understand as well and are prepared to make the sacrifices required.

Investors also expect entrepreneurs to take their companies as far as they can with their own resources. Investors do not like entrepreneurs who hedge their financial bet on the company. If they invest their money, they want to know that the entrepreneur has invested his money too. Entrepreneurs who retain a safety net of cash outside the company make some investors nervous and, thereby, reduce the likelihood they will receive funding. *See: Entrepreneur, Ethics, Zeal.*

Commitment Letters are documents issued by lenders to companies after they have decided to make a loan but before they are ready to complete the formal loan documents. Commitment letters are usually short and describe only the essential terms of the pending loan.

Most commitment letters obligate the lender to make the described loan only if the company meets all of the conditions identified in the letter. Once the conditions are met, the commitment is further documented with more complete (lengthy) loan, security, and guarantee agreements that contain many terms and conditions not specified in the commitment letter.

Commitment letters serve a useful purpose. By setting out the general terms of the loan, they solidify each party's commitment to move forward with the deal. They also insure that the parties have, in fact, come to terms with one another on the major points of the deal.

Commitment letters should not be treated lightly. They should be reviewed as carefully as the final, formal loan documents they precede. Even though many of their provisions may not be legally binding (at least until all the conditions are met), some may be enforceable against the company in any event. Also, these letters set the tone for how negotiations of the formal loan agreements will proceed. Both parties will expect the deal to be completed in the manner set out in the letter. As a result, it can be very difficult to negotiate and close a loan that includes terms significantly different from those contained in an earlier commitment letter. *See: Bridge Loans, Investment Memorandums, Letter Agreements, Letters of Intent.*

Common Stock is what most people think of when they think of owning part of a company. It is the security most frequently issued by companies and represents an ownership interest in a company. In most cases, common stock carries the right to vote for directors and to vote on other matters affecting the company. It also entitles holders to receive notice of shareholder meetings and to attend them. Rights to review corporate records or receive financial reports also customarily accompany common stock ownership.

Certificates are usually issued to holders of common stock (and other company securities) to evidence their existence. Figure 1 is an example of a common stock certificate.

Common stock can pay cash dividends based on company earnings but only after preferred stockholders receive their dividends. Dividends are usually paid at the discretion of the company's board of directors but are the exception, not the rule, with most growing, privately held companies. Holders of common stock participate last in company liquidations. Company creditors, debenture holders, and preferred stockholders get paid in that order, before holders of common stock.

Common stock can be issued in one or more classes. One frequent company structure authorizes the issuance of two classes of common stock, which differ only in the number of directors each class is entitled to elect. This arrangement can be used to insure an investor a seat on a company's board of directors while, at the same time, insuring that control of the board will remain with management. For example, Class A stock might be issued to management and give its holders the right to elect three directors. Class B stock, which entitles its holders to elect only one director, is then issued to the investor. Even if the investor

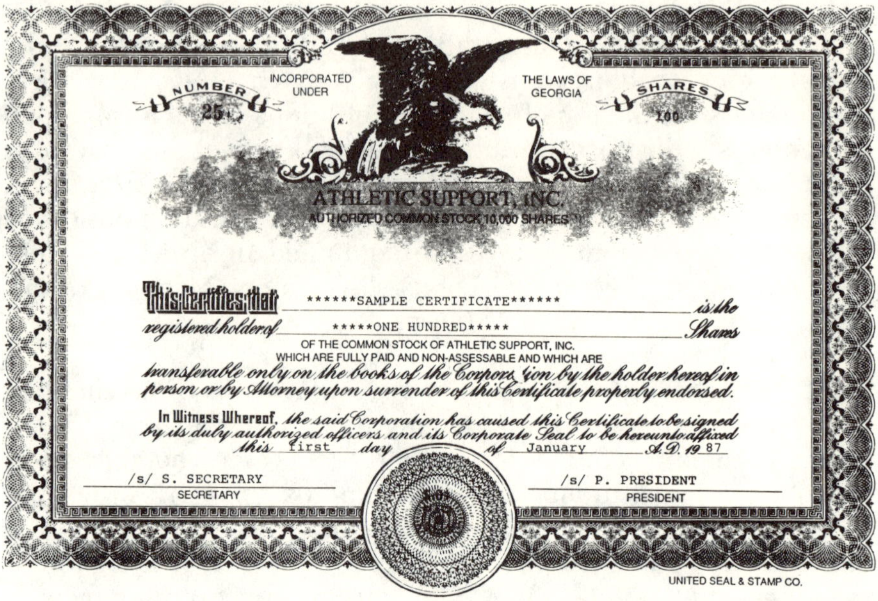

NUMBER 25

INCORPORATED UNDER THE LAWS OF GEORGIA

SHARES 100

ATHLETIC SUPPORT, INC.

AUTHORIZED COMMON STOCK 10,000 SHARES

This Certifies that ******SAMPLE CERTIFICATE****** is the registered holder of *****ONE HUNDRED***** Shares

OF THE COMMON STOCK OF ATHLETIC SUPPORT, INC.
WHICH ARE FULLY PAID AND NON-ASSESSABLE AND WHICH ARE
transferable only on the books of the Corporation by the holder hereof in person or by Attorney upon surrender of this Certificate properly endorsed.

In Witness Whereof, the said Corporation has caused this Certificate to be signed by its duly authorized officers and its Corporate Seal to be hereunto affixed this first day of January A.D. 1987

/s/ S. SECRETARY
SECRETARY

/s/ P. PRESIDENT
PRESIDENT

UNITED SEAL & STAMP CO.

Figure 1 A common stock certificate

holds twice as many shares of stock as do the Class A shareholders, he can still elect only one director. In this way, even if management holds less than half of the company's stock it can still control the company and its board of directors. *See: Board of Directors, Control, Cumulative Voting, Debentures, Equity, Junior Common Stock, Options, Preferred Stock, S Corporations.*

Compensation and Bonus Plans are company policies that provide money or other benefits to company officers and selected employees in excess of their salaries.

Most companies seeking venture capital cannot afford fancy compensation and bonus plans, particularly those that require them to use cash. At the same time, however, growing companies need incentives to attract and keep valuable employees. In many instances, they need their key employees more than their established competitors need theirs. This is because the smaller size of the entrepreneurial company makes each employee more important. Unfortunately, though, the entrepreneurial status of the company also means less job security and, usually, lower salaries.

To offset these hiring disadvantages, most start-up companies use their stock and its relatively low market value. They do so by offering important employees the opportunity to acquire equity in the company. The attraction for the employee is the chance to purchase large quantities of stock at today's low prices in anticipation of the company growing and the stock increasing in value.

Young companies take advantage of their cheap stock by fashioning compensation and bonus plans around the right to acquire shares of company stock. The most widely used plans are ones that allow key employees to purchase company stock or acquire options to purchase it in the future.

Often, the grants of stock or options are conditioned in ways that encourage the employee to remain with the company after the stock is purchased. For instance, shares of stock purchased pursuant to a plan may not "vest" immediately. Instead, they may vest over a period of years. During that period the company may have an option or obligation to repurchase the unvested shares from the employee at cost if he leaves the company for any reason. The company may even have rights to repurchase a departing employee's vested shares for some predetermined price. All of these conditions are designed to reward the employee who stays with an increasing interest in the company's equity and to penalize those who leave.

With stock option grants, the company may make them exercisable at today's low prices but contingent upon some future event. The employee's right to purchase shares may be restricted until he has been with the company for a year or until the company attains certain sales goals. Once the conditions are met, the employee can purchase the stock until the option's expiration date. If the conditions are not met, the option dies and the employee gets no stock.

Other plans commonly used include issuing "phantom stock" and granting options to purchase special classes of stock. Grants of stock bonuses to employees from a pool of shares set aside for that purpose are used also. The variety of plans available to attract important employees is limited only by the imaginations of management and its advisers. A good adviser can help management select an incentive plan (or plans) that reward employees in ways that secure their attention, enthusiasm, and tenure with the firm. *See: Golden Handcuffs, Incentive Stock Options (ISOs), Junior Common Stock, Phantom Stock Plans, Stock Committee, Vesting Schedules.*

Confidentiality Agreements are contracts used to protect trade secrets and know-how from being misused or misappropriated by those who have access to them. When they are used, they can help companies prevent competitors from learning valuable secrets. For many start-up and technology-based companies, the secrets these agreements help protect are among the most valuable properties they have. Often, those secrets constitute the essential difference between them and their competitors. Having written contracts that obligate employees to maintain the secrecy of a company's techniques, processes, or know-how can mean the difference between maintaining a competitive advantage or giving it away to competitors.

In some cases, confidentiality agreements can even cover "negative know how." That is, they can prohibit the transfer of information about mistakes the company made in perfecting its technology or project, information many would not normally think of as secret or important. Restricting "negative know how," however, can help insure that a company's competitors will have the opportunity to make the same time-consuming mistakes the company made, and thereby delay the introduction of competitive products.

State laws generally permit companies to prevent others from using their secrets only as long as they treat the secrets as confidential and take reasonable precautions to prevent them from being disclosed to others. Depending upon the nature of the secrets, these necessary precautions might include restricting access to confidential data or setting aside a safe or room for storage of secret documents.

In most cases, written confidentiality agreements should also be required from everyone who has access to company secrets. The importance of these agreements and of complying with the company's other secrecy procedures should be impressed upon new employees and consultants. Departing employees should be reminded of their secrecy agreements. No one should be given access to a company secret before he signs a confidentiality agreement.

No venture capitalist wants to invest in a company that has

not taken steps to protect its valuable secrets. Most will carefully review a company's arrangements to protect its secrets. And most will expect management and other company employees to be bound by written confidentiality agreements. Many will engage local counsel to be sure the agreements are enforceable. Because of this and the fact that the state laws that govern the enforceability of these agreements vary widely and are quite specific in their requirements, care should be taken when drafting a confidentiality agreement. To be sure of its enforceability, it should be prepared or reviewed by experienced legal counsel. *See: Employment Contracts, Patents, Software Protection, Think Capital, Trade Secrets.*

Consultants are professionals who perform specific services on behalf of company management for a fee. Many start-ups hire consultants to obtain specific expertise and to delay the expense of hiring additional full-time employees. Consultants do not earn fringe benefits, as employees do, and thus can be less expensive in the short run. They can also be hired by task and thereby be used when a full-time employee would not be economical.

One common use of consultants is to assist in the preparation of a business plan. Another is to assist in conducting market research or to advise in developing a company's product, manufacturing process, or marketing strategy. Sometimes, companies hire persons to consult whom they are interested in hiring full-time in the future. This allows the company to get services it needs and evaluate a person for staff employment at the same time. (As with company employees, consultants should always be required to sign confidentiality agreements when they are given access to company secrets.) Consultants' services can be paid for in a variety of ways.

Consultants who are hired to help raise money should be used carefully. Regardless of their claims, do not expect them to replace management entirely in the fund-raising process. Even with the best consultant or broker, investors will want to meet and measure management's knowledge of its business plan and its ability to make the company succeed. They can only do this if management participates actively in the preparation of the business plan and in discussions with investors. *See: Brokers, Consulting Agreements.*

Consulting Agreements generally refer to contracts with consultants. They can be written or oral and cover a variety of concerns. Whenever practical, these agreements should be in writing and set out the scope of the consultant's obligations to the company and his fee arrangement. If the consultant's duties give him access to company secrets, the agreement should contain secrecy provisions. If they require him to interact with company customers or suppliers, the limitations on his authority should be carefully delineated.

Some investors require companies to enter into consulting agreements with them as a condition to funding. These contracts usually require the company to pay a monthly or quarterly fee to the investor for advice management would probably obtain anyway by virtue of its relationship with the investor. The real purpose of most of these consulting agreements is to increase the investor's return and give him access to management. Investors who require consulting agreements often tie the consulting fee to their cost of monitoring the company. Some investors believe consulting agreements improve their communication with management. They argue that managements feel fewer reservations about asking for investor advice when they are paying for it.

Most investor-consultants give companies little value for their consulting dollar. At the same time, the fee required to be paid for their "consulting services" increases the company's cost of capital and decreases its available cash. Whenever possible, these consulting agreements and their fees should be avoided. When avoiding them is not possible, the consulting fee should be reviewed carefully and included in the company's calculation of its true cost of capital. *See: Cash Flow, Consultants, Financing Agreements, Management Agreements, Pricing.*

Control is the ability to direct the actions of a company. It includes the power to determine company strategy and to select the people who will carry out that strategy. In a corporation, control consists of the ability to elect or persuade a majority of the board of directors. Control can be assured through ownership of enough shares of stock to elect more than half of the company's directors. In most cases, this means owning more than 50 percent of the company's common stock.

Raising capital affects management's control in several ways.

When enough stock to elect a majority of a company's board of directors is sold, management continues to direct the company only as long as the investor consents. Even when less stock is sold, contractual provisions required by an investor as a condition to funding can also change control by reducing management's unrestricted freedom to run the company. These provisions usually entitle the investor to participate in certain management decisions and to receive detailed and regular financial reports. Some contractual rights affect control by giving investors the right to manage the company if performance standards are not achieved.

As a rule, venture capitalists are more interested in obtaining a high rate of return on their investment than in obtaining control of a company. Most want control only to the extent that they believe is necessary to protect their investment. Few are interested in running the day-to-day affairs of a company.

Even when an investor acquires the ability to elect a majority of a company's board, there are ways management can retain operating control. A shareholders' agreement requiring the investor to vote his stock for a slate of directors that is controlled by management is one example. Management contracts are another. These can be used to insure management of at least minimum representation on the company's board of directors or of the right to direct the company's activities as long as it does so within agreed-upon parameters. Classes of common stock can also be created to insure that control stays with management. By issuing a second class of common stock to the investors that only has the right to elect a minority of the company's directors, management can retain majority control of the company's board of directors even when it sells a majority of the company's outstanding capital. A combination of these devices can be used to keep control in management's hands.

Most investors insist on some influence over a company's affairs as a condition to funding and require a seat on the company's board of directors. Few will want to control the board, however, unless they lack confidence in management's abilities. Most will expect to receive regular financial reports from company management.

Investors will say that they are not interested in control. They will say that as long as management runs the company successfully they will not interfere. Nonetheless, management's definition of success may differ significantly from that of its investors. And investors may develop independent reasons for moving a company in a direction that does not interest management. The only way for management to assure its control is through ownership of enough stock to elect a majority of the company's board of directors or through a binding written agreement with the investors. *See: Board of Directors, Common Stock, Cumulative Voting, Management Agreements, Shareholders' Agreements, Voting Agreements, Voting Trusts.*

WHY IT PAYS TO KEEP THEM

Although incorporating a business requires a board of directors, nobody requires you to have a single outside director. An entrepreneur can fill up a board, required to sport a minimum of three directors in most states, with aunts, uncles, [and] brothers . . . as some entrepreneurs have done. Although that may guarantee that no one ever asks an embarrassing question, it also deprives an entrepreneur of the business advice and financial credibility outside directors can bring to a growing company.

Ideally, outside directors offer experience and perspective that can rescue entrepreneurs preoccupied with day-to-day issues and routine fire fighting. Many bring particular expertise—in marketing, finance, or product development—that the entrepreneur may not have in abundance. Adds Charles Hartman, general partner at CW Group Inc., a New York venture capital firm: "You really need a board set up to say unkind things to you, to tell you when you're not doing a good job."

Directors are also crucial to the fundraising process. Banks, underwriters, and institutional investors all want companies to have one or two independent directors, preferably well-known business figures who have themselves managed major ventures successfully, before they fork over their cash. "It certainly is a significant factor in our judgment of the readiness of a company to go public," says Alan Herzig, managing director of corporation finance at the San Francisco offices of investment bank L. F. Rothschild, Unterberg, Towbin Inc. For companies that aren't "perfect," says Herzig, the absence of good, outside directors can be a critical swing factor that could lead to rejecting a company for an underwriting. "It's a factor," agrees Richard Spillane, portfolio manager for Nautilus Fund, a Boston-based mutual fund managed by Eaton Vance Corp. that specializes in emerging growth companies. "It's not an absolute block, but it's definitely a factor in the equation. . . . I look at the board of directors, and if I see some good people I get a warm, glowing feeling." If not? Well, there are always other companies to search for.

—From an article by Edmund L. Andrews in the June 1986 issue of *Venture*

Convertible Securities are equity or debt investments that can be exchanged for something else of value upon the happening of some future event. The most common convertible securities are debentures and preferred stock that are convertible into common stock. The election of the holder is usually all that is required to convert.

Convertible securities are a nice way for investors to hedge. They allow them to acquire a debt instrument, with its rights to interest and principal payments, without sacrificing the chance to participate in the company's capital appreciation. When a company does well, the investor can convert his debenture into stock that is more valuable. When a company is less successful, he can retain his debenture and receive his interest and principal payments.

Most venture capitalists like convertible securities, particularly convertible debentures, because they help preserve their capital and give them the potential of profiting from increases in the value of the company's stock. By giving their holders an option for removing money from a modestly successful company, convertible debentures allow investors to continue making venture capital investments even when their portfolio companies are not successful enough to allow them to liquidate their investments through public offerings. Contrary to popular opinion, most venture capital investments do not generate large profits for their investors. Most portfolio companies fail or succeed modestly. Deal structures that include convertible debentures can enable venture investors to retrieve their capital from their modest successes for reinvestment in other companies. *See: Cashing Out (or In), Debentures, Downside, Equity, Liquidity Agreements, Upside, Appendix A—A Few Words About Tax Reform.*

Copyrights are protections afforded to writing by federal law. They prevent unauthorized copying or duplicating of protected works. The protections are available to writings of all kinds, including computer software.

Copyrights protect the expression of ideas and are often contrasted with trade secrets, which protect ideas themselves but not their expression. The distinctions are important. Companies cannot publish their secret processes in a magazine with a copyright notice and expect to keep others from using the process. The copyright will prevent only the duplication of the way in which those ideas were expressed in the magazine. By the same token, there are things such as mass-marketed video games and monitor displays for which copyrights provide valuable protections that trade secrets cannot. And, where the use of a secret process requires copying of the expression of that process, as with most computer software programs, copyrights can, for many practical purposes, protect the process itself.

Copyrights can be obtained for computer software in object code or source code. They can also be obtained for documentation, manuals, and display screen configurations. Copyrights are available to software that is mass-marketed or sold under restrictive license.

Securing copyright protection requires careful compliance with the federal copyright rules. Whenever copyrights are used to protect a valuable asset, companies should engage qualified counsel to assist them in making the application. Particularly when the asset is software, management should understand the advantages and disadvantages to copyrights and the best application procedure to follow before sending a program printout to Washington. Qualified lawyers can help management determine whether copyrights, trade secrets, or a combination of the two is the best protection for a company's asset. They can also plot a strategy for obtaining those protections. *See: Software Protection, Trade Secrets.*

Corporate Venture Capital refers to the fact that many large corporations have separate subsidiaries that make venture investments. These corporations often focus, like specialty funds, on companies within their industry or industries into which they would like to expand.

Corporate venture companies evaluate investment proposals in much the same way as traditional venture capitalists do. They conduct extensive due diligence and look for a high rate of return from their investment. In addition, venture corporations frequently look for companies and products that can fill a market niche the corporation's parent wants to enter or that can develop technology the parent needs.

Corporate venture capitalists can make good partners for companies with good products who need assistance in marketing them. Often, the corporate partner can lend its marketing expertise and give the company access to distribution channels that accelerate its growth. Sometimes a corporate partner can lend technological assistance to a company as well. Because they are often able to provide some specific strategic assistance, managements should explore the additional "value added" the corporate investor can bring to the table and contract in the financing agreement for those investor services the company needs. *See: Specialty Funds, Value Added, Venture Capitalists.*

IN THE LAND OF THE GIANTS

Fred L. Luconi talks with the vision gained by sitting on top of $12 million in capital. He knows money isn't everything. "When we built the business plan for this company, we had a strong idea of what it would take to get this product into the market," says the president of Applied Expert Systems Inc. As much as dollars, Luconi wanted investors who would buy his expert system for financial planners themselves and also market it to others.

His list of investors is short on venture capital partnerships and long on corporations. Luconi's financing, including $8 million in a second round that closed in May, comes from The Travelers Insurance Co., TRW Inc., Chemical New York Corp., and Beneficial Corp.

Like a lot of other entrepreneurs, Luconi has found that it can pay to walk with giants. Direct strategic investments by corporations in venture capital–backed companies, the method that Venture Economics Inc., Wellesley Hills, Mass., uses to track the increasing activity of corporations, have climbed steadily. The total reached 245 investments in 1985 from just 30 in 1980.

Behind this growth lies an extraordinary—and possibly temporary—concurrence of interest among corporations, entrepreneurs, and venture capitalists that is changing the form of private venture partnerships and the structure of the venture capital industry. Large corporations are often looking for a window on technology—knowledge of new methods or new products in their field before they come to market. Backing an entrepreneur can reduce the time it takes to get a product to market.

Du Pont & Co.'s approximately $5 million investment in ImagiTex Inc., for example, was "very much initiated by [our quick] time to market," says Jeffrey D. Glidden, vice-president of finance at ImagiTex. "We effectively have a product now," says Glidden. "They could develop a product from scratch, and it could take them two or three years."

To an entrepreneur a corporate investor can mean money, marketing, and management advice. "We did two venture rounds with a very positive group of venture investors" that included American Research & Development and Hambrecht & Quist, says ImagiTex' Glidden. "Rather than do a third round of venture, we wanted to find an investor who could bring us access to technology and markets and access to operating management rather than just money." Du Pont Vice-President Mark A. Suwyn sits on ImagiTex' seven-person board. "He understands the market and the opportunity even better than we do in some ways," Glidden notes. Du Pont will market the MSR 2000, a proprietary electronic imaging system built by ImagiTex.

—From an article by Jim Jubak
in the September 1986 issue of *Venture*

Co-Sale Agreements are clauses usually contained in financing agreements that require management members to share any future sale of their stock to new investors with the present ones. They are usually entered into at the insistence of the outside investors as a condition to their providing funding.

The purpose of a co-sale agreement is to prevent important management members from selling out (perhaps at a large profit) and leaving the investors "holding the bag." While co-sale agreements do not prevent management shareholders from selling their shares at a profit, they do force them to share the benefit of their sale with the investors by allowing the investors to include their shares in the sale.

In practice, co-sale agreements work like this: Whenever a management shareholder is approached and has the opportunity to sell his shares of company stock, he must notify the investors and tell them the terms that have been proposed. Then the outside investors have an opportunity to sell some of their shares to the purchaser. If the outside investors elect to include some of their shares in the sale, the management shareholder will reduce the number of his shares being sold so that the purchaser obtains the number of shares he originally offered to buy. The number of shares the outside investors are entitled to include is usually a predetermined percentage of the total number of shares being sold. Often, that percentage reflects the relative number of shares held by the investors and the selling management shareholder.

The operation of co-sale agreements raises some interesting securities law questions. For instance, does the participation by the outside investors in the management shareholder's sale of shares create an obligation on the management shareholder to provide more formal disclosure to the buyer of the shares than he would otherwise have had to make? Certainly, it creates an obligation on the part of the participating outside shareholders to be as candid with the buyer as the management shareholder is required to be. Just as certainly, the management shareholder has a separate responsibility to the participating outside shareholders to make full and accurate disclosure to them about the offer and the condition of the company. How to fulfill this obligation can be a troublesome question in a real world where companies have extensive activities and even investors who sit on a company's board of directors may not have a full or accurate understanding of the company's operations.

What happens if the buyer of the shares obtains rights against both the management shareholder and the outside selling shareholders because of an inadvertent misrepresentation or omission made by the management shareholder? Has the management shareholder created additional liabilities for himself to the participating investors by permitting them to participate in the sale? (Probably yes.) Does the management shareholder risk incurring liability as a selling shareholder if the participating shareholders make a misrepresentation that entitles the purchaser to rescind the purchase or obtain damages? (Again, the answer is probably yes.)

Because co-sale agreements create so many difficult securities questions, which in turn can create substantial liability for management shareholders, they should be avoided whenever possible. When they cannot be avoided, they should be accompanied by cross-indemnification agreements, which make each party responsible for any liabilities created by their misrepresentations or failure to comply with the requirements of the applicable securities laws. Co-sale agreements should be for as short a term as possible and expire after a term of months or years. They should terminate automatically when the company goes public.

Management shareholders should try to limit co-sale rights by making them nontransferable. Participating sellers should also bear a percentage of the cost of consummating a sale. These costs could be significant if the sale requires the preparation of an offering circular or other significant disclosure document.

Whenever possible, management should negotiate a minimum number of shares that it can sell in any twelve-month period without triggering the co-sale rights. After all, the rationale for the co-sale provision is to prevent management from selling out wholesale and leaving the investor with an unmanaged company. Sales of small numbers of shares should not diminish management's interest in the company. Gifts of shares and use of the shares to secure a legitimate debt should be excluded from the co-sale obligation. In all events, any sales made under a co-sale agreement, whether the outside investor chooses to include his shares or not, should be made only on the advice and with the assistance of counsel. Otherwise, management and the outside investors these rights are designed to protect may find themselves being exposed to unexpected and unwanted liabilities. *See: Blue Sky Laws, Exits, First Refusal Rights, Reg D, SEC (Securities and Exchange Commission), 10b5, 33 Act.*

CPAs (Certified Public Accountants) are professionals who, by training and certification, are qualified to audit a company's financial statements. These audits can help attract some (but certainly not all) investors and are essential for going public. CPAs can be sole practitioners or members of a larger firm.

Companies that do not have an accountant who is experienced in working with emerging growth companies should consult with an outside accountant to establish a company accounting system that is appropriate to their business. Even a company with a good accountant can usually benefit from the counsel of an accounting firm that is experienced in representing emerging growth companies. Such firms can help management decide what types of books and records the company should keep and what types of regular reports management should receive to help it manage its business and attract investment. These firms can also help management design a bookkeeping system that anticipates rapid growth and provides mechanisms to make it easier to manage the problems such growth inevitably brings.

Many accounting firms also help companies prepare projections and draft business plans. Many have valuable contacts in the business community and can provide introductions to potential investors. Some even assist start-up companies on a reduced-fee or delayed-billing basis. A relationship with a good accounting firm can also provide a reference for venture capitalists to consult. *See: Audits, Reports and Records.*

LEARNING TO COUNT ON YOUR ACCOUNTANT

If you're on the verge of taking your company public, you'll need to rely heavily on accountants. CPAs can assist in crunching numbers for the prospectus and all related documentation required by the Securities & Exchange Commission. They can also help you evaluate the track records and terms offered by different underwriters, and put you in touch with securities lawyers. And they can establish internal controls and systems to keep your reporting timely and accurate after you've completed your offering, structure compensation packages, and advise you on computerized financial services.

Entrepreneurs "can't go public at a decent price without an opinion from a well-recognized public accounting firm," says William Lerach, partner in the San Diego office of Milberg Weiss Bershad Specthrie & Lerach, a securities law firm. (Over 87% of 193 IPOs with share price $5 and above went with a Big Eight firm, according to a month-long *Venture* study of IPOs in 1985.) Big Eight firms typically subject the financial statements of IPOs to at least three levels of senior partner review—that's usually enough, along with their reputations, to reassure most underwriters and prospective investors, as well as the SEC, which requires disclosure of all materials (including balance sheet and profit and loss statements) relevant to the offering.

Going public begins with audits. The process includes reviewing such internal controls as your cash disbursement and accounts payable and receivable systems, and testing transactions and account balances that are "material" to your company. If you have bought an expensive piece of equipment, for example, an accountant will want to see the purchase order, the canceled check, and the actual machine.

Accountants necessarily are fussy people. Audited financials require them, for instance, to observe inventory firsthand each year. If they can't, CPAs must qualify their opinion of the financial statements when filing with the SEC, which can mandate a delay until reliable inventory records have been established. Accountants recommend that startups considering an IPO have inventories verified at least two years in advance of their target date. The process takes one to three days and costs $250 to $1,000, according to Big Eight sources. Similarly, acquisitions that are considered "material" to a company—for example, anything that cost more than 10% of total assets—must be audited separately for at least one year. Without such an audit, filing can be put off for months or years.

The standard registration statement—form S-1, used for offerings of any size, but generally for those exceeding $7.5 million—demands [audited] balance sheets for the previous two years and audited income statements for the past three fiscal years. (For S-18 filings limited to $7.5 million in proceeds, audited income statements are required for only two years.) Prior audits by another accounting firm must be reviewed for compliance with SEC regulations. If a company hasn't been audited in past years, IPO accountants must reconstruct the financial past as best as they can.

Only rarely is a company preparing to go public so disorganized that an audit is impossible. More often, startups have at that point simply outgrown their record-keeping systems. Typical problems of such companies include unreconciled bank accounts, poor accounts payable systems, and uncollected receivables that haven't been written off. Often, new companies fail to keep close track of inventory values, notes payable, and underlying collateral, sometimes pledging the same assets more than once. On occasion clear records of issued stock and options may not exist.

Accountants can also help you by filing what are known as supplemental schedules—a more detailed balance sheet as well as income statement information—for plants and equipment, land and leasehold improvements, allowances for bad debts, and total depreciation expenses. In the prospectus, CPAs render their opinion, either "clean" or qualified, that no material financial information has been misstated or left out. They must draft and send to underwriters a "comfort letter"—explaining how charts, graphs, and all statistical data were derived, and giving updated financial information—no more than three days before a prospectus hits the Street.

The entire auditing process takes about three to six months. You can save time if your records are in ace condition. Count on spending $25,000 to $200,000, depending on the complexity of the job: that is, the condition of your records, the nature and size of your business, and the difficulty of reporting details about acquisitions and divestments.

—From an article by Michelle Bekey in the April 1986 issue of *Venture*

Cumulative Voting refers to a particular method of voting shares of stock that can be provided for in a company's governing documents. It allows a shareholder to cast all of his votes for company directors (determined by multiplying the number of his shares by the number of director positions being filled) for just one director. Cumulative voting can be used to insure a minority shareholder that he will have a seat on a company's board of directors.

In a normal voting arrangement, a shareholder with 30 percent of the voting stock can never be assured of any representation on a company's board of directors. This is because each director position is voted on separately. As each position is voted on, the 70 percent shareholder can outvote the 30 percent shareholder and, thereby, elect all of the directors.

With cumulative voting, the result is different. Instead of electing each director separately, all the director positions are voted on at once with the top vote-getters taking seats on the board. If three positions are being filled, each shareholder gets three votes for each of his shares. He can vote them in any fashion he wants.

With three positions open, a shareholder with 30 shares gets 90 votes (three times 30 votes), while a shareholder with 70 shares gets 210 votes (three times 70 votes). If the 30 percent shareholder votes all of his 90 votes for one candidate, that candidate is guaranteed to be one of the top three vote-getters because the remaining 210 votes can only give two other candidates more than 90 votes. Since the three candidates receiving the most votes are elected to the board, the 30 percent shareholder is assured of being represented on the board. *See: Common Stock, Control, Management Agreements, Minority Shareholder, Shareholders' Agreements, Voting Agreements, Voting Trusts.*

Cure Periods refer to provisions in agreements that allow a defaulting party to "fix" the cause of a default. In a financing agreement, a cure (or sometimes "grace") period provision might state that if the company fails to perform a required task, such as meeting goals that are a condition to obtaining more funding from the investor, the company will, nonetheless, be given an extra thirty days in which to perform that task before it is held to be in default of the agreement. If the company meets the goal within the cure period, the investor becomes contractually bound to provide the next round of funding. *See: Benchmarks, Default, Stage Financing.*

D

Deal refers to the final agreement between management and an investor for the funding of a company. The terms of the deal are set forth in financing agreements that both sides have reviewed and negotiated carefully. A deal is normally very different from the offer, the counteroffer, or the final offer. In some cases, the deal is quite different from what either management or the investor originally envisioned. The time required to complete a venture capital deal can vary from several weeks to several months.

In conversation, entrepreneurs and investors speak of good deals, bad deals, sour deals ("the deal went sour"), sweet deals (a deal that is particularly lucrative), side deals (a secondary deal enabled by the first deal), and raw deals (deals in which one party thinks he has been outmaneuvered). No matter how a deal is described, it involves at least two parties and their attorneys, all of whom may characterize it differently. *See: Closing, Deal Breakers, Deal Flow, Financing Agreements, Negotiation, Structure.*

Deal Breakers are those individuals who are so interested in something other than closing a deal that they hinder or stop a financing without good reason. No one wants a deal breaker near an important negotiation.

Deal breakers can be hard to distinguish from friends and counselors who try to help management get a good deal. They come in assorted varieties:

- *The hard-liner* believes that the best way to negotiate is to take firm positions and not discuss the issues. He presents a proposal on a take-it-or-leave-it basis and acts annoyed when a legitimate issue is raised by the other side. The hard-liner's intransigence results in a dead deal even when the parties' respective interests could have resulted in a good deal for both sides. The best deals are usually made between parties who discuss their concerns intelligently and search creatively for common ground on which a deal can be based.

- *The minutiae master* wears everyone out with his obsessive concern for detail. He wants to document every detail regardless of its practical importance to the deal. This sometimes disguises the fact that he does not understand its economics. He is often heard repeating phrases such as "we did it this way on the last deal" or "this is our standard language, we always insist on it."
- *The best dealer* is obsessed with getting the best deal. Instead of working to get the best deal available, he insists on a deal that is so good for him and so bad for the other party that it cannot be made. This person often appears as an adviser to a businessman who is unsure of himself and does not completely understand the economics of the proposed transaction.
- *The last dealer* wants the current deal to be exactly like the last one he worked on. It doesn't matter to him that this deal is different: He understood the last deal and will do everything he can to force this one into a format with which he is familiar. Since his last deal is different from the present deal, the other side will object. If he goes unchecked, the deal will die.

Deal breakers are hard to distinguish in some cases from advisers who have the parties' best interests at heart. This is because their deal breaking is related to some hidden agenda, such as fulfilling their personal idea of what a tough negotiator is or hiding their inexperience with the funding process. By contrast, good negotiators are not constrained by personal agendas that are unrelated to the goals of the negotiation. They are able to keep the goals of their party clearly in focus throughout the negotiations and work diligently, using all their creativity and experience, to obtain the best deal. For the entrepreneur, distinguishing between an adviser who is a deal breaker and one who is a good negotiator can mean the difference between success and failure. *See: Deal, Deal Flow, Negotiation, Shopping, We Always Do It This Way.*

Deal Flow refers to the never-ending stream of business proposals that come to most venture capitalists for review. It is common for a big venture capital firm to receive more than 100 business proposals each month. Therefore, it is not unusual for a venture capitalist to invest in less than 1/2 percent of the deals arriving at his doorstep.

Deal flow explains why an outstanding business plan is so important. Also, it explains why venture capitalists can often insist on the structure of the deals they will accept. The best way an entrepreneur can address this inflexibility is to approach more than one venture firm at a time. Few venture capitalists will object or lose interest in a company's proposal when an entrepreneur takes this approach. Soliciting more than one venture capitalist can create healthy competition among investors and enhance a company's bargaining position. In the best case, several capitalists will bid against each other to fund an attractive deal. This happened frequently in computer-related financings of the early 1980s, resulting in excellent deals for the computer entrepreneurs, and rude awakenings for the investors several years later. This is not to say, however, that companies should shop their business plans indiscriminately to a large number of investors. To do so shows a lack of sophistication on management's part and can discourage interest from investors. *See: Business Plan, Business Plan Format, Shopping, Summary.*

Debentures are one form of corporate note, under which a company borrows money and agrees to repay it, with interest. They represent a legitimate alternative for companies to raise funds without selling equity. Many investors fund both debt and equity and use debentures to reflect the debt portion.

Investors sometimes use debentures to increase their return on investment. This happens when they characterize a portion of their equity investment as a debenture while computing the amount of stock they require on their total equity and debenture investment. When this is done, the investor receives money as a debt repayment without reducing his potential return from the stock purchase. If the investment is only moderately successful, the debenture also helps the investor reclaim a portion of his money for investment in another company.

How can characterizing a portion of an investment as a debenture benefit investors at the expense of management? Assume, for example, that an investor agrees to provide $600,000 in return for 30 percent of a company's outstanding stock. The investor wants to pay $100,000 for the stock and $500,000 for a debenture. The debenture proposed will have a term of ten years, and the company will not have to repay any principal or interest until then. In the meantime, if the company generates enough profits to pay off some of the debenture without hurting cash flow, then the company will begin to do so.

The investor's preference for this structure is clear. If he invests all $600,000 in the stock and the company succeeds, his initial investment may pay back $2 million, for example, making his profit $1.4 million. If, instead, he puts $100,000 in the stock and $500,000 in a debenture, his profit will be more than $1.9 million because in addition to the $2 million he also gets paid back his $500,000, with interest. In the first case his return on his stock investment is 2.3 to 1; in the second case it is more than 19 to 1!

But does it matter to the company? Should the company begrudge the investor a higher return as long as it does not cost more? Consider the following:

The investor argues that the structure does not hurt the company or management. The company still gets $600,000. If it does well and meets its projections, the company can pay back the debenture early. If the company does not do well enough by the tenth year to pay back the debenture, it probably will not matter because, he says, management will probably have abandoned the project by then anyway. It is a corporate debt, after all, and if the company cannot make the payment, it will not be doing well enough to keep the entrepreneur's loyalty anyway. There's no personal liability (at least, not now), so management should not care.

The proposed structure does allow the company to use the $500,000 without making interest payments during the start-up years of its operations. It may even help the company to borrow other funds as long as the debenture holder's rights are subordinated to another lender's. It will not, however, improve the company's balance sheet to the same extent or give a lender as much comfort as an equity investment will.

The terms of a typical debenture require a company to start

repayment after three or four years of operations (if the company is generating enough cash). If the company is expanding at that point, as everyone hopes it will, management may need cash to support larger inventories or more ambitious marketing efforts. Therefore, if management agrees to the investor's proposed structure, the company may incur the expense of further borrowing *earlier* than it would have had to if the original investment had been all for stock.

Thus, the use of a debenture reduces the value to the company of the venture capitalist's investment. It may not reduce it below what is needed to get the company started, but it does reduce it in a measurable way. As a result, companies should try to structure debentures they issue in ways that reduce and delay their adverse effects. Here are some ways to accomplish this:

- *Make the term as long as possible.* The longer the company has the money to use before it has to repay the loan, the more like equity it is to the company. (This also applies to interest payments and early principal payment required by the terms of the debenture. These principal "prepayments" typically become due when the company exceeds its projected profits.) To the extent possible, these obligations should be delayed even if they are made contingent upon the success of the company's operations.
- *Reduce the portion of the investment made as a debenture and make required prepayments small.* Ideally, any prepayment obligation should be small, start late, and be at management's option. If the investor wants interest on optional prepayments that the company chooses not to make, payment of that interest should not be required until late in the term of the debenture. The financing agreements should make it clear that any failure to make prepayments or interest payments before the end of the term will not give the investor any rights to require earlier payments under the debenture.
- *Persuade investors to subordinate their debentures to other debt of the company.* This will make it easier for the company to borrow additional cash, which, in turn, makes it easier for the company to succeed. Success of the company, after all, is the primary goal of management and the venture capitalist; without that success the debenture is worthless.

- *Negotiate a right to force the investor to convert the debenture if certain events occur.* For example, if the company meets its performance goals, give management the option to force conversion of the debenture into equity and thereby improve the company's debt-to-equity ratio and make it easier for the company to borrow from outside lenders. Management may choose not to exercise the option if new equity is cheaper than new debt, but the option could prove valuable in the right situation.

You can also try to convince investors to make the company's payments on the debentures contingent on company success and not require an absolute obligation for the company to repay the debenture at the end of ten years. But do not expect an investor to be too sympathetic to this suggestion. Without a definite repayment obligation, the IRS may treat repayments under a debenture as dividends to the investor. This means unwanted taxable income to the investor and reduces the debenture's after-tax value. As long as the IRS recognizes the debenture as a legitimate debt, repayments of principal create no income and no taxes to the investor.

The use of a debenture does not decrease the risk to the venture capitalist that he will lose all of his money if the company fails. It does, however, increase the size of his reward if the company succeeds. At the same time, the debenture decreases the value of what the company receives from the venture capitalist. This being the case, there is a strong basis for management to argue that the venture capitalist should be entitled to less stock for his investment when a debenture is included in the funding structure.

Do not confuse debentures with convertible debentures. "Straight" debentures do not give investors any option to buy additional stock. Convertible debentures do. If a venture capitalist requests convertible debentures, be sure the number of shares the company is willing to sell equals the number he buys outright plus the number his convertible debenture entitles him to buy. *See: Convertible Securities, Debt Service, Leverage, Structure, Subordinated Debt, Appendix A—A Few Words About Tax Reform.*

Debt Service is the amount of money a borrower must pay to his lender in order to keep his loans out of default. It consists of the interest and principal payments required to pay off the loan.

Debt service payments reduce cash flow, which explains why equity investments, which do not require repayments, are often preferable. Debt service also explains why certain types of venture companies, such as SBICs, MESBICs, and BDCs, usually structure their fundings as loans with warrants instead of as straight equity purchases. These types of companies rely on borrowed funds to provide all or most of their capital. By using loans when they invest, these venture firms are able to use the debt service payments from their portfolio companies to repay their loans and stay out of default. *See: BDCs (Business Development Corporations), Cash Flow, Default, Debentures, Leverage, MESBICs (Minority Enterprise Small Business Investment Companies), SBICs (Small Business Investment Companies).*

Default is the failure of one party to fulfill its obligations to another party under an agreement. Company defaults usually give substantial rights to the investor. Depending on the nature of the default and terms of the contract, those rights could empower an investor to withhold funding, to take over the company, or to accelerate the company's obligation to pay off debt.

Whenever possible, management should try to limit an investor's default rights to circumstances that involve "material" defaults so that inconsequential, technical defaults do not cause the company to be penalized. Rights to remedy or "cure" defaults can often be obtained and written into an agreement. These cure rights permit a company to correct defaults and avoid the severe penalties they can involve. *See: Benchmarks, Cure Periods, Projections.*

Demand Rights are contractual agreements that entitle an investor to *force* a company to register his shares of company stock so that he can sell them to the public. Demand rights are often contrasted with piggyback rights, which allow an investor to *include* his shares of stock in a public offering that the company voluntarily conducts for its own benefit.

Most venture capitalists require companies to grant them demand rights as a condition to their investing. Demand rights enable the investor to liquidate his investment when he wants by forcing the company to register his shares for sale to the public. This registration process, however, is expensive and time-consuming. And a public sale at the wrong time can reduce the future value of the company's shares. Because this can increase a company's cost of raising equity in the future, the number of demand rights granted and the conditions under which they can be exercised are usually heavily negotiated issues. The outcome of those negotiations can seriously affect the value of a funding and the future success of a company. *See: Piggyback Rights, Registration Rights.*

Dilution (Percentage) is a decrease in the percentage of a company's outstanding stock represented by a fixed number of shares. Percentage dilution occurs to existing shareholders whenever a company issues shares of stock to a new shareholder. It results from the increase in the total number of company shares outstanding caused by the sale of new ones. This increase reduces the percentage ownership each share represents in the company. As a result, existing shareholders who do not purchase new shares find themselves owning a smaller percentage of the outstanding equity.

For example, if management owns all eighty thousand shares of a company's stock and the company issues twenty thousand new shares to another investor, management's percentage ownership in the company will be reduced from 100 percent to 80 percent. Its 80 percent of the stock may be worth more than the 100 percent it owned before the new investor bought twenty thousand shares, but, nonetheless, management's stock ownership has been diluted.

Percentage dilution is almost inevitable in venture capital financings. In fact, few entrepreneurs manage to retain a majority of the stock in their company by the time it goes public. Still, 25 percent of a $50 million company with publicly traded stock is worth a lot more than 100 percent of a privately held company worth $5 million. Not only is it more than twice as many dollars, but it is also in a more liquid form, which itself adds value to the stock.

The most important factor about percentage dilution is how great it is and how much money the company receives for the stock it sells. In general, for a growing company, the longer outside equity financing can be delayed, the less percentage dilution management will suffer. *See: Antidilution Provisions, Dilution (Value), Going Public, Pricing, Restricted Securities.*

Dilution (Value) is an accounting concept. It refers to the difference between what an investor pays for his shares of company stock and their book value immediately after the transaction. Whenever an investor pays more than book value for his shares he suffers value dilution.

Assume, for example, that an investor buys twenty thousand shares at $10 per share when eighty thousand shares are already outstanding and the book value of the company is $50,000. The investor's $200,000 investment will be added to the $50,000 to increase the company's book value to $250,000. Dividing the company's new book value by the number of outstanding company shares gives the per-share book value. In this case, the $250,000 book value divided by one hundred thousand shares (the investor's twenty thousand plus management's eighty thousand) gives a per-share book value of $2.50. The investor who paid $10 per share suffers a $7.50 per-share value dilution. At the same time, management's shares experience an increase in book value from $.62 per share ($50,000 divided by eighty thousand shares) to $2.50 per share.

Venture investors expect value dilution. They know that book value is only one method of measuring a company's worth, and that, in most cases, it is a conservative measure. Most investors are more interested in the fair market value of the shares they purchase and the company's prospects for success. *See: Antidilution Provisions, Dilution (Percentage), ROI (Return on Investment).*

Directors' Indemnities are pledges of a company's credit to protect the members of its board of directors against liabilities they might incur when acting on behalf of the company. Most states permit corporations to provide these indemnities for their directors. Usually, the indemnities apply only when the directors are acting in good faith. Most states exclude from protection actions taken by directors that are willfully fraudulent or grossly negligent.

Venture capitalists usually require these indemnities to be included in a company's bylaws before they invest in a company or join its board of directors. A common indemnity provision reads like this:

> *Indemnification of Officers and Directors.* The corporation shall indemnify any current or former director, officer, employee or agent of the corporation, or any persons who are or were serving at its request as a director, officer, employee, trustee or similar functionary of another foreign or domestic corporation, trust, partnership, joint venture, employee benefit plan or other enterprise, against any and all liabilities and expenses actually and necessarily incurred by such person in connection with or resulting from (a) any threatened, pending or complete action, suit or proceeding, whether civil, criminal, administrative, arbitrative or investigative, (b) an appeal in such an action, suit or proceeding, or (c) an inquiry or investigation that could lead to such an action, suit or proceeding, all to the full extent permitted by law. Such indemnification shall not be deemed exclusive of any other rights to which such person may be entitled, under any bylaw, agreement, insurance policy or vote of shareholders, or otherwise.

See: Board of Directors, Board Committees, Bylaws.

Downside is the risk of loss of capital in any investment. While the downside in almost every venture investment includes some possibility that the investor will lose all of his money, most investors use the term in a limited sense. They use it to describe a realistic appraisal of the probable risk in the situation. Investors often talk about the downside in terms of possible scenarios the company's operations might follow. Some try to quantify the likelihood that the company will fail and the amount of money (or percentage of their investment) they will lose if it does. In the final analysis, however, there is usually as much "gut feel" in an investor's estimation of downside as there is hard analysis. For any company, the more likely it is to fail and the more money its investor stands to lose in a failure, the greater its downside and the less likely it is to attract an investor.

Venture investors use a number of deal-structuring devices to reduce their downside risks. Often, they delay part of their funding obligation and make it contingent upon the company meeting a predetermined benchmark. This allows the investor to postpone risking some of his money until the company has proven its ability to meet a goal. The later rounds of funding are put in at less risk when the company is more established. Taking collateral and guarantees also reduces the downside by increasing the probability that the investor can salvage something if the company goes under. Preferred stock and debentures do the same thing by giving the investor a preference over common stockholders when a company is liquidated.

Other investor practices also reduce the downside. Investor due diligence not only helps the investor pick good companies but also helps him avoid losers. Board of director seats and required reports from management help investors identify and, they hope, correct problems early. Puts, buy-sells, and registration rights can liquidate an investment before all is lost or help an investor get his money out of a modestly successful company and into something else.

Managements can reduce the downside too. When they do, they increase the chance of getting funding at a reasonable price. The best way they can reduce the downside is to anticipate strategic and operating problems and address them realistically in the business plan. This won't eliminate the downside entirely, but it will increase the investor's comfort and help management deal better with problems as they arise. Since most of the deal-structuring devices that reduce the investor's downside tend to increase the risks of management shareholders (by delaying needed funding, making it contingent on future events and giving preferences to the investor when the company fails), precautions that reduce everyone's risk (such as good planning) not only help attract new investors but also enhance the value of the management's shareholdings. *See: Business Plan, Business Plan Format, Collateral, Convertible Securities, Debentures, Due Diligence, Exits, Liquidity Agreements, Negotiation, Pricing, Stage Financing, Structure, Upside.*

Due Diligence is the independent investigation of a company, its management team, and its prospects for success by an investor before funding is provided. It is usually intensive and thorough and often takes months to complete.

Due diligence customarily includes background checks on the management team, independent verifications of statements made in the business plan, and studies of the company's product and market. It includes extensive questioning of management and other company personnel. Most venture capitalists will talk with company suppliers, customers, competitors, and others who know the company and its industry.

Entrepreneurs should conduct due diligence too. They should investigate their industry and their partners thoroughly to gauge their company's prospects and the depth of experience and commitment of each of its principals. Business plans should not be completed without giving careful attention to the assumptions and "facts" that support the company's profits and cash flow projections.

Just as important, entrepreneurs should conduct due diligence investigations about the company's potential investors. Selecting the right investor for a company can mean the difference between success and failure. A disreputable or reluctant investor can slow and even prevent company success. Conversely, an honorable investor can help management by giving it the benefit of his experience with growing companies and his contacts with financial institutions. This can be as valuable as cash.

One way to learn about a particular investor is to ask bankers, lawyers, and accountants about his reputation. If a publicly held venture capital fund is considering investing, a good deal of information about it can be obtained from the Securities and Exchange Commission. If it is privately held, management can usually obtain a copy of the offering circular it used to raise funds by simply asking the investor for one. The National Venture Capital Association, National Association of Small Business Investment Corporations (NASBIC), *Venture's Guide to International Venture Capital* (the bulk of which is about venture funds in the United States), and *Pratt's Guide to Venture Capital Sources* by Stanley Pratt can also provide valuable information about the size of a fund and the types of investments it makes.

Once it has begun investigating a company, most venture firms will give an entrepreneur a list of the companies in which it has invested. These companies can provide valuable insights into the operations of the fund and its desirability as a business partner. Appropriate questions to ask the founders of these companies are:

- Was the firm easy or difficult to work with?
- Was it prompt in making investment decisions?
- What type of participation in management did it require?

- Are its officers honest and candid?
- Were they reasonable in their negotiations?
- Have they provided services promised to the company?
- Have they helped or hindered company success?
- Are they responsive to company needs?
- How has the firm reacted to company problems?
- Is it flexible?
- Has the firm participated in later rounds of financing?
- Did it help identify further investors?
- Did its performance live up to its promises?

The more specific the questions are, the more valuable will be the information obtained. Questions to and about the venture capital firm are appropriate and demonstrate management's concern for the future. Questions about how long it will take the investor to make a decision and whether it has the funds and freedom to make an investment are particularly appropriate. *See: Adventure Capitalists, Audits, Business Plan, Downside, Ethics, Five Factors, NASBIC (National Association of Small Business Investment Companies), National Venture Capital Association, Stage Financing, Three Questions.*

HANDS-ON VENTURE CAPITAL

When the Friday meeting turns to new investments, the atmosphere gets charged with gossip, character assessment (and assassination on occasion), and the hard bargaining of street peddlers. Nearly every partner looks at some aspect of each deal. Frank Bonsal heard about Seattle's Summation Inc. (formerly Personal Scientific Corp.) from Howard E. Cox, a general partner at Greylock Management Corp., a Boston venture capital firm. [Partners] Bonsal, Marks, and Rea looked at the business plan and concluded that the product, a computerized programmer for test equipment, did have a potential $1 billion to $4 billion market. [Partners] Kramlich, Rea, and McConnell visited the company's Seattle plant to talk at length with key personnel. Once they returned, McConnell worked the phone, calling his network about the entrepreneurs, the viability of the product, its market, and the competition. A month later, McConnell provided a blow-by-blow description of his due diligence. Other partners seemed skeptical about the market. What about the Summation Inc. product is proprietary? Is the present management good enough to pull it off? NEA finally put in $1 million for 10% of the company.

Like most other venture capitalists, NEA arrives at a price on a deal by working backward. Using information on the potential size of the market, the industry, and possible competitors, the partners estimate the approximate value of the company five to seven years from now. If that value is, say, $100 million, then an investment today of $1 million should garner 10% of the company, allowing for a 60% return on the investment.

Money may be the subject of the most haggling—and the subject most on entrepreneurs' minds—but it's the easiest part of the deal. It isn't enough to find the right price, the right company, and the right entrepreneur. The question is whether the deal can be sold to the right investors and whether the venture capitalists can get the proper representation on the board of directors. "Sometimes we have to walk away from a deal if we can't sell it to others," says Marks.

During that morning's meeting, NEA will walk away from two deals for reasons that never cross the minds of most entrepreneurs. In both cases it's not the entrepreneurs but the other investors who fail to pass muster. In one, the California investment banking firm leading the deal won't provide management help, or much in the way of monitoring. NEA passes, even though the price is tempting and the company is one the partners have watched for some time.

The round of questions about the other investment gets exceedingly personal. The lead investor is a prominent venture capital firm. Both Kramlich and Prothro want to know which partner at the firm will handle the investment and take the investors' board seat. On one prior occasion NEA had put money into a deal, relying on the senior partner most likely to handle this deal for the other venture firm to safeguard the investor's money. It's not just that NEA lost its stake when the company went into bankruptcy. It's also that several partners feel the lead venture firm simply didn't stay on top of the situation. NEA passes on that deal too. "You want partners who know and understand the business the company is in," says Art Marks. "You want to make sure that the lead investor can handle problems as they arise."

—From an article by Udayan Gupta about New Enterprise Associates (NEA), a venture capital firm with main offices in San Francisco and Baltimore. The article appeared in the January 1986 issue of *Venture*.

E

Earnouts refer to acquisitions or leveraged buyouts in which the purchaser, usually management, finances part of the company's purchase price by borrowing from the seller. In the purest form of the arrangement, the purchaser is required to pay the earnout portion of the purchase price only from the profits of the company. If the company does not earn enough profits under the new owners to pay off the seller, the seller may become entitled to take the company back, receive certain minimum payments, or increase the purchase price. The term *earnout* is also used to refer to venture capital financings in which a portion of the funding is provided by a loan that is repaid only from company profits. *See: Earnups, Leveraged Buyout (LBO).*

Earnups are arrangements whereby an investor acquires most of a company's capital stock but gives management the opportunity to increase its stock ownership by managing the company successfully. Usually, earnups are accompanied by a contract that allows management to control the operations of the company as long as the company meets specified goals. Earnups are less a financing device than they are a technique for attracting good people to manage a company. They are sometimes used in a leveraged buyout by the outside investor to entice existing management to remain with the company. If management can keep the company profitable and meet its goals, it often can earn a substantial equity position in the company. Earnups assign little value to management's role in putting together the funding used to purchase the company. Instead, they reward management for making the company succeed after the purchase or funding. *See: Earnouts, Golden Handcuffs, Leveraged Buyout (LBO), Management Agreements, Vesting Schedules.*

83(b) Election is an option shareholders have under Section 83(b) of the Internal Revenue Code. It enables a shareholder to elect to be taxed on the difference between his purchase price for unvested shares and their fair market value when he purchases them instead of on the difference between his purchase price and their value when they later vest.

Anyone who receives stock that is in connection with his performance of services for a company should know about section 83 of the Internal Revenue Code. Unless an 83(b) election is made, section 83 can require that shareholder to pay taxes at ordinary income tax rates when the restrictions on his stock lapse on the difference between the value of his stock then and the price he paid for the shares. This tax must be paid regardless of whether the shareholder actually sells his stock when the restrictions lapse.

Section 83(b) entitles the shareholder to make an election within thirty days after he purchases the shares to prevent this unwanted attribution of income. The election (basically, filing the proper form) causes the shareholder to be taxed at the time of the purchase, instead of the date of vesting. The tax is based on the difference between his purchase price and the fair market value his shares would have had on the date of the purchase if they had been fully vested. If, as is often the case in early stage companies, the initial low purchase price for the shares can be tied to the actual market value of those shares at that time, the practical effect of making an 83(b) election can be to prevent the attribution of income to the shareholder when the vesting provisions expire, without creating any taxable income to the shareholder at the time of the purchase of the shares.

Failure to make an 83(b) election can have disastrous effects. If, as everyone involved hopes, the company increases in value during the vesting period, the shareholder who failed to make the election will have to pay taxes on the difference between the increased value of the shares on the date they vest and the amount he paid for them. At the same time, the shares are likely to be illiquid (unsalable) because of restrictions that apply to unregistered securities. As a result, the shareholder may owe the federal government a substantial tax payment (caused by his failure to make an 83[b] election) without having the means to pay it.

The provisions of section 83 and of section 83(b) are complex and cannot be completely explored here. They apply in situations when a casual observer would not think they should. As a result, any person who receives or purchases securities that are subject to vesting or other similar restrictive provisions should consult with a qualified attorney or accountant to determine whether the filing of an 83(b) election is appropriate. *See: Restricted Securities, Vesting Schedules.*

Emerging Growth Companies (EGCs) are what venture capitalists are eager to add to their investment portfolios. They are companies that promise to grow fast and create a healthy return on investment for their investors. This is customarily achieved when the company, now just "emerging" as an attractive investment, does well enough to support a public offering or attract a corporate purchaser in three to eight years. EGCs are usually in industries whose stocks tend to sell at high multiples of company earnings; thus, it takes fewer dollars of earnings to support a high-stock price when the investor later sells.

High-tech companies are not necessarily emerging growth companies. While it is true that high-tech companies have attracted a lot of venture capital investment, it is not because they are high tech. They have succeeded in obtaining funding because they tend to be in industries that support high price-to-earnings ratios.

EGCs include any company that presents good potential for rapid and sustained growth (growth in excess of the industry average or the gross national product). Low- or no-tech companies with the potential for rapid and sustained growth are being funded. The venture capitalist's primary concern is final return on investment when the company stock attains liquidity, not the glamour of high tech. *See: High Tech, Price-Earnings Ratio, ROI (Return on Investment).*

VENTURE'S FAST-TRACK 100:
FROM $42 MILLION TO $1.9 BILLION

For five years *Venture* has published its Fast-Track 100 and for five years the top two spots on our list have been held by Apple Computer and the Price Co. This year's ranking of the 100 largest founder-managed companies started within the past 10 years resembles the lists of previous years in other ways: Namely, computer and computer-related companies account for almost half of the Fast-Track, followed by health-care service and product companies.

Of the 48 computer-related companies on the Fast-Track, 12 produced disk drives, 10 manufactured components, 8 marketed general computers, 7 sold scientific and engineering computers, 5 published software, 3 are developing local-area networks (LANs), and 3 are involved in computer distribution and sales.

The second biggest category on the Fast-Track 100 was the health care field, which contributed 10 companies to the list. Four produce medical equipment and products; three are hospital chains; two are health maintenance organizations; and one is a regional health plan company. The third largest category contained eight wholesale and retail operations, including three club membership warehouses.

—From an article by Michele H. Fleischer
that appeared in the May 1986 issue of *Venture*.
A complete list of the Fast-Track 100 is reproduced in Appendix C.

Employment Contracts are agreements between a company and its employees that set forth the terms of their tenure. They are used for a variety of purposes, including attracting key people to join a company by guaranteeing their salary or describing their benefits. They can also be used to define job duties or to bind an employee to secrecy and noncompetition agreements. Employment contracts can provide protections against arbitrary firings. If properly written, they can even help companies avoid expensive fights over trade secret infringement claims made by former employers of newly hired company personnel.

Employment contracts with key employees are important to many investors. Young companies usually depend more on the talents of a small group of people than their larger, more established competitors do. Because of this, most investors require assurances that a company's key people will remain after it is funded. They want to know that the people they evaluated will stay around to run the company with their money. At the same time, entrepreneurs often want protection against being fired when new investors are brought in. It is no surprise, then, that an important negotiation in many venture financings deals with who will enter into employment contracts and what the terms of those contracts will be.

Employment contracts do not always make sense for a company, however. As a general rule, employment contracts should be avoided unless they serve a specific company purpose. Giving an employee a contract that guarantees his employment for a period of time does not further company interests unless it is necessary to secure an important benefit for the company, such as convincing the employee to take the job. Because of the personal-service nature of employment, employment contracts are usually ineffective at forcing an employee to stay with a company. They are even less effective at keeping an employee interested in doing a good job. At the same time, however, employment contracts can cause management to retain an employee longer than it wants or to pay a departing employee a premium to leave.

Investors' preferences for contracts with management does not mean they like rich employment contracts. They expect entrepreneurs to sacrifice present earnings for the prospects of long-term capital appreciation. Managements that crave large salaries and elaborate executive benefits can scare away venture capitalists. Contracts that insure management employment for too long or in circumstances that could jeopardize a shareholder's investment also cool investor enthusiasm.

Venture investors want the freedom to remove management if it proves to be ineffective. At the same time, managements want some security against arbitrary firings. Employment contracts are designed to reconcile these different points of view. *See: Compensation and Bonus Plans, Confidentiality Agreements, Golden Handcuffs, Noncompete Agreements, Vesting Schedules.*

Entrepreneur is someone who accepts the many risks inherent in operating an enterprise in pursuit of profit. The term can apply to anyone who forsakes the relative security of a job for the challenge of building a successful company. Most entrepreneurs invest great amounts of time and effort, at considerable sacrifice to themselves and their families, for the privilege of starting their own business and being their own boss. Entrepreneurs come from all walks of life and have different degrees of experience and ability.

What do venture capitalists look for in an entrepreneur? What type of people do they like to invest in? Here are a few characteristics venture capitalists like to find in an entrepreneur:

- *Achievement.* Investors look to past experiences as a prime indicator of an entrepreneur's prospects for success. Someone who has been successful in the past is more likely to be successful in the future. Obviously, the best achievement an entrepreneur can have is to have started a business in the same industry. Next to that, success and advancement in a large company are preferred.
- *Knowledge.* Knowledge of the industry and where the new product will fit is essential. An accurate study of the industry may give an entrepreneur this knowledge, but actual experience in it is a real plus. Knowledge about working with people and the ability to put together a good management team is important.
- *Energy.* A venture capitalist must be convinced of an entrepreneur's ability and willingness to work hard to make the company a success. A tenacious entrepreneur with enthusiasm for his company is a must. Surveys show that entrepreneurs work long hours.
- *Intelligence.* What an investor looks for here is rationality, insightfulness, and creativity. Advanced degrees from universities are nice and may evidence intelligence, but what a venture capitalist really wants is an entrepreneur who can analyze a complex problem, understand it, and arrive at an appropriate solution quickly.
- *Flexibility.* No one wants to invest in a blockhead! A flexible entrepreneur is one who can adjust his approach to meet unexpected problems. He is one who can accept criticism and advice from others, including his investors. Most important of all is the entrepreneur's ability to learn from his mistakes and grow with the increasing demands of his expanding company.
- *Management ability.* A successful company's management will be faced with personnel and management problems that would stretch the patience and creativity of the best of managers. A good manager must be able to work with and motivate his people. He must also keep a tight rein on cash flow, cash control, manufacturing, and sales.

- *Integrity.* Investors want an entrepreneur who is honest and open with them and with himself. This integrity includes an honest appraisal by the entrepreneur of his strengths and weaknesses as well as a realistic appraisal of his product and its prospects for success in the marketplace.

All entrepreneurs have faults. The more of these "ideal" characteristics an entrepreneur has, however, the more likely it is that his company will get funded. Investors consider these characteristics carefully when they evaluate business proposals. *See: Commitment, Due Diligence, Ethics, Five Factors, Management Team.*

ENTREPRENEURS ARE DIFFERENT

I am convinced that the major reason researchers have such difficulty pinning down the origins of entrepreneurial behavior is that they keep looking for *differences*, asking why some people are more "entrepreneurial" than others. But I suspect that all humans have a bit of the entrepreneur in them. Most of our ancestors were entrepreneurs or we wouldn't be here today. In order to be successful at hunting, fighting, and establishing new communities, many of our ancestors had to be able to tolerate ambiguity, to imagine multiple alternative outcomes or futures, and to be comfortable with the status of "misfit."

Harvard Business School research (summarized by John Kao in the *American Banker,* March 16, 1984) finds no single, unitary, entrepreneurial psychology. Rather, that research has identified some recurrent traits or themes among entrepreneurs:

- A high tolerance for ambiguity
- High levels of creativity
- An ability to tolerate paradox in one's personal style, for example to be highly intuitive and at the same time attentive to detail in a highly disciplined fashion.

That research sounds intriguing, but we should be cautious in shouting from the roof tops whatever new findings are unearthed in studies focusing entirely on entrepreneurs.

One midwestern entrepreneur club, for example, polled its membership and found very little except that they had strong mothers. This complements a *Venture* survey of its readers (November 1985) that found entrepreneurs describe some kind of childhood deprivation—emotional, physical, or financial—in the father-child relationship.

According to a Gallup poll summarized by Ellen Graham in the *Wall Street Journal* (May 20, 1985), entrepreneurs are often loners or misfits. They tend not to be joiners or team players and are far more likely to have been fired from jobs than top executives. These findings are especially trustworthy because they represent the results of three samples comparing the opinions of entrepreneurs in young, rapidly expanding companies with those of both businessmen in more well established companies with slower growth rates and executives in Fortune 500 posts.

Joseph Mancuso, president of the Center for Entrepreneurial Management in New York, says that entrepreneurs are misfits, out of step. "Corporate executives get to the top by offending the least number of people, while the entrepreneur gets to the top by stepping over those in his way."

One consistent finding in both academic studies and public opinion polls is that entrepreneurs are not high rollers, but tend to be moderate risk-takers. And a Gallup poll found that "protecting the company from risks" was their most important job characteristic. Even their investments are not any riskier than those of non-entrepreneurs.

Denial of the possibility of failure, eternal optimism in the face of both success and failure, feeling exhilarated by the stress and challenge of launching an enterprise—these characteristics all sound like a description of some kind of inspirational or religious experience. A *Venture* survey (January 1986) confirms the religious strain among entrepreneurs, finding that of 1512 respondents, nearly seven out of ten (69%) from both smaller and larger businesses believe that the strength they gain from religion helps them cope better with business-related problems. The specific characteristics of a particular religion may be less important than one of the chief functions of religion generally, which is to assert a faith in optimism in the face of life's uncertainties.

From this perspective, entrepreneurs may be misfits only in the sense that their optimistic faith is more resilient and harder edged than that shown by other contemporaries. Given the opportunity for entrepreneurship and the economic climate in which it can grow, most humans might choose this way of life over working in a large organization.

—From a speech by John Crothers Pollock, Ph.D.,
chairman, New World Decisions, Ltd.,
delivered to a *Venture/Adweek* Seminar
for advertising agency professionals

Equity is ownership. It is what is sold to investors to get them to fund a company and what is retained by the entrepreneur to reflect the value of what he has created. It represents the value of a company as a going concern. Equity is the most permanent form of investment in a company. It does not require repayment and so does not deplete company cash, as debt repayments do.

Usually, equity takes the form of stock ownership and is different from rights a person may have under a note, debenture, or other debt instrument. Convertible debentures have characteristics of both debt and equity. They are treated as debt until the holder elects to convert them. Then they lose their debt characteristics and become equity.

Equity has an element of magic. Some of the most outrageous, unlikely, seemingly ridiculous business ventures have been undertaken with the object of creating equity. The pursuit of equity is as deeply a part of the American entrepreneur as is the pursuit of happiness. *See: Cash Flow, Common Stock, Convertible Securities, Debentures, Equity Penalties, Preferred Stock, Appendix A—A Few Words About Tax Reform*

Equity Penalties are agreements, usually contained in written contracts, that increase an investor's percentage of ownership upon the occurrence of a specified event, such as the failure of the firm to reach a sales level on a given date. By increasing the investor's share of the company, equity penalties decrease the share of other investors, including management's.

Be extremely wary of equity penalties. They include any arrangement that results in management's stock ownership percentage decreasing if the company fails to achieve its goals. Equity penalties can be in the form of investor options, specialized antidilution protections for outside investors, or restrictions that prevent management shares from vesting.

Few investors ask for equity penalties at first—the issue usually works its way into the deal at a later point. The first hint that an investor wants equity penalties often comes when he suggests to management that if the company does not meet the projections in its business plan, then his investment will not be a good one.

To get the funding, management probably made a good sales

pitch to the investor. In the course of its many discussions, management probably reassured the investor several times that the company's projections were reasonable and attainable. Now the investor suggests that if the company does not meet its projections, his return on investment will not be high enough to justify his investment. The fair thing to do, he says, would be to increase his equity percentage if the company fails to meets its projections.

At this point, most entrepreneurs get heartburn. They have spent a lot of time with the investor and have become accustomed to thinking of the deal as done. If they refuse this "reasonable" request, they might lose their funding. The temptation to concede is great. But is the request reasonable? Should management concede the investor's request? Usually not.

Most investors know how difficult it is to accurately project results and do not really expect management to concede this issue. After all, the value of management's investment also diminishes if company projections are not met. And one reason the investor is getting so much equity for his money in the first place is because of the risky nature of the investment.

When an investor insists on equity penalties and management has neither the time nor inclination to look for other investors, it should nonetheless try to get the investor to require "extra" equity only if the company does not attain 70% or 80% of projected results. Management should also try to work in a time cushion. If the projections show the company reaching a certain result on January 1, for example, management should try to get until April 1 to reach 80% of the projections.

Finally, management can suggest that if it makes sense for the investor's percentage to increase if the company fails to make its projections, that it also makes sense for his percentage to decrease if the company exceeds them. Investors will often concede the fairness of this proposal and console themselves with their original offer for a fixed percentage of the company. *See: Benchmarks, Business Plan, Earnouts, Earnups, Negotiation, Projections, Vesting Schedules.*

Ethics are critically important in venture capital transactions. The relationship of entrepreneur and venture investor is so intertwined that when one acts unfairly the other almost always suffers. Even when the parties carefully document their agreements, either party can be ruined by the unethical behavior of the other.

Investors recognize the need to deal only with people they can trust and direct a good bit of their due diligence work toward determining whether an entrepreneur is honest and trustworthy. Entrepreneurs should be just as careful to examine their investors' reputations.

An unfair or reluctant investor can cause real problems for a company. If he fails to provide funding or delays or reduces the funding he agreed to provide, he can steal a company's promise and starve it for cash. This cash shortage can delay expansions and product developments. It can cause the collapse of companies that are not yet profitable. At the very least, it distracts management from the day-to-day management of the company and forces it to deal, instead, with the cash crisis created by the investor.

What is more, this same cash crisis often prevents the company from enforcing its contracts against its investor. Even if the company's contracts require the investor to fund, the company may be unable to force the investor to live up to his bargain. This is because the investor's unwillingness to fund takes away the two assets management needs most to force him to do so: money and time. In many cases, the company simply cannot afford to spend its money or time trying to force an unwilling investor to fund. Even if it could, the actions required to do so would be a serious drain on the company and might frighten other investors away. After all, how many investors want to put money into a company that is suing its prior investor?

At the same time, the investor may frustrate management further with new demands that make it difficult for the company to obtain money from other sources. As a result, just when management needs to concentrate its efforts on building its company, it is forced, instead, to find cash and deal with an uncooperative investor who has acquired significant rights in the company. The best way to avoid these problems is to be careful when selecting investors, to investigate their reputations, and to try, when possible, to deal only with people who are trustworthy. *See: Adventure Capitalists, Cash Flow, Due Diligence, Stage Financing, Unlocking Provisions.*

CONNED!

Each day Nikolaus J. Heilman and his partner Robert Clark hoped for the phone call that would put Heilman on a plane from Seattle to Miami and $6 million. Their bankers stood on alert, ready for a loan of what seemed to be Arab money from an account in the Cayman Islands. An air pollution control system was to be only the first of four products for their Island Research & Development Co.

But each day the phone rang with a new snag. Steven Taylor Russell, the money broker from Harlingen, Tex., who was pulling the deal together, explained that the last details were taking longer than expected. Russell had been working hard to close the deal, he reported, flying between Houston and Miami to meet with the lenders' agent. It would take just a little longer: Key people in Miami had gone on vacation. Be patient just a little longer: Russell had injured his finger moving a piano. A new date was set. Another snag, something about documentation. More flying back and forth. Then, in June, 1985, Russell stopped calling, Heilman and Clark say. His secretary got more and more vague about his whereabouts. Russell, they believed, had fled to parts unknown.

According to Heilman and Clark, Russell didn't disappear alone. He took along $7,500 from Heilman and Clark, what Russell had called their nonrefundable share of the cost of clearing the financing. Says Clark: "That $7,500 hurt."

These two entrepreneurs believe they had just been snookered in an advance-fee scheme. The scamster operates on the premise that the lure of millions with the right staging and not-half-bad acting can induce even the shrewdest of business owners to part with modest thousands. The majority of victims, say law enforcement officials, are entrepreneurs who have already been turned away by conventional lenders. The usual sting is several thousand dollars, but one scheme took a group of Louisiana businessmen for $400,000.

The real price to victims includes blown opportunities as well. W. W. Robinson, a Richmond, Va., developer of thin-film technologies for metal surfacing, walked away from $2 million in venture capital to pursue an offer of $8 million. Richard Matherson of Oakland, Calif., figures his misadventure cost him $50 million when he had to delay and scale down his energy project. Donald McMeans of Willingboro, N.J., lost control of a TV station he had founded. Robin Lawrence of La Jolla, Calif., dropped efforts to buy a hotel in Plymouth, Mich. "I got so much egg on my face after working so hard to earn the respect of the owner and the broker," recalls Lawrence. "I felt so empty inside. I just washed my hands of the whole deal."

Telling the cons from the legitimate deals is a hard call even for prosecutors, which explains why so few advance-fee artists are brought to trial. Legitimate brokers routinely charge an up-front fee to cover expenses, and it's often nonrefundable. Who's to say whether the entrepreneur fell victim to a scam, lost his money through an incompetent broker, or simply had a deal fall through?

If one flaw seems to be common among victims, say experienced money raisers, it's not so much gullibility as a lack of knowledge of how to raise money. According to Burt Alimansky, an investment banker and co-founder of the New York Venture Group, unsophisticated entrepreneurs invariably approach all lenders. Heilman and Clark, for example, had concentrated on four commercial banks and a brokerage, not good financing sources for technology-oriented startups. After so many dry wells, these entrepreneurs are then so thrilled by the prospect of financing that they fail to ask two critical questions: Why would this person want to invest in my project, and do I want this person as an investor?

—From an article by E. S. Ely
in the April 1986 issue of *Venture*

Exits are how venture capitalists liquidate their investments and take their profits. The three most common exits are: public offerings of company stock, sales of company stock or assets to a corporation, and liquidity agreements. The exit formula, or how the entrepreneur envisions the investor will eventually liquidate his investment, is a critical section of the business plan. Entrepreneurs must demonstrate that they understand and anticipate the investor's exit. They must be ready to answer the investor when he asks, "How and when do I get out?" The best answer is, "In five years via a public offering or a merger with Beatrice, at five times your original investment." The time period, corporate buyer and multiple can be changed to suit the deal. *See: Business Plan Format, Buy-Sell Agreements, Cashing Out (or In), Co-Sale Agreements, Downside, Going Public, IPOs (Initial Public Offerings), Liquidity Agreements, Puts, Appendix A—A Few Words About Tax Reform.*

F

Factoring is a form of receivables financing. The factor (or lender) pays the company a discounted portion of the company's receivables and then collects those receivables directly from customers as they become due.

Factoring differs in popularity by industry. It is perhaps most widely used in the garment industry, in which orders are shipped well before the season when they are to be sold, but vendors cannot (or do not) pay for the merchandise until it is sold. A factor will buy the invoices from the manufacturer at a discount. The manufacturer receives the factor's money and shows the invoice as paid. The factor collects the full face value of the invoice and accepts the risk of doubtful accounts. *See: Collateral, Inventory Financing, Receivables Financing.*

Financing Agreements are the final contracts that document the outcome of the negotiations between the entrepreneur and the investor. In a typical financing of debt and equity, the financing agreements might consist of a stock purchase agreement, a registration rights agreement, a shareholders' agreement, a loan agreement, a note or debenture, and the stock certificates issued to the investor.

Financing agreements are usually long and involved. Their provisions identify the amount of funding and the conditions under which funds are released. They spell out the types of securities the investor receives and any special shareholder rights he has negotiated for. Financing agreements also contain provisions that govern the ongoing relationship of the investor and management. Many contain penalties if the company's results do not meet expectations.

Because of their breadth and the far-reaching effects their provisions can have on a company and its continued viability, financing agreements should be reviewed carefully. Each provision should be considered for its long-term impact as well as its short-term benefits. A convenant that seems appropriate today may haunt an entrepreneur in three years if he does not consider its long-term effects. *See: Boilerplate, Closing, Convertible Securities, Debentures, Investment Reps, K.I.S.S., Lawyers, Letters of Intent, Management Agreements, Promissory Notes, Negotiation, Registration Rights, Reps and Warranties, Shareholders' Agreements, Structure.*

First Refusal Rights are agreements, usually in writing, that give an investor the opportunity but not the obligation to participate in future company financings. Except when they are granted to avoid giving an investor another, more onerous right, first refusal rights should generally be avoided. They do not guarantee a company any funding and often make it more difficult to find new investors.

As a practical matter, however, many venture investors insist on some sort of first refusal right as a condition to their investing. Some use first refusal rights like options to secure the opportunity to purchase more shares in the future. Some use them for antidilution protection. The first refusal rights enable them to retain and increase their ownership in a company by purchasing shares at then current rates. Others use them to exercise control over who the company's other investors will be.

First refusal rights are usually structured in one of two ways. One variation allows the company to negotiate with others for needed capital, but only if it gives the first investor a right of "first refusal" to provide the desired financing on the same terms management negotiates with its other investor. Under this variation, management can discuss but cannot close a funding with another investor until the first investor declines to take the deal. The other type of first refusal right requires the company to present the first investor with the opportunity to invest on terms suggested by the company. If the first investor does not make the investment, the company is then free to negotiate with others to provide the funding on terms no more favorable to the new investor than those presented to the first investor.

Both variations impair a company's ability to raise money. The first form can make it very difficult because most potential investors are reluctant to negotiate with managements when they know the deal they make can be taken away from them by another investor. In fact, many investors will not even talk with a company's management unless it has the ability to close the deal it is offering.

The second variation also chills a company's ability to obtain financing because it requires the company to construct an investment proposal for the first investor before it has had an opportunity to shop around to see what the best available deal is. It requires the company to begin looking for money earlier because the first investor must be given time to evaluate the investment proposal. If the first investor declines to make the requested investment, the company is still restricted in how much equity it can sell to obtain the money needed.

In general, rights of first refusal should be avoided and investors should be comforted, when possible, with company exhortations of loyalty and the reality that money is hard to find. If the right of first refusal is insisted upon, the second form of right of first refusal is generally preferable, because under that scenario, once the company has presented its investment proposal to the first investor, it is free to go and negotiate with others. Unlike the first variation, the company will be able to tell those other investors that it can close the deal it is negotiating.

Sometimes an investor will accept the addition of a twist to the second type of first refusal right that makes it more palatable to management. This requires the first investor who rejects the company's offer to either make a binding offer of his own to fund the company or release it completely from the right of first refusal. If the investor waives the first refusal right, the company is free to negotiate with others. Even if the investor does not waive his refusal rights, the company can proceed to try to negotiate a better deal with outside investors. If it cannot make a better deal, it can still accept the first investor's offer. *See: Antidilution Provisions, Buy-Sell Agreements, Co-Sale Agreements, Options, Warrants.*

Five Factors refer to criteria venture capitalists use when evaluating a company. Knowing something about these criteria can improve an entrepreneur's odds of getting funded by helping him focus his business plan on the factors that matter most to investors.

Stanley E. Pratt, publisher of the *Venture Capital Journal* and noted venture capital authority, identifies five principal factors venture capitalists look for in a company. Those factors are: management, management, management, market niche, and product or service.

Mr. Pratt recommends this list to make a point. Many entrepreneurs overemphasize their product or service when making a presentation to an investor. They fail to realize that investors tend to be more interested in a company's ability to build a business than they are in its particular product. Most experienced venture investors have seen plenty of good, even spectacular, product ideas fail. At the same time, most investors have seen companies succeed in ways they did not anticipate when funding was solicited. It is the management team, therefore, that many investors consider to be the single most important ingredient for a successful company.

Venture capitalist Frederick R. Adler, who is managing partner of Adler and Company, a firm that manages several venture funds, identifies five different factors his company uses when investigating a company. The potential for large long-term profits is the first factor. To fulfill the requirement a company must be able to forecast significant, profitable growth over an extended period of time.

The second criterion relates to whether the company has the right technology at the right time. A product that is too revolutionary or not revolutionary enough might not qualify. Technology that is easily replicated would fail too, especially if large competitors exist with superior channels of distribution. The third criterion is potential for high profits. High profits improve cash flow and make it easier for companies to grow. Companies in markets that are intensely price-competitive might not qualify under this criterion unless their products can be produced for significantly less than their competitors'. This criterion can be hard to meet when a market does not already exist for the company's product. When this is the case, investors cannot be certain of profit margins or even of the company's ability to build a profitable market.

Management is the fourth criterion. All investors look for companies with complete and well-rounded management teams. Investors like managers who are not only competent, but who are flexible and open-minded. The characteristics Adler and any looks for when evaluating a manager are: judgment, essiveness, sincerity, experience, and charisma. The fifth, d last, factor considered is what value added the investor can bring to the company. Money is important, but the investment potential of a company is enhanced if the investor can offer the company something more in the way of experience or contacts. *See: Business Plan, Business Plan Format, Commitment, Entrepreneur, Management Team, Value Added, Windows.*

VENTURE CAPITALISTS BET ON MANAGEMENT FIRST, PRODUCT LATER

A new survey of the investment criteria used by 100 professional venture capital firms revealed that the entrepreneurs' "capability for sustained intense effort" was the most important of the 24 factors listed in the survey questionnaire. The survey, conducted by New York University's Center for Entrepreneurial Studies, asked 100 venture capital firms to rank on a scale of 1 to 4 the factors they considered before investing in venture proposals. Ranking just after "capability for sustained intense effort" was "thorough familiarity with the market targeted by the venture" and "demonstrated leadership ability in the past." At the bottom of the ranking were "the venture will create a new market" and "I will not participate in later rounds of investment."

Here is a list of the 10 criteria most frequently rated essential by the survey respondents:

Item	*Percent*
Capable of sustained intense effort	64
Thoroughly familiar with market	62
At least ten times return in 5 to 10 yrs	50
Demonstrated leadership in the past	50
Evaluates and reacts to risk well	48
Investment can be made liquid	44
Significant market growth	43
Track record relevant to venture	37
Articulates venture well	31
Proprietary protection	29

The failure to satisfy these criteria in most cases means the venture is "disqualified" for investment.

The study did contain some surprising findings. For example, the entrepreneur's personal compatibility with the investor was not cited as a major consideration for investment. Also, the respondents said familiarity with the entrepreneur's reputation was irrelevant.

—From an article in the July 1985 issue of *Venture's Capital Club Monthly*

Franchising refers to a form of licensing that businesses use to expand their bases of business and generate revenue. It is generally characterized by the license from a franchisor to a franchisee of a trademark and system of doing business. In return for the license, the franchisee pays the franchisor an up-front fee, which is often substantial, and agrees to pay the franchisor a percentage of sales or some other royalty in the future.

For the right kind of business, franchising can reduce the need for venture capital by enabling the franchisor to obtain capital from its franchisees. In most franchising arrangements, the cost of expanding to a new unit is borne by the franchisee. The franchisor advises the franchisee in the best methods of establishing his unit of the business and charges him a fee to cover the cost of providing that advice and to make a profit. After the business begins operating, the franchisee pays the franchisor a percentage of sales or other agreed-upon royalty.

Franchising does not usually replace the need for outside equity. Capital is almost always needed to develop the franchise system and protect the trademark. In many cases, franchising is pursued only after the company has owned and operated a few successful units of its business itself. This operation takes time and usually requires considerable capital to fund. Traditional venture capital sources are receptive to funding businesses that plan to grow through franchising.

Establishing a franchise program requires the preparation of an extensive franchise disclosure document, which provides information about the franchisor and the franchise program. Careful compliance with both federal and state franchise and business opportunity laws is a must. Failure to comply with all of the requirements can result in significant liability to a company and its managers. *See: Licensing, Trademarks.*

G

Geography refers to a simple fact: Companies that are conveniently located to their market and to an investor's headquarters are more likely to get funded than those that are not.

Venture capital funds invest more than money in companies —they invest time and expertise as well. They invest their time in monitoring a company's progress and in providing it with the benefit of their experience with growing companies. An investor's experience and business contacts can be valuable to a company. As a consequence, venture firms operate most efficiently when the companies they invest in are located relatively close to their headquarters. The next best case for a venture investor is to have his investments located in clusters that allow him to monitor several investments on one trip. (One venture capital investor we know of invested only in cities from which a round trip could be completed in one day.)

When selecting venture capital firms to approach, geography suggests that a company should stay as close to home as possible. When approaching a fund located a long distance away, management should be sensitive to the fact that the venture investor may want to make a joint investment with a local fund or one that has a portfolio of investments near the company's headquarters. Companies located away from suppliers and customers should be careful to describe to investors how they plan to overcome the inconveniences this causes. The business plan is the best way to address these problems and their solutions. *See: Networking, Syndications, Value Added. But see also: Shopping, Specialty Funds.*

Going Public refers to a company's first sale of its securities (usually common stock) to the general population of equity investors. It is accomplished by registering those securities with the federal Securities and Exchange Commission and state securities commissions and then selling them to the general public. The sale itself is usually conducted by a professional underwriter. Going public is a goal of many companies that seek venture capital. It enables them to raise money from the public and creates a market for subsequent sales of their stock. It also creates an easily ascertainable market value for shares.

Many entrepreneurs think longingly about going public. They see it as a confirmation of the success they have worked long and hard to attain. They believe that the money and other benefits generated by a public offering are worth the effort and expense required to complete it.

But going public is not always the right decision and does not always indicate success. Seeking funds from private investors or from traditional lending sources may make more sense.

Determining whether going public makes sense requires consideration of a number of factors including timing, company history, prospects for future growth of the company and the industry, and management's personality. The advantages and disadvantages of going public should be weighed carefully before a decision is made to seek funds in the public markets. Among the advantages management should consider are:

Lower cost of capital
Capital for continued growth
Increased shareholder liquidity
Future financings
Enhanced ability to expand
Improved company image

Lower cost of capital. Going public is often triggered by management's belief that it can raise more money and get a better price for its stock by selling to the public than to a venture capitalist or other private investor. When this is true, a public offering can raise money at less cost and with less dilution of management's shareholdings.

Going public becomes cost effective for most companies when they finally meet the profile required to attract institutional investors to the offering. While this profile varies according to market conditions, it generally requires sustained growth and profitability over a significant period of time, a company valuation of at least $10 million, prospects for continued growth at a rate greater than the industry average, and an offering of at least one hundred thousand shares at prices of $10 or more. When a company matures to the point of meeting this profile, its ability to attract institutional investors often boosts the price of its stock high enough to make going public the most economical way to raise capital.

Capital for continued growth. Perhaps the most obvious benefit of going public is the proceeds (cash) of the offering. These moneys can be used for a variety of company purposes as long as they are disclosed in the company's offering documents. Typical uses are: to increase working capital, to acquire new divisions or technologies, to increase marketing efforts, to pay for research or plant modernization, or to repay debt.

Increased shareholder liquidity. Going public makes it easier for company shareholders to sell their shares by creating a public market for the company's stock. Shareholders who register their shares in the company's offering hold freely tradeable shares once the offering is completed. Even the shares which are not registered in the offering become more liquid. Because of the offering and the periodic reporting requirements it imposes on the company, they often qualify after a prescribed period of time to sell limited numbers of their shares under Rule 144. If they want to sell more shares than Rule 144 permits, they can benefit from easier and less expensive methods available for registering their shares that are available to public companies. (*See: Restricted Securities.*)

Future financings. Most public offerings raise a significant amount of equity capital and thus dramatically improve the company's net worth and debt-to-equity ratio. This, in turn, makes it easier for a company to borrow money from commercial lenders at competitive interest rates. Also, an existing public market for the company's stock makes it easier for the company to sell additional equity. If the company's stock does well (that is, increases in price), the company can offer for sale additional shares of stock or a new class of stock.

Enhanced ability to expand. The market created by going public makes it easier for a company to expand through acquisitions and mergers. Because registered shares can be converted into cash, a public company can often use its stock instead of cash to acquire a company or other valuable property. With the proper deal structure, the use of shares instead of cash can ease the immediate tax burden of the seller caused by the sale of his company and, thereby, make the acquisition easier and less expensive to close. Liquid stock also makes a company's stock and option plans more valuable and, thereby, makes it easier for a company to attract and retain the key employees it needs to help it grow.

Improved company image. Going public, with all the financial disclosure and investor relations planning it requires, usually attracts the attention of the business and financial press. Free publicity, coupled with the perception that going public is a significant milestone of success, enhances a company's image.

This improved image can make it easier for management to deal with suppliers and customers. Many privately held companies that compete with public ones find their customers and suppliers reluctant to deal with them on equal terms because of their lack of operating history and the confidentiality of their financial data. Going public can erase this distinction and make it possible for the company to compete more effectively.

The advantages of going public can be substantial, but they can be outweighed by the disadvantages. It depends on management's goals and the circumstances of the company. Among the disadvantages that should always be considered are:

Expense
Loss of confidentiality
Periodic reporting
Reduced control
Shareholder pressures
Restrictions on stock sales

Expense. Going public is expensive. The underwriter's discounts alone can amount to as much as 6 to 10 percent of the total proceeds of the offering. (In a $5 million offering, this can be as much as $500,000.) Other expenses, which include the underwriter's out-of-pocket expenses (typically not included in the underwriter's discount), filing fees, transfer agent fees, legal fees, printing fees, and accounting fees, can add another $150,000 to $350,000 to a company's cost of going public. Most of these expenses must be paid at the closing of the offering.

Going public also subjects a company to annual and quarterly financial reporting requirements imposed by the Securities and

Exchange Commission. Complying with these requirements increases the company's costs of doing business. Time and money are required to generate the information necessary for these reports.

Loss of confidentiality. Going public forces a company to prepare and distribute to potential investors a complete description of the company, its history, its strengths, its weaknesses, and its future plans. *Detailed* disclosures of financial information are required. Information about the shareholdings and compensation arrangements of management and holders of large blocks is made public. All of this information must be updated and supplemented in reports required by the Securities and Exchange Commission. Once information is filed, it can be obtained by competitors, employees, customers, suppliers, union organizers and others.

Periodic reporting. Going public subjects a company to a number of periodic reporting requirements with the Securities and Exchange Commission. These requirements include annual and quarterly financial reports (on forms 10-K and 10Q) as well as prompt reporting of material events that affect the company (on form 8-K). For most companies, these and other reporting requirements, which force the company to maintain audited financial statements, increase the company's cost of doing business by imposing more stringent accounting practices and by making additional demands on management's time.

Reduced control. A public offering can reduce management's control over a company if outsiders obtain enough stock to elect a majority of the company's board of directors. Whenever this is true, outside shareholders can remove members of the management team. (This is not a risk inherent only in public offerings, however. Any sale of voting stock to raise money reduces the percentage ownership of management. Sales of a majority of the company's voting stock to a few private investors, in fact, may make management's ability to retain control less certain than a public offering, which distributes those same shares to a greater number of investors. The larger number of shareholders in a publicly held company can make concerted action by the outsiders more difficult.) Public companies are more susceptible to unfriendly takeover because their shares are easy to accumulate.

Shareholder pressures. Even managements that retain voting control over their companies find that going public subjects them to pressures that can affect the way they run their businesses. Many entrepreneurs find that shareholder expectations and the quarterly reporting requirements of the Securities and Exchange Commission combine to create significant pressures on a company to continually improve its performance on a quarter by quarter basis. Failure to meet these shareholder expectations can cause the market value of the company's stock to decline, making it more expensive for the company to raise money or acquire other companies using its stock. This pressure to meet short-term goals can tempt management to forgo necessary long-term planning when it includes present-day sacrifices that will be reflected in the company's quarterly reports.

Restrictions of stock sales. Only those shares registered and sold in the offering become freely tradeable. Nonregistered shares remain subject to the same trading restrictions as they were before the offering. Moreover, the Securities and Exchange Commission imposes additional restrictions on the ability of major shareholders and company insiders to sell company stock.

The factors that should be considered when contemplating a first public offering are numerous and complex: This discussion does not cover them all. Entrepreneurs should consult with their accountants, attorneys, investment bankers, and other advisers before taking their companies public. *See: Control, Investment Bankers, IPOs (Initial Public Offerings), Penny Stock, Private Placements, Public Offering, Restricted Securities, Unit Offerings, Appendix A—A Few Words About Tax Reform.*

THE COST OF GOING PUBLIC

Going public has its price, at least from the point of view of the security issuer—the company. With information supplied by *New Issues*, a Ft. Lauderdale, Fla., newsletter, and Securities Data Co., New York, *Venture* collected and examined the prospectuses of every new issue in 1985. We discovered that total expenses—including all fees paid to underwriters, attorneys, accountants, and printers—can range from as little as 6.4% of the offering, as in the case of Alco Health Services Corp., Valley Forge, Pa., which raised $75.2 million, to as much as 41.4%, as Intercell Corp., Cortez, Colo., did to raise only $255,000. Our survey did not attempt to assess share performance after an IPO, the primary concern of investors.

Just what entrepreneurs pay to go public is determined by their industry group, the size of the offering, the underwriter that supports them, the quality of their company, and general market conditions. Businesses with a high degree of risk and not much of a track record—including blind pools, which are investment vehicles, not operating companies—may never find a welcome at the top underwriters for their IPOs or hope for a share price above a few dollars and a total offering exceeding $5 million. Such companies shell out at least 10% to 15% of their proceeds, a portion of their total expenses, to their underwriting troup. By contrast, older companies with solid operating histories and good prospects for growth can easily sign on with national underwriters, for whose services they pay only 5% to 8% of their total offering.

How are the costs apportioned? In firm commitment deals, a part of the proceeds goes to the managing underwriter and the syndicate of other brokerages that sign up to sell a portion of an IPO. Whereas the underwriting group must purchase a stipulated number of shares at a discount to the offering price, the selling group has no such obligation. Its compensation is a discount on the shares it sold. Known as the gross spread, this portion of the expenses includes management and underwriting fees and selling concessions—discounts at which shares are allocated to the underwriting group, including individual salespeople—and can range from 5% to 15% of the total offering.

Other costs of going public are printing and engraving expenses (some $155,000) for preliminary and final prospectuses and legal and filing fees ($50,000 to $350,000), which may include blue-sky registration of the offering in those states where the securities will be sold. Accounting fees run $25,000 to $200,000, depending on the complexity of the audit.

But less obvious costs lurk in many smaller deals. Some underwriters charge a nonaccountable expense allowance—compensation for, say, office and administrative outlays—that ranges from 1% to 4% of the total proceeds. Once in a while, firms affix investment banking consulting fees of $24,000 to $48,000 for "general financial matters." Underwriters often pick up more of a company's stock at a discount to the market price by taking warrants.

Even among similar companies the dollar cost of going public varies tremendously. While quality companies can usually find major investment banking firms that charge comparatively lower fees for taking them public, less proven companies end up with small underwriters that cost more on a percentage basis. Consider the quite different fates of two specialty ice-cream makers, Ben & Jerry's Homemade Inc. and American Foodworks Inc.

Ben & Jerry's smacked of quality: The eight-year-old Waterbury, Vt., firm earned $408,500 on revenues of $6.1 million for the 12 months ended June 30, 1985. Both its quality and its high profile drew the interest of Tucker, Anthony & R. L. Day Inc., a New York underwriter, which priced the deal at $13 a share to raise $6.5 million for 29.3% of the company. Ben & Jerry's paid $769,343, or 11.8% for its proceeds, $520,000 (8%) as a gross spread and $249,343 (3.8%) for other expenses.

J. Brooks Securities Inc. (now Brooks Weinger Robbins & Leeds Inc.), New York . . . offered American Foodworks a best-efforts unit deal. It consisted of one share and one warrant, priced at 1¢ a unit to raise $650,000. In addition to $90,000 (13.8%) in legal, accounting, and printing costs and $65,000 (10%) in underwriting fees, American Foodworks paid Brooks $26,000 (4%) in a nonaccountable expense allowance.

Although it's more expensive as a percentage to raise smaller amounts of money, there's another way of looking at costs—in real dollars. Ben & Jerry's gave up a total of only 11.8%, but that amounted to $769,343. American Foodworks parted with almost 28% of its offering to go public. In actual dollars that came to $181,000. Says Laurence M. Teicher, chairman and president: "It was a fair deal. We considered private financing, but the cost would've been even higher."

—From an article by David P. Sutton and Tom Post in the April 1986 issue of *Venture*

Golden Handcuffs refers to the combination of rewards and penalties given to key company employees that compensates them so generously for staying and punishes them so severely for leaving that it would be absurd for them to quit the company.

There are two ways to keep valuable people with a company. One is to reward them if they stay. The other is to penalize them if they leave. Many companies combine both approaches by mixing generous economic incentives with noncompete agreements and vesting schedules. If the combination of these incentives and disincentives is effective, they can act as golden handcuffs that prevent the employee from leaving. They do so by raising the employee's expectations of wealth so high that he cannot meet those expectations with another employer, particularly when he considers the restrictions and penalties caused by his leaving. *See: Compensation and Bonus Plans, Employment Contracts, Incentive Stock Options (ISOs), Noncompete Agreements, Phantom Stock Plans, Vesting Agreements.*

Golden Rule differs from the one taught in the Bible. In venture capital, the golden rule is "he who has the gold makes the rules." Many venture capitalists live by this axiom. Since they are providing the cash, they expect to lay down the terms of the financial deal. *See: Deal, Deal Flow, Leverage, Negotiation, Structure, We Always Do It This Way.*

H

High Tech is a glamorous phrase used to describe any endeavor that involves the application of sophisticated technology. Many people think of venture capitalists as people who fund high-tech companies. The fact is, however, that most venture investors are more interested in return on investment than in the glamour of sophisticated technology. Many do invest in high-tech companies, but only when they are also emerging growth companies that promise rapid growth and a healthy return to the investor. *See: Emerging Growth Companies.*

I

IDBs (Industrial Development Bonds) are tax-free bonds issued by a government or designated authority for the purpose of assisting a company in raising funds to finance a physical plant construction or improvement within the geographic jurisdiction of the authority.

A company must meet certain qualifications to use an IDB. The government or authority issues and sells the bonds (often to a cooperating financial institution) and then lends the proceeds to the company. As a rule, IDB financing is relatively inexpensive because of the low financing rate made possible by the tax-free nature of the bonds.

Since holders of the bonds do not pay federal (or, in some cases, state) taxes on the interest, the amount of interest needed to sell the bonds is less then a corresponding taxable bond. For example, if similar taxable bonds carry an interest premium of 15 percent, a tax-free IDB may carry an interest premium of only 10 percent. The cost to the company of borrowing money through taxable bonds is 15 percent while the cost to the company using an IDB is only 10 percent.

IDBs appear to be on their way out. While Congress has vacillated on the question of IDBs in the past, current laws restrict IDBs to manufacturing facilities and schedule their extinction for December 31, 1989. What's more, recent tax reform changes have made IDBs less attractive to institutional purchasers and more difficult to sell in the public market. *See: Debentures.*

Incentive Stock Options (ISOs) are rights to purchase company securities, usually common stock, which are issued to company employees and others the company wants to attract or keep involved. ISOs accomplish this by giving the holder the right to purchase company shares in the future at present-day prices. If the company is successful, theoretically in part because of the efforts of the option holder, and its stock increases in value, the option holder can purchase shares of company stock in the future at a price far below the then fair market value of the shares. By creating this potential "windfall," the incentive stock option motivates the holder to work hard to make the company succeed.

Usually, ISOs are issued pursuant to guidelines adopted by the company's board of directors. These guidelines are commonly referred to as plans.

Federal tax laws recognize two types of ISO plans: qualified stock option plans and nonqualified stock option plans. Preferential tax treatment is given to the holders of options issued under qualified plans. The preference is that there is no realization of income for federal income tax purposes when the option is issued by the company or exercised by the holder. Holders of nonqualified stock options realize income, at ordinary income tax rates, when they exercise their options if the fair market value of the shares purchased exceeds the price they paid for the shares under their option. Depending on the holder's tax bracket and amount of the difference between what the holder paid for the stock and what its fair market value was when purchased, the holder's tax liability could be substantial.

By contrast, qualified stock option holders realize no gain upon the exercise of their options and, consequently, incur no federal tax obligation until they later sell their stock at a profit. No income is realized when the option is issued or exercised. When the stock is later sold, the gain realized is taxed at capital gains rates.*

Obtaining the benefits of qualification with the IRS requires careful planning and close attention to detail. Qualified stock options may be issued only pursuant to a plan that meets the requirements set out by the Internal Revenue Service. These in-

* The 1986 Tax Reform Act increased long-term capital gains rates up to the level of ordinary income rates. We make the distinction here because capital gains rates have changed frequently in the past. If those rates are reduced in the future (they have historically been lower than ordinary income rates) the difference between paying taxes at ordinary income rates when a nonqualified option is exercised and being able to defer those taxes on a qualified option until the stock is sold and then only pay lower capital gains rates will make qualified options even more attractive.

clude having the plan approved by the company's shareholders within twelve months after it is adopted by the company's board of directors. Qualified plans must also identify the types of employees who may receive options and the total number of shares that may be subject to options issued under the plan. Each option may have a term of no more than ten years and must be issued within ten years after the date the plan is adopted. Options may be issued only to employees. Except in certain limited circumstances, employees must exercise their options while they are employed by the company or within three months thereafter.

Further, qualified options may not be transferred except on death and their exercise price must be at least as great as the fair market value of the underlying stock at the time the option is issued. For any employee who holds 10 percent or more of the company's stock, the exercise price must be at least 110 percent of the fair market value of the company's stock when the option is issued, and the option term cannot exceed five years. The total fair market value of stock subject to qualified options that can vest in one employee in one year cannot exceed $100,000. If less than the total $100,000 in value is not used in a given year, however, a portion of the unused part may be exercised in later years.

Plan administrators (usually management) must be careful whenever they accept a note in lieu of cash payment when a qualified option is exercised. The note must be a full-recourse note and must bear interest at least equal to minimum rates established by the IRS. If it does not, the IRS-imputed interest rules will apply. This will require the employee to pay tax on the imputed interest and may, because imputed interest is not included in the option exercise price, cause the latter to fall below fair market value. If it does, the option will not be treated as qualified.

Any incentive stock option plan that does not meet all of the requirements of a qualified stock plan is treated by the IRS as nonqualified. This means the employee will not receive the tax advantages of holding qualified options. However, they also will not be subject to the $100,000 value limitation or to the requirement that they be employees. Nor must the term of their options be tied to employment. And, below-market interest rate loans used to exercise options will not have a disqualifying effect. If the employee is sufficiently wealthy to pay the taxes, or if the term of the option is long enough to permit him to exercise the option after the company's and his stock becomes tradeable in the public market, the nonqualified stock option may still create a viable incentive for the employee.

Nonqualified options issued to employees also entitle the issuing company to take as a deduction against its income tax obligation an amount equal to the compensation income attributed to the employee upon the exercise of the option. The amount of this deduction is the same as the amount of income attributed and taxed to the option holder upon exercise of the option, the difference between the option exercise price and the fair market value of the shares purchased. In order to obtain the deduction, however, the company must be sure to withhold the proper amount from the employee's income. This can usually be done by withholding cash or stock.

The use of options to create incentives for employees must be carefully considered so that the use of qualified or nonqualified options can be tailored to fit the employee's and the company's needs. Qualified stock options can be used to advantage in most situations and can benefit the employee by giving him the opportunity to share in the future appreciation of the company's stock without adverse tax consequences. To qualify the options the employee receives, however, the company and its management must be careful to structure the option plan to meet all of the IRS's requirements. This usually means engaging a qualified professional to establish and administer the plan.

Also, certain individuals, particularly those who are attempting to shelter income from federal taxation, must be careful to consider the alternative minimum tax (AMT) consequences of obtaining rights under a qualified plan. The difference between the holder's exercise price for the shares in a qualified plan and the fair market value of those shares when he exercises the option is a tax preference item that may become subject to the 21 percent alternative minimum tax. The application of the AMT rules can make qualified options less attractive to these individuals. Those persons with AMT concerns should consult their tax adviser before accepting qualified stock options. *See: Board Committees, Compensation and Bonus Plans, Golden Handcuffs, Junior Common Stock, Options, Phantom Stock Plans, Warrants, Appendix A—A Few Words About Tax Reform*

Incubators refer to centers that assist entrepreneurs in getting businesses started. They are called incubators because they are designed to help an entrepreneur hatch his idea into a thriving business. Unlike technology development centers, incubators do not restrict their assistance to companies that utilize advance technology. They accept high-tech, low-tech, and no-tech companies as participants.

There are a number of incubators throughout the country that offer entrepreneurs a variety of services. There are privately run incubators and incubators that are associated with universities, government agencies, and regional development authorities. The services they provide include inexpensive facilities; free or reduced-cost consulting services from accountants, lawyers, or business consultants; assistance in obtaining government grants and identifying sources of capital; and assistance in marketing and public relations. Entrepreneurs can identify incubators in their locale by contacting their local chamber of commerce, reading local business publications, or by inquiring of their accountant, banker, or lawyer.

Entrepreneurs should take care to evaluate a center before joining one. The number, quality, and costs of services provided vary from center to center. It is appropriate, when considering an incubator, to meet with and question the center's director about the services available and the qualifications of the persons providing them. It is also helpful to speak with entrepreneurs who are working with the incubator and (even more helpful) those who have left it.

Incubators can provide valuable services, but beware of "incubator syndrome." The services incubators provide can sometimes sound so good and complete that they lull unprepared businessmen into making the entrepreneurial jump too soon or into relying too much on the center. Joining an incubator is no substitute for entrepreneurial initiative, training, or self-evaluation. Entrepreneurs must remember when joining a center that their personal efforts and resourcefulness are the key to making their business succeed. An entrepreneur with incubator syndrome permits his initiative and judgment to be replaced by those of the consultants who provide assistance at the center. Even if those consultants are superbly skilled and dedicated, they cannot replace the entrepreneur or make his business succeed. Incubator syndrome can be deadly to a new business. *See: Commitment, Entrepreneur, Technology Development Centers.*

U.S. INCUBATORS PROLIFERATE

Business incubators—potent economic development tools that nurture fledging firms into small businesses—are being introduced across the country.

Small business incubators are facilities that support new and small firms by providing affordable space, shared office services and management assistance.

Business incubators organized to nurture such enterprises bring under a single roof a number of new and emerging businesses. The period spent in the incubator gives entrepreneurs time to develop management skills which are essential for the successful transition of a start-up to an ongoing, viable small business. The experience, skills, business contacts and access to capital gained while a tenant resides in an incubator helps a firm avert the failure that befalls the vast majority of small businesses within their first few years.

Private incubators run by venture and seed capital investment groups, or by large corporations and real estate development partnerships, usually are concerned with high economic reward for investment in tenant firms and added value through development of commercial and industrial real estate. Such private groups also generally are concerned with new technology applications and other technology transfer.

A third category of incubator operators include universities, which share some of the same concerns as public and private operators. Universities also are concerned with faculty research in connection with incubators, faculty consulting and, for some universities, the opportunity to invest in incubator firms.

Additional information on incubators across the country is available from the National Business Incubation Association. Contact Carlos Morales, Executive Director, National Business Incubation Association, 6914 Andover Drive, Alexandria, Virginia 22307 (703) 765–0927.

—From an article in the December 1985 issue of *Venture's Capital Club Monthly*

Integration refers to the combining of two or more securities offerings under the rules of the federal Securities and Exchange

Commission. When it occurs, it can cause serious securities problems for an issuing company and its management.

This is because the federal securities rules treat the combined offerings as one and require that all of the securities sold in both offerings be registered for sale to the public or qualify under a single exemption from registration. If a company conducts two or more offerings (i.e., closes two venture fundings), they may be integrated if they are not sufficiently distinct and separate in the eyes of the SEC. This integration can void the exemptions from registration that were relied upon by the company even though it intended for the offerings to be distinct and separate. If the exemptions are voided, the company and management may become subject to significant liability.

Potential integrations of previous offerings with a company's present efforts to raise capital can also delay its ability to raise money without a public offering. Because of this, it is important to determine what constitutes an offering whenever securities are sold.

Factors that the Securities and Exchange Commission considers when determining whether two or more offerings will be integrated into one include:

- whether they are part of a single plan of financing
- whether they involve the issuance of the same class of security
- whether they are made at or about the same time
- whether the same type of consideration is received for the security
- whether the offerings are made for the same general purpose

There are certain "safe harbors" that can be relied upon to avoid integration if the issuing company is careful to comply with their requirements. These safe harbors should be taken advantage of whenever possible. If the requirements are met, they can prevent integrations and the liabilities they create. In any event, experienced legal counsel should be retained whenever company securities are sold. It can guide the company safely through the many peculiarities (including avoiding integration) contained in the complex federal and state securities laws. *See: Private Placements, Reg D, Restricted Securities, Safe Harbors, SEC (Securities and Exchange Commission), 33 Act.*

Inventory Financing refers to loans that are collateralized by a company's product before the product is sold; that is, while it is still in inventory. It is often contrasted with receivables financing or factoring, when the company's accounts receivables are used to obtain funding. *See: Factoring, Receivables Financing.*

Investment Bankers are financial institutions and individuals who assist companies in raising capital, often through a private placement or public offering of company stock.

Sometimes companies use investment bankers to help identify available financing options or obtain introductions to venture capitalists. Because their business is raising money for companies, investment bankers can help a company analyze its funding needs and identify the most likely or appropriate types of sources for obtaining the money. This is not to say, however, that an investment banker can always sell a company's business plan to a given investor. If they are experienced with the stage of financing a company needs, they can often be helpful in packaging and introducing a business plan or offering circular. If they do not do a regular business in the stage of financing being sought, they are less likely to help significantly.

Many venture capitalists believe investment bankers are unnecessary, even disruptive, to a venture funding. They prefer, instead, to deal with an entrepreneur without the intercession of an investment banker. Many entrepreneurs share this view and look to investment bankers only when they prepare to take their companies public. Then, an investment banker's ability to underwrite (or sell) the company's stock can make its services indispensable. Choosing the best investment banker to underwrite a company's initial public offering is an important part of conducting a successful public offering. *See: Going Public, IPOs (Initial Public Offerings), Stage Financing, Underwriters.*

Investment Memorandums are letters that commit an investor to acquire company securities and describe the terms of the purchase. People often use the phrases *letters of intent, commitment letters,* and *investment memorandums* interchangeably to refer to short letters of understanding that precede formal financing documentation. *See: Commitment Letters, Letters of Intent.*

Investment Reps are written representations (reps) of the conditions under which an investor has purchased company securities. They customarily appear in financing agreements or in separate "subscription agreements."

Investment reps help complete a funding quickly and cheaply. They do so by giving management the information it needs to obtain an exemption from the time-consuming and expensive registration requirements of the federal and state securities laws. Investment reps should always be required when restricted securities are sold. Used in connection with a proper exemption from registration under applicable securities laws, these representations can help protect a company and management from serious securities liabilities. Some common investment reps acknowledge that the investor:

- has purchased the company's shares for investment only and not with a view of reselling them
- has made such independent investigation of the company as he has deemed necessary or advisable
- has been given free access to company information
- is sufficiently sophisticated about investments to judge the merits of investing in the company or has hired someone who is so sophisticated
- meets certain minimum wealth standards
- will not sell the shares purchased without first complying with applicable securities laws in a manner acceptable to company counsel.

See: Blue Sky Laws, Investors, Legend Stock, Private Placements, Reg D, Restricted Securities, 33 Act.

Investors are those individuals and firms who supply money to a company in return for the prospect of capital appreciation. Federal and state securities laws restrict the number and type of investors a company can sell its securities to without conducting an expensive and time-consuming registered public offering. Unless the number and nature of the investors qualify the company for an exemption, the company's securities cannot be sold without a registration.

The exemptions most commonly used when a venture capitalist is the investor rely on the venture capitalist qualifying as an "accredited investor" under the securities acts. These "accredited investors" are persons or entities that the statutes recognize as having sufficient wealth, sophistication (or access to sophisticated advice), and access to company information to fend for themselves when examining and investing in a privately held company.

Often, sales to these investors can be made without having to prepare an elaborate private offering circular. By contrast, most of the exemptions that permit private companies to sell their securities to investors who are not accredited require the preparation of an offering circular and close attention to the number of investors solicited, their states of residence, and various state "blue sky" limitations on the number of investors who may reside in each state.

Whoever the investors are, company management should be careful to conduct its stock offering to investors in a manner that complies with all the rules of an exemption from the registration requirements of the federal and state securities laws. Overlooking a single detail can create significant liability for the issuing company and its management.

Whenever an exemption requires a company's investors to qualify as accredited, management should investigate the credentials of the investors to determine whether they meet all of the requirements. The financing agreements should also contain representations from the investors that they are accredited, that they have had adequate access to the company and its management, and that they are capable of bearing the loss should the investment fail.

Elsewhere in this book, we have discussed the value of dealing with good investors, and the negative consequences of dealing with poor ones. Being accredited does not mean an investor is good or ethical. It means simply that he has sufficient wealth and sophistication to fend for himself. Generally, he is someone who has enough other investments that losing his money on one deal will not break him. It is not true, from an entrepreneur's point of view, that money from anyone is better than no money at all. Entrepreneurs should be careful whom they allow to buy a piece of their company! *See: Blue Sky Laws, Ethics, Investment Reps, Private Placements, Reg D, 33 Act.*

IPOs (Initial Public Offerings) refer to the first registered offering of company securities to the general population of equity investors. They are registered with the Securities and Exchange Commission and with the securities commissions of the states in which the company's securities will be offered and sold. The registration of an IPO requires the preparation of a detailed offering memorandum (usually on SEC Form S-1) which contains an extensive description of the company, its reasons for conducting an offering, a description of the securities being sold, an analysis of the risks inherent in investing in the company, and a description of how the company will utilize the proceeds of the offering. Disclosures regarding the stockholdings and compensation arrangements of management and persons with significant stockholdings in the company are also required. Detailed audited financial statements must be provided too.

Conducting an initial public offering is a painstaking and time-consuming project that requires extensive due diligence by the company's counsel, accountants, and underwriters and a serious time commitment by management before, during, and after the offering. The offering process usually takes at least three to six months to complete. Typically, these months of preparation include an extensive review of company documents, the preparation of audited financial statements, numerous due diligence meetings between company personnel and the company's advisers, and several drafting sessions (often referred to as "all hands meetings") for the offering memorandum. The preparation also includes filings and discussions with the Securities and Exchange Commission and with state securities commissions to secure proper registration for the offering, and a "road show" during which the underwriter and company officials take their offer "on the road" to sell the company's securities.

Although IPO schedules vary widely from company to company and are sometimes compacted or expanded to respond to the perceptions of the company's underwriter as to the best time to sell the company's stock, a representative IPO schedule might look something like this:

IPO Schedule

Day 1 Organizational all hands meeting to set schedule and assign responsibilities.

Day 2 Begin due diligence interviews and documents review. Distribute officers and directors questionnaires. Begin selection of transfer agent, printer and others. Begin preparation of offering circular by company counsel and required financial statements by the company's outside accountants.

Day 30 Distribute first draft of offering circular.

Day 40 First all hands drafting session to review and revise offering circular. Second draft is recirculated ten days later.

Day 60 Second all hands drafting session.

Day 70 Final all hands drafting session to make any final revisions and sign offering circular.

Day 75 File offering circular with the Securities and Exchange Commission. Issue press release.

Day 85 Begin road show to sell securities. Proceed with state securities registrations.

Day 110 Receive comment letter from Securities and Exchange Commission. Prepare response or amendment to offering circular, as appropriate.

Day 120 Determine offering price. Complete state securities filings. File amendment to offering circular if necessary.

Day 135 Effective date, offering commences.

Day 140 Closing. Company issues securities. Offering proceeds transfer to the company.

Of course, the schedule only outlines some of the major undertakings involved in an initial public offering. The process also involves directors' meetings, extensive due diligence meetings, and the negotiation and execution of contracts with underwriters and others. Often, the process includes the preparation and adoption of employee stock incentive plans or substantial corporate "cleanup" to get the company's books, records, and systems into proper order to become public. *See: Blue Sky Laws, Going Public, Penny Stock, Private Placements, Public Offering, SEC (Securities and Exchange Commission), 33 Act, Appendix A—A Few Words About Tax Reform.*

J

Junior Common Stock is a class of common stock established by a company's articles of incorporation and action of its board of directors that entitles its holders to lesser rights than the company's regular common stock does. Typically, junior common stock is given much weaker voting, dividend, and liquidation rights than the company's regular common stock, often equal to only one-tenth of those conferred by the latter. Usually, junior common stock becomes convertible share for share into regular common stock upon the company attaining certain predefined goals. Failure to reach those goals cancels the convertibility feature.

Junior common stock is seldom used today. A few years ago, however, it was a common mechanism to grant additional share rights to management as an incentive for outstanding performance. The reduced rights of the junior common stock (or sometimes options to acquire junior common stock) allowed holders to contend that the shares were worth less than their regular common stock counterparts. This, arguably, allowed management to purchase these shares at prices considerably below the market value of the company's regular common stock without having the IRS contend that they were purchasing the junior common stock at below its market value. As a consequence, the argument followed, the IRS would not require the holder to pay taxes on the differences.

By making the junior common stock convertible share for share at a later date, management could eventually trade in its less valuable junior common stock for the company's regular common stock. In order to create an incentive for management and to prevent the IRS from claiming that the convertibility of the junior stock was so certain that the shares should be valued at the higher regular common stock value when they were purchased (and the holder should pay taxes on the difference between what he paid and the fair market value of what he bought), the event that permitted management to convert its shares was usually a future performance goal that would be significant for the company and difficult for management to attain.

It was a nice mechanism to reward management for outstanding performance. Unfortunately, however, in 1984 the Financial Accounting Standards Board announced that in accounting for junior stock transactions accountants must include as compensation paid to the management shareholder by the company an amount equal to the difference between what that holder paid for his junior stock and the value of that stock at the time such conversion became reasonably certain. This would create an expense on the books of the company granting the junior stock rights when it became apparent that it would meet the conversion goals.

Ironically, even though this accounting treatment does not affect the underlying value of the company, by reducing earnings for accounting purposes it can have an adverse effect on the company's valuation in the marketplace since these valuations are often premised, in part at least, on some multiple of the company's earnings. This lower company valuation can in turn reduce the market price of the company's shares and, consequently, make it more difficult for the company to raise money by selling its shares at full value. As a result, junior stock incentives are much less prevalent today than they were just a few years ago. *See: Common Stock, Dilution, Earnups, Golden Handcuffs, Incentive Stock Options (ISOs).*

K

Key Man Insurance is life insurance purchased by a company or investor on the life of an important member of a company's management team. It insures the life of a man who is "key" to making the company a success. Many investors insist on key man insurance as a condition of financing.

K.I.S.S. is short for "Keep It Simple, Stupid!" This may not be artfully phrased, but it is an important principle to keep in mind when negotiating a financing package.

There are many factors that complicate a venture capital funding. Many of those complications are necessary and unavoidable to insure the best deal and lowest cost to the company. Others, such as registration requirements, are usually imposed by the investor. Nonetheless, management should always be wary of the tendency to overcomplicate matters.

In general, the simpler a company's relationship with its investor the better. Remember, management has to run the company after it gets funded. The less time it has to spend figuring out the cute twists and complications of the company's deal with its investor, the more time it will have for the productive work of making the company a success. *See: Financing Agreements, Structure.*

FINDING A PERFECT MATCH

Clarity and simplicity. Get every issue on the table without sacrificing simplicity. "I advise against overcomplicating the structure of the financing," says Grover Wickersham, a principal in Niesar & Wickersham, a San Francisco Bay area firm that specializes in entrepreneurial companies. "Aside from the unforeseen consequences it could have, it may require so much explanation to new prospective investors that they may get scared off, making it hard for the company to raise additional funds."

"A major problem for investment bankers is simply disentangling the mess created by early-stage financing once the company has grown to the point where it needs us," says director of research Joseph Arsenio of Birr, Wilson in San Francisco. "Implicit promises—of preemptive rights, for example—always create problems, especially when the founders don't want to honor them." From the very beginning, according to Arsenio, a company should keep in mind where it wants to be in five years.

Often, the investor will ask for a "put," permitting him to exercise his rights at a given time. "That could cause a cash drain on the company when it least needs one," says Dennis O'Connor, whose Lexington, Mass., law firm O'Connor, Broude & Snyder deals almost exclusively with emerging companies. "The entrepreneur might try to condition the put on certain levels of performance or even limit it to the original amount invested." Where the angel [investor] insists, a mutually protective clause could be written. "A staged put/call could be arranged," suggests Frank Marco of the Hartford law firm Shipman & Goodwin, "so the angel could 'put' his investment in, say, four years, but if he did not, the entrepreneur could 'call' it after four-and-a-half years." That way, the company could clean up its balance sheet and get the angel out before the investment became too valuable to buy back.

Angels frequently seek further protection. Noncompetition agreements prevent the entrepreneur from leaving to start another business in the same field. Buy/sell covenants bind the founder to sell stock back to the company if he or she should leave, preserving enough equity in the firm to attract another topflight management team.

Antidilution agreements bind the entrepreneur to preserve the angel's percentage stake in the company whenever future stock is sold. "The entrepreneur is better off without them," Marco says. "When he goes looking for more funds, the market may be bad or he may not quite have fulfilled his projections. It could be harder to sell new stock, if you have to then revalue the old." Giving the angel the right of first refusal on the next round of financing can have similar effects. "What new investor would want to go through a whole round of negotiations with a company, knowing that the company will pass the deal right back to the original investor?" wonders O'Connor

—From an article by Wilham Bryant Logan
in the March 1986 issue of *Venture*

L

Lawyers are those persons who have graduated from a school of law and passed a bar examination in the state in which they practice. That said, know there are lawyers who understand corporate finance and venture capital financings, and those who do not.

A lawyer who knows corporate finance can be a real help to a start-up company's financing efforts. One who does not cannot, and probably will be expensive and more distracting than helpful. The easiest way to determine whether a lawyer understands financings is to interview him and ask him about his experience.

Venture capitalists almost always use lawyers to prepare and even negotiate their financing agreements. Nonetheless, some venture investors discourage entrepreneurs from employing counsel to represent them in negotiating financing terms and finalizing documents. Others encourage entrepreneurs to keep things simple and hire a lawyer only after the deal has been agreed to and to limit the lawyer's function to that of reviewing the financing agreements prepared by the investor's lawyers.

The theory these venture capitalists espouse is that while they need a lawyer to protect themselves from making bad deals and taking unnecessary risks, the entrepreneur needs none. But does it really make sense that a venture capitalist who has completed dozens of financings needs a lawyer while an entrepreneur who is new to the whole venture financing process needs none? Of course not.

The venture capitalist who advises the entrepreneur not to seek professional advice usually does so from personal motives. Certainly, the deal will go easier and better for the venture capitalist if the entrepreneur forgoes the advice of counsel and negotiates from a position of inexperience.

The negotiation and documentation of venture capital financing involves a number of issues of importance to the entrepreneur. Many of these issues are ones that are apparent only to a person experienced in corporate finance who understands the legal and practical implications of the way these issues are resolved. In general, it is wise to enlist the aid of counsel before the terms of the financing are fixed. If a letter of intent or investment memorandum precedes the formal financing agreements, it is probably best to secure counsel before the letter of intent is signed. *See: Letters of Intent, Negotiation, Structure.*

DON'T CALL JUST ANY LAWYER

Although most stock purchase agreements tend to be boilerplate and go off without a hitch, entrepreneurs have come to rely more and more on their lawyers. "I wouldn't put a deal together without outside counsel," avows an entrepreneur, himself an attorney. "Lawyers have a perception of today's market: They can put a note of reality on valuations."

More fundamentally, venture attorneys introduce entrepreneurs to receptive backers (and deal with venture capitalists—the lead investors), handle the negotiations, and draft the necessary documents, a process that can take three months or more. They can play a vital role even earlier on by helping entrepreneurs make fail-safe exits from their employers and assisting them with their business plans. And they can continue to advise young companies up to and beyond their IPOs.

When it comes to financing, lawyers can put startups on more or less equal footing with venture capitalists, who are intimately familiar with the ins and outs of [financing] agreements by virtue of doing a dozen or so deals each year. With entrepreneurs, who may go through the process once or twice in a lifetime, "You have a much greater educational role to perform," asserts Paul Jacobs, a partner at Reavis & McGrath. "Typically, when an entrepreneur shakes hands, he's thinking about the $4 million he's getting for 50 percent of his company. The first time he realizes the complexity of the transaction is when the term sheet comes to him."

It's in contending with term sheets—the two-to-five page documents that "define who gets what" in a deal, according to Richard Testa, a partner at Testa Hurwitz [& Thibeault]—as well as with other contractual complexities, that lawyers can help entrepreneurs navigate a course to the completion of an agreement. The perils of deal making can include structuring various classes of stock and wrestling with a host of relatively new clauses designed to protect investors, including antidilution protection, forced buyouts, and demand registration rights. "Entrepreneurs are at an absolute disadvantage without someone competent to handle the negotiations," asserts Testa. Venture capitalists, too, have come to depend on such lawyers.

As a rule, startups find venture attorneys through referrals from other entrepreneurs, lawyers, accountants, or venture capitalists.

—From an article by Michelle Bekey
in the January 1987 issue of *Venture*

Lead Investor is the company's principal provider of capital. When more than one investor participates in a company's financing, the one who puts together the syndicate of investors who provide the company's funding is referred to as the lead investor. Often, the lead investor serves as the syndicate's representative on the company's board of directors.

Sometimes, however, all or most of the investors in a syndicate will want to be represented on a company's board of directors. When this is the case it is usually because the syndicate members have distinctly different motivations in investing and do not feel comfortable having their interests represented by the lead investor. Sometimes the desire for more than one seat on the board springs from a lack of confidence in the lead member.

Whatever the reason, management should resist attempts to place too many members of a single syndicate on its board of directors. With divergent motivations, too many venture board members can create a serious distraction to the business of running a company. More people add more experience to a board, but too many people in any decision-making group make decision making more difficult. Too many directors, particularly if a large number represent outside investors, can make decision making impossible. *See: Board of Directors, Control, Syndications.*

Legend Stock refers to a certificate of equity ownership that carries a description, usually on its face or back, of the restrictions imposed upon the ability of the holder to sell or otherwise transfer its ownership. Most legend stock carries one section identifying the restrictions imposed by state law and another identifying those imposed by federal law. If the holder of the stock has entered into a shareholders' agreement or agreed to some other restriction on his ability to own or resell his securities, these will also typically appear on his stock certificate.

The purpose of legending stock certificates is to alert potential purchasers to the restrictions imposed upon the stock. The absence of restrictive language on a share certificate, however, does not necessarily mean that the stock is freely tradable and unrestricted. The legends may have been left off by accident. If they were, the purchaser may acquire fewer share rights than he anticipated unless he investigates to determine what restrictions apply. *See: Restricted Securities, Shareholders' Agreements, Vesting Schedules, Voting Agreements.*

Letter Agreements are binding contracts that appear in correspondence form. Often, they are used to facilitate the immediate transfer to a company of some portion of a larger financing. Like letters of intent, which are generally binding in only a few particulars, letter agreements often contemplate additional documentation before additional funding is provided. For example, an investor may agree to lend a company $1 million of which $100,000 is needed immediately. This amount can be advanced when the letter agreement is signed while the remaining $900,000 is held pending completion of the final documentation. The $100,000 will be covered by the letter agreement until the longer, final agreements are completed and signed. *See: Bridge Loans, Investment Memorandums, Letters of Intent, Financing Agreements.*

Letters of Intent are writings in correspondence form signed by a company and an investor that set out the broad parameters of the business deal between them. Letters of intent tend to be short and almost always anticipate additional formal documentation before funds are actually transferred.

Intent letters do not appear in all venture capital financings. Some venture capitalists prefer to proceed directly from negotiations to formal financing agreements. When intent letters are used, they always precede the formal documentation and often provide for interim working arrangements or bridge financing.

Letters of intent can be completed quickly, usually in an afternoon, and serve several purposes. First, by putting the business deal into writing they assure both parties that the other party agrees to the major terms of the deal. Also, they usually establish a time frame for finalizing the details and getting the necessary documentation completed. Letters of intent highlight the agreements of the parties. In so doing, they tend to solidify each party's commitment to the financing and often make it easier for the parties to agree on the peripheral issues that have to be dealt with in the definitive financing agreements.

Although many people think of them as unenforceable expressions of intent, letters of intent usually contain some agreements that are binding. Some contain agreements regarding how the company will be operated until funding is provided. Others contain binding agreements for bridge loans or other immediate funding to hold the company over until the formal financing agreements can be completed.

Most intent letters have three things in common: They contain binding agreements by management and the company not to negotiate financing with others for thirty days or more; they allow the investor full access to company records and facilities; and they require the company to continue to operate its business in the ordinary course. Many further require management and the company to make representations about the company's business plan, financial statements, and management's stock ownership.

When preparing a letter of intent, management should be careful to understand which provisions of the letter are binding and which are not. The alteration of only a few words in a letter of intent can mean the difference between a binding obligation and a simple statement of intent.

Management also should be careful to understand the full implications of the proposed funding. Intent letters set the tone for the negotiations of the final financing agreements. Because of this, it can be very difficult to change a poorly considered term of an intent letter even though that term may appear only as an expression of intent.

Managements that plan to use an attorney or other adviser in connection with the final financing agreements should consult with that adviser before the letter of intent is negotiated and signed. Many entrepreneurs, however, sign intent letters without first consulting their advisers. Some do so with the belief that they can fix what they do not like in the final documents. Others feel compelled to sign immediately when presented with an investor's letter to show their good faith and to get the deal moving. Most are disappointed later when the investor resists fixing the deal or when they discover the full impact of concessions they have made. These disappointments can usually be avoided by taking twenty-four hours to consider the letter before signing. During this time the entrepreneur can meet with his advisers to be sure he fully understands the investor's offer and has addressed the business issues that need attention. *See: Bridge Loans, Commitment Letters, Financing Agreements, Investment Memorandums, Lawyers, Letter Agreements, Negotiation, Structure.*

SAMPLE LETTER OF INTENT

February 2, 1987

Virden NewCo, Inc.
New Business Street
Atlanta, Georgia 33333

Attention: Harold Peters and Paul Carrot

Gentlemen:

This letter is to set forth our understanding regarding the investment by Nokomis-Atlanta Ventures Ltd., a Georgia limited partnership (the "Investor") of $1,500,000 in Virden NewCo, Inc., a Delaware corporation (the "Company"), whose sole shareholders are Harold Peters and Paul Carrot (collectively, the "Shareholders"). Except with respect to paragraphs, 8, 9, and 10, the provisions of this letter are not intended to be legally binding.

1. Upon execution and delivery of the Agreement described in paragraph 7 by the Company and the Shareholders, the Investors will immediately (i) pay to the Company the sum of $850,000 and (ii) execute and deliver to the Company subscription agreements in Company's standard form subscribing for a total of 16.7% of the total issued and outstanding common stock of the Company after such issuance. The Company shall thereupon issue to the Investor 1,500 shares of its common stock, $.01 par value, equal in number to 16.7% of the issued and outstanding shares of common stock of the Company immediately after the issuance thereof.

2. In addition to the investments set forth in Paragraph 1, the Investor will invest an additional $650,000 in the Company in return for common stock which increases the Investor's percentage of the issued and outstanding capital stock of the Company

immediately after such issuance by 8.3% (so that the Investor's total percentage ownership at that time will be 25% of the issued and outstanding capital stock of the Company). This subsequent $650,000 investment will be made only after the Company has achieved certain agreed upon benchmarks, including without limitation benchmarks relating to the receipt by the Company of its first order, the first shipment of Company product and the first collection on account by the Company.

3. The Investor and each of the Shareholders will agree to vote their shares of common stock in the Company to elect a slate of directors nominated by the Shareholders, which slate of directors shall always include at least one nominee of the Investor. This agreement shall be evidenced by a written voting agreement and expire upon the earlier of January 1, 1990, the sale of the Company to any third party, or the sale by the Company of shares of its common stock in a public offering. All shares of common stock of the Company issued to the Investor and the Shareholders will be marked to bear appropriate restrictive legends, including reference to this voting agreement.

4. The Company shall use the $850,000 provided pursuant to paragraph 1 only to fund product development, marketing and inventory expansion associated with the Company's software crash prevention program (the "Failsafe System"). Each of the Shareholders also agrees to submit to a physical examination at the Investor's request for the purpose of enabling the Company to acquire key man insurance. The Company further agrees to purchase key man insurance on each of the Shareholders in amounts reasonably required by the Investor.

5. The Investor shall be entitled to one demand registration, at the cost and expense of Investor, and to participate as a selling shareholder in any public offerings of the common stock of the Company initiated by the Company upon reasonable terms and conditions to be agreed upon and set forth in the Agreement described in Paragraph 7 below.

6. As an inducement to the Investor to enter into this letter and the subsequent Agreement contemplated herein, the Company and the Shareholders, jointly and severally, represent and warrant that (i) the total issued and outstanding capital stock of the Company consists of 7,500 shares of the Company's common stock, $.01 par value, issued and outstanding all of which are held by the Shareholders, (ii) to their knowledge, the business plan of the Company heretofore delivered to the Investor (the "Business Plan") and all other written information provided to the Investor by the Company do not contain any untrue statement

of material fact or omit to state any material fact which is necessary in order to make the statements contained therein not misleading in light of the circumstances under which they are made, (iii) to their knowledge, the financial projections contained in the Business Plan have been prepared accurately based on the assumptions described therein, (iv) the Shareholders have no rights (and know of no other party having any right) in or to the Failsafe System other than by virtue of their stock ownership in the Company and (v) that within 14 days after the date of this letter the Shareholders will each have entered into written agreements in form reasonably acceptable to Investor (A) not to use or disclose any of the confidential information or trade secrets of the Company, including information relating to the Failsafe System, except for the benefit of the Company and in the ordinary course of Company business, and (B) not to compete with the Company for a period of two years after their employment with the Company terminates for any reason.

7. The terms and conditions governing the transactions described in Paragraphs 2 through 9 hereof are to be set forth in a definitive agreement (the "Agreement"), which shall be subject to the approval of all of the parties and their counsel. Such terms and conditions shall include among others:

(a) warranties, representations and indemnities including those usually given in transactions of the nature herein contemplated, satisfactory to the Investor relating to the Company's structure, organization, business, operations and financial condition;

(b) the usual conditions which must be satisfied before parties to transactions of the type contemplated are obligated to close, including, but not limited to, obtaining of any required consents relating to material contracts, the absence of any litigation or other legal proceeding relating to this transaction or the Company; and

(c) provisions relating to compliance with all applicable securities laws.

8. All the parties agree to use their reasonable best efforts to complete the aforesaid Agreement within 30 days. Neither the Shareholders, the Company nor the Company's management will enter into any negotiations with any third parties for the provision of the moneys described herein during the aforesaid 30 day period.

9. Following execution of this letter, the Company will

provide the Investor and its agents with full and complete access to its property, books and records and will allow the Investor and its agents to talk to personnel, customers and independent providers of professional services to the Company. The Investor agrees to hold all information obtained by virtue of such access in confidence and not to release it to third parties without the prior written consent of the Company.

10. From the date of execution of this letter, the Company will operate its business in the manner described in the Business Plan and will use its best efforts to (i) secure at least $600,000 in borrowed funds for the Company (even if such borrowing requires the personal guarantees of the Shareholders), (ii) maintain its business as a going concern and (iii) maintain its business relationships.

If the foregoing accurately describes your understanding of our agreements, please sign, date and return the enclosed copy of this letter to me.

Sincerely,
NOKOMIS-ATLANTA VENTURES, LTD.
(the "Investor")
By:______________________________
Floyd Williams, General Partner

Read and Agreed to this
5th day of February,
1987:
VIRDEN NEWCO, INC. (the "Company")

By:______________________________
Its:
SHAREHOLDERS:

____
Harold Peters

____
Paul Carrot

Leverage refers to using debt instead of equity to increase company funds. Usually, leverage is used to avoid "giving up" equity. The cost of preserving equity is the debt service payments required to service the company's loans. These payments reduce earnings and require funding themselves. A company that has high debt in relation to its equity is said to be highly leveraged.

Leverage is used also to refer to a strong negotiating position caused by a compelling need of the other party. If a company cannot meet a large loan payment without an investor's funding, that investor may use his leverage to obtain concessions from the company he might not otherwise obtain. *See: Bridge Loans, Cash Flow, Debt Service, Leveraged Buyout (LBO), Negotiation.*

Leveraged Buyout (LBO) refers to the purchase of a company that uses borrowed money for a substantial portion of the purchase price. If the purchasers are management, the acquisition is sometimes called a "management buyout" or a "management leveraged buyout."

The phrase usually refers to a purchase of a company by its management using moneys borrowed from the seller or a third-party lender for part of the purchase price. The remainder of the purchase price usually comes directly from management and outside investors, often venture capitalists.

Three factors generally are considered essential to conducting a successful leveraged buyout: the ability to borrow significant sums (leverage) against the company's assets; the ability to retain or attract a strong management team; and the potential for each participant's (including management's) investment to increase substantially in value. The ability of a company to support significant leverage depends upon whether it can service the principal and interest payment obligations that accompany that leverage. This, in turn, requires a company that is capable of generating large sums of cash on a regular basis or that has substantial assets that can be sold to pay off the debt. This usually means a company with a history of operations sufficient to support the borrowing required to fund the deal.

Attracting a strong management team usually means that the division or company being purchased has a strong management team in place that requires few or no changes to make it complete. It is, after all, the investor's and lender's confidence in management's ability to run the company profitably and to expand its operations that make the buyout possible. Attracting and keeping good management also means cutting them in for a significant portion of the deal. In other words, management usually acquires a healthy percentage of the company's equity. This motivates them to stay with the company and make it grow.

The potential for increase in value of the company's stock comes not only from the ability of strong management to build on an existing base of business but also on the very fact of leverage. The heavy borrowing undertaken to complete a buyout is customarily made directly by the company. This borrowing, because it is large in comparison to the value of the assets of the company, decreases the "value" of the company's stock, enabling management and the outside investors to acquire it at lower prices that reflect the company's value as reduced by the leverage. The leverage results in the common stock having a "value" that is low in comparison to the underlying market value of the company's assets and its historical level of earnings. As the company's debt is paid off, the value of its stock increases, creating wealth for the investors. (It also helps if the underlying assets of the company were significantly depreciated when purchased so that they appear at low book values on the company's financial statements.)

As might be expected, sophisticated cash flow analysis is essential to structuring a successful leveraged buyout. Failure to properly project the company's ability to service the debt placed on the company to accomplish the acquisition can doom a buyout to failure. This, coupled with the number of parties typically involved in a buyout and the variety and complexity of the financial structures needed to accommodate the divergent interests of the parties involved almost always requires the involvement of experienced professionals. These include leveraged buyout specialists, investment bankers, accountants, and lawyers.

Leveraged buyouts often involve sensitive negotiations by company management with the principals of its parent corporation. These negotiations can be difficult because company management must weigh the risk to its job security created by suggesting a leverage buyout against the necessity of conducting those conversations to determine whether the buyout is possible. Price negotiations can be particularly sensitive since management, not the parent company, is often better equipped to evaluate the company, and management has an incentive to keep the price low. These conflicts can make negotiations intricate and sometimes require the use of an intermediary in the initial stages. *See: Debt Service, Earnouts, Earnups, Leverage, Appendix A—A Few Words About Tax Reform*

A BUYOUT CUTS EXPENSIVE APRON STRINGS

When Herbert Kirby came aboard as general manager of Allied Chemical Corp.'s Agricultural Products Group in 1983, he inherited a substantial headache. The fertilizer manufacturing division had lost $39 million on sales of $167 million the year before. But Kirby got more than he bargained for when, less than six months later, Allied reacted to mounting losses with an ultimatum: Sell the division or close it. Kirby, 52, instead engineered a $75 million buyout. He's now president and CEO of Arcadian Corp., Parsippany, N.J.

Less than two years after the June 1984 buyout, the business has increased sales and returned to profitability. The magic was possible only after freeing Arcadian from the apron strings of its parent. Under an existing agreement, Arcadian was locked into a contract for a key ingredient in its product that called for paying four times the going rate. Its rent to Allied was more than twice what it pays its new landlord. And Kirby is attempting to rebuild market share by adding to sales staff and distribution centers that Allied had dismantled.

Kirby met with E. F. Hutton to shop for a buyer. But, when no suitor offered more than 35% of the division's estimated $175 million book value, Kirby and Hutton began making plans for a leveraged buyout. They predicted that without Allied's overhead and with a rebuilt sales and distribution team, the division could produce profits in excess of $10 million in 1984 on sales of about $200 million. Says C. Clarke Ambrose, Hutton executive vice-president: "We saw the turnaround coming before Allied did. Energy costs were on the decline and demand for fertilizers was up."

The buyout was structured through AAC Holdings Inc., a Delaware company whose sole asset is 100% of Arcadian. Financing involved $50 million in credit from General Electric Credit Corp. and ITT Financial Services. Allied provided an additional $20 million, half in a 10-year balloon note at 12% interest and the rest in Arcadian preferred stock. The remaining $5 million is held in equity, 65% by Hutton and 35% by 40 Arcadian employees, including Kirby himself.

In its first fiscal year ended September 1984, Arcadian hit its profit goal on $204 million in sales. For its most recent year, ended September 1985, profits fell slightly on $200 million in sales, but its share of the liquid fertilizer market grew to 16.4% from 12.5% in 1983. Kirby projects sales of $210 million in the current fiscal year, and an 18% share of market.

After paying off $10 million of Arcadian's $20 million debt to ITT, Kirby is now negotiating to restructure the company's remaining $60 million debt. The goal is to remove restrictions agreed to at the time of the buyout, such as caps on inventory to be used as collateral and limits on capital spending. The move would also reduce expensive interest payments.

—From an article by Ian Gittlitz
that appeared in the April 1986 issue of *Venture*

Licensing is an arrangement whereby an inventor grants another person or company the right to make and sell his invention. In many cases, licensing is a viable alternative to starting a company and raising capital. Licensing of an invention can be very profitable to the inventor if the invention succeeds in the marketplace and the license agreement is properly structured.

In general, an inventor who licenses his technology to another stands to earn less from his invention than one who builds a new company to exploit it. This is because the inventor transfers the risk and cost of developing and marketing his invention to the licensee. On the other hand, because the inventor does not undertake the time-consuming job of starting and financing a new company, his time is available to explore other interests and develop other products, which may provide additional commercial successes.

Sometimes an inventor does better to license his product rather than trying to build a new company around it. If the product requires a large capital investment or if the marketplace for it is dominated by a strong competitor, the inventor may be more successful licensing his invention than trying to raise venture capital to start a new company. If the channels of distribution are particularly hard to penetrate or name recognition is especially important to his type of product, it may make more sense to license. In short, when the entrepreneur conducts his market research, he should consider carefully whether his product is one that can be successfully developed and marketed by a new company or whether there are factors that indicate that licensing would be more fruitful. See: *Business Plan Format, Franchising, Market Research, Patents, Software Protection, Trade Secrets.*

Limited Partnerships are a form of business organization that combines attributes of corporations with those of partnership. Like corporations they can provide investors with the protection of limited liability. Like partnerships they can give management and the investors flexibility in allocating profits and losses among partners.

Limited partnership is the structure most frequently used by venture capital firms to raise money. They enable investors to receive the profits and losses generated by the fund's investment without the intervention of corporate income tax. At the same time, they give investors the flexibility needed to attract competent fund managers by funding their expenses and salaries and providing them with a percentage of profits for incentive. Limited partnerships are also used by young companies to transfer company losses to investors as a method of attracting equity (transferring losses reduces the investors' after-tax cost of providing the equity).*

Limited partnerships have two types of partners, general and limited. Limited partners traditionally provide funding to the entity and, by virtue of their limited partnership status, receive limited liability much like that of a corporate shareholder. The general partners do not receive limited liability and customarily manage the business. Limited partners, unlike corporate shareholders, are generally prohibited from becoming involved with the active management of the partnership. If they do become involved, they risk being treated like general partners and becoming personally liable for the actions of the entity.

Limited partnerships must be structured carefully. Obtaining the tax benefits of a limited partnership depends upon close compliance with Internal Revenue Service rules that govern, for tax purposes, the differences between corporations and partnerships. A limited partnership must qualify as a partnership to obtain the special tax treatment.

* The ability to use these losses has been curtailed. See Appendix A—A Few Words About Tax Reform.

There are generally four factors the Internal Revenue Service looks at when determining how to tax a limited partnership: 1) unlimited personal liability for the debts of the entity; 2) lack of centralized management; 3) limited duration; and 4) restricted transferability of ownership interest. If a limited partnership meets fewer than two of these standards, it may be characterized and taxed as a corporation. To avoid this result, limited partnership agreements usually try to qualify under criteria (3) and (4) by making the partnership terminate after a specified period of time and restricting the rights of limited partners to transfer their partnership interests. Whenever a limited partnership is used, management should consult with its attorneys and accountants. Only they can insure management of obtaining the tax results desired. *See: R & D Partnerships, S Corporations, Appendix A—A Few Words About Tax Reform.*

Liquidity Agreements allow a stockholder to convert his investment in stock or debentures into cash. They usually appear as provisions in a written contract between a company and its investor. Liquidity agreements are common in venture capital financings, particularly when the investor is uncertain whether the company will ever be able to offer its stock for sale in public markets (i.e. "go public"). Since many venture capital investments end up being less successful than the business plan predicted, these options can be very important to investors.

Common liquidity agreements include puts, which enable an investor to force a company to repurchase his shares for an agreed-upon price, and buy-sell agreements, which enable an investor to force management to either purchase his shares or sell its to him. These buy-sell arrangements make it easier for an investor to liquidate his investment even when management chooses to sell its shares. This is because it is usually easier to sell a controlling interest in a company than it is to sell a minority interest (which is what most outside investors hold).

Convertible debentures also increase investor liquidity and provide an escape when a company is not living up to expectations. They do so by giving the investor the option of not converting his debenture into shares of the company's common stock. If the company does not do well enough to give the investor a "healthy" profit upon the sale of the common stock he would obtain by converting his debenture, the investor can choose to forgo converting to the company's stock and collect instead the interest and principal repayment on his debenture.

Demand registration rights that enable an investor to force a company to register his shares for sale are also a form of liquidity agreement. Debentures and promissory notes used in a financing structure provide liquidity by allowing investors to withdraw a part of their investment as a nontaxable return of debt. Any agreement that makes it easier for investors to get their money back is a liquidity agreement.

All liquidity agreements should be considered carefully before they are agreed to. Each, in creating liquidity for an investor, creates a corresponding company or management need for funding. If the provisions are not carefully considered, this need for funding could come at a time when it is particularly costly or unavailable. In this situation, a liquidity agreement could cripple a company or even force management out. *See: Buy-Sell Agreements, Cashing Out (or In), Convertible Securities, Co-Sale Agreements, Debentures, Demand Rights, Exits, Piggyback Rights, Puts, Registration Rights.*

M

Management Agreements are contracts that determine the manner in which a company will be managed. They can be in the form of shareholder agreements, which guarantee the election of a management-controlled board of directors, or in the form of a contract between the company and management to operate the company for a specified term. Management agreements usually provide for their cancellation if the company fails to operate according to plan.

The term *management agreements* is misused by some venture capital firms to refer to consulting or management participation agreements they require a company to sign as a condition to funding. These management agreements usually require the company to pay the investor a regular fee and give him the right to obtain financial reports and participate in management decisions.

Most venture capitalists do not require these management agreements. Instead, they work their rights to participate in management into their financing agreements and do not charge a separate management fee. Whenever a management fee is required by an investor, management should consider it as a part of its cost of capital. *See: Consulting Agreements, Financing Agreements, Pricing, ROI (Return on Investment).*

Management Team refers to the group of individuals who are collectively responsible for the decision making and growth of a company. In many entrepreneurial companies the management team consists of the founders and one or two key individuals hired after the company was incorporated. Most venture capitalists prefer to invest in management teams rather than in individual entrepreneurs. This is because few individuals possess the ability or stamina that is necessary to create and manage an emerging growth company alone.

Investors usually look to the three or four people who are essential to a company's success as its management team. Most prefer to invest in companies whose management teams are complete. Because of this, the chances of obtaining venture capital are improved greatly by presenting a complete team in the business plan.

Companies with gaps in their management teams should be ready to explain what plans they have to fill the vacant spots. Most investors will want to know about these plans and how present management believes it can fill the important vacancies. Some venture capitalists help entrepreneurs fill those spots, but, as a rule, it is better to present an investor with a complete management team or with concrete plans to identify and attract additional team members.

In fact, a substantial risk many young companies face is the inability to identify and retain key personnel. Especially in high-tech fields such as bio- or medical engineering, few persons with the requisite skills may be available. Thus, presenting a business plan that lacks key players may make an investor reluctant to invest. *See: Entrepreneurs, Five Factors.*

Market Research is empirical information that helps to determine whether the company's product will sell and whether the marketplace for the company's product is large enough to support the product sales projected by the company. Every venture capitalist bases his investment decision, at least theoretically, on market research.

Market research requires an investigation of the market in which the company's product will compete and an analysis of how the company's product will fit into it. It identifies who the company's competitors are, what their present and future products will look like and sell for, and how price-sensitive its customers are. It also determines who the potential company suppliers will be and whether product components will be difficult to obtain.

Market research should include reviews of available industry data, including industry magazines and reports by industry experts. Annual reports by competitors should also be digested. Personal interviews and discussion should not be overlooked.

Some of the most insightful information can be obtained by a telephone conversation with a potential competitor.

Venture capitalists conduct thorough market research and expect thorough research from the entrepreneurs they consider for their portfolios. The thoroughness of management's market research and the conclusions drawn from it should be fully reflected in the company's business plan. Unless the research is thorough and reflected in the company's business plan, few venture capitalists will invest.

If market research is new to company management, experienced consultants can be hired to help focus the questions and to conduct the research. Another way to determine what questions to research is to review one or two business plan formats and draw questions from there. *See: Business Plan, Business Plan Format, Due Diligence.*

MESBICs (Minority Enterprise Small Business Investment Companies) are government-chartered venture firms that can invest only in companies that are at least 51 percent owned by members of a minority group or persons recognized by the rules that govern MESBICs to be "economically disadvantaged." These funds must have private capital of at least $300,000. MESBICs borrow government moneys to increase (leverage) the size of their funds just as SBICs do. As a result, most of the investment characteristics of SBICs also apply to MESBICS. *See: SBICs (Small Business Investment Companies).*

Mezzanine Financing is a venture capital investment provided to a company that is already producing and selling a product or service, in order to help it achieve a critical objective (such as increasing inventories to accomplish greater sales) so the company can go public.

Because it is usually the last round of venture financing before a company goes public, management should consider carefully the costs and benefits involved. Mezzanine financing should only be undertaken if it promises to *decrease* the company's overall cost of financing or if the market for public offerings is so poor that going public is not a viable alternative.

Many times companies will accept mezzanine financing even though a public offering of its stock is possible. Usually, the company forgoes the public offering on the theory that one more round of private financing will enable it to increase its sales and profits to a level that will support a higher price for its stock in a subsequent public offering.

A theory espoused by many underwriters and investment bankers is that there are important psychological break points in initial public offerings below which the company's stock will not attract institutional investors and other important investors. Without their interest, the theory goes, the stock will have fewer potential buyers and will obtain a lower price.

Many investment bankers believe that a company needs to offer at least one hundred or two hundred thousand shares of its capital stock to support the active trading of its shares that is necessary to support a good price. A price of between $10 and $20 is considered ideal to attract the large investment banking firms and institutional investors. A price below $5, the theory goes, decreases the attractiveness of the company's shares. Since the number of company shares can be changed easily by stock splits, the critical factor in determining a viable price of a company's stock usually becomes the size of the company, its earnings history, prospects for continued and dramatic growth, and the price-earnings ratio its shares can command.

Sometimes mezzanine financing can move a company into a position in which its stock will attract a significantly larger audience and healthier price. By accepting mezzanine funding management hopes to make its stock more appealing to investors and to decrease the company's overall cost of financing by making its first round of public financing significantly less costly. A large increase in the price the public is willing to pay for a company's stock means the company will have to issue far fewer shares to raise funds than it would if its shares supported a lower market value. *See: Going Public, Investment Bankers, Penny Stock.*

Minority Shareholder refers to an investor who does not own enough stock to elect a majority of a company's board of directors and so cannot control the manner in which the company is run. However, in some cases, a minority shareholder may represent a "swing" vote in battles for control or may have contractual rights to participate or veto certain actions within a company. *See: Control, Shareholders' Agreements, Voting Agreements.*

N

NASBIC (National Association of Small Business Investment Companies) is an organization that maintains a directory of investment firms that are licensed by the United States Small Business Administration. Obtain a copy of the list by writing: NASBIC, 1156 15th Street, N.W., Washington, DC 20005, or by calling (202) 833-8230. *See: National Venture Capital Association.*

National Venture Capital Association is a trade association of venture capital companies. Most members are not affiliated with the SBA. It maintains a list of members. Obtain the list by writing the association at 1655 North Fort Myer Drive, Arlington, VA 22209, or by calling (703) 528-4370. *See: NASBIC (National Association of Small Business Investment Companies).*

Negotiation is the discussion, sometimes lengthy, of the terms of investor financing. It begins when management makes its first contact with an investor.

Whether that contact is face to face or made through the mail, the first impression management makes sets the tone for the dialog with the investor. A solid presentation by management sets the groundwork for a positive exchange with the investor by improving his perception of the company and its management. This, in turn, can help reduce a company's cost for funds and improve the terms of the company's deal.

Most venture capitalists prefer to make a funding proposal to management rather than react to a proposal prepared by the company. Their proposal is made only after they complete their due diligence, during which management's opinions and expectations about financing are solicited. Usually the proposal is specific as to amount of money, timing of investments, and the number and types of company securities the investor desires.

Once the proposal is made, management's negotiating position is reduced to that of reacting to the proposal and trying to convince the investor to modify those terms that are unacceptable. This can prove difficult, especially when a company's need for money is acute and there are no other offers on the table. Therefore, one good strategy for improving management's bargaining position and the results of its negotiation is to begin the search for money early and to approach several investors simultaneously. The entrepreneur who waits until the last minute before he approaches investors seriously compromises his ability to negotiate effectively.

Another good strategy is to convince the investor that the company presents an exceptional and extremely rare opportunity. (This too is usually best done before the investor makes his funding proposal.) The care management takes in preparing its plans and presentations to investors pays off in better financing packages and easier negotiations. An investor's impression of the company and his judgment as to its value usually have more to do with the price he requires for his funding than all the persuasion attempted during the negotiation of the actual financing agreements. As a result, much of management's most effective negotiation usually occurs when it is selling its concept to the investor—long before formal negotiation of the terms of that financing begins.

That is not to say, however, that management should relax once a funding proposal is made and accept whatever price and structure an investor proposes. Most investors are interested in getting the best deal they can and will propose a price and structure very favorable to themselves. Managements should expect this and analyze the investor's proposal carefully, using the analysis as the basis for its negotiation with investors.

Most investors expect a reasoned, issues-oriented negotiating approach from management in which management and the investor openly address the concerns of both parties and search creatively for solutions that build a workable deal. Negotiating effectively in this context requires an understanding of venture capital deals and structures, of the needs and concerns of the company and its management, and of the perspective of the investor.

A major purpose of this book has been to provide entrepreneurs with more knowledge about the venture capital dealstructuring process so that they can understand better the compromises and concessions they are asked to make. A better understanding helps management identify and articulate its concerns with objectionable parts of an investor's proposal, which, in turn, makes it easier for the parties to discuss the open deal points and arrive at acceptable compromises.

Obtaining a better understanding of a given deal and its short-term and long-term effects on the company and its management involves more than just reading one book and looking closely at the investor's proposal. It also involves getting qualified professional help from someone who has done venture deals before and can give management an independent appraisal of the proposed deal. This person should be able to guide management in suggesting effective solutions to many of the problems identified in the deal proposal. He should be conversant with the applicable securities laws so he can direct the deal's structure in a way that avoids securities problems for management and the company.

In most cases this person should be a lawyer. It simply is not true for most entrepreneurs that they can negotiate a commercially reasonable financing package without the help of a qualified professional. In most cases, the professional investor has vast deal-making experience, while the entrepreneur has little or none in structuring a funding. This, coupled with the far-reaching and often prejudicial effects of many common venture deal provisions, makes it almost foolhardy to complete a venture deal without qualified professional help.

And, while it is true that most venture investors use a reasoned analysis approach in their negotiations, entrepreneurs should not be so naive as to believe that investors will not also use deceptive tactics and pressure strategies to get the deal they want. While most effective deal makers find that an open, analytical approach makes for the best deals, some also view games and pressure tactics as a legitimate part of the negotiating process. Many of these investors mix these tactics into an otherwise straightforward negotiation. They may include delay, refusals to discuss reasons *(See: We Always Do It This Way)*, and last-minute demands for concessions to "get the deal done." An adviser who is practiced at venture deal making usually can distinguish these tactics from the heart of the negotiating process so they can be dealt with effectively.

The discussion in the *Equity Penalties* entry describes one last-minute demand tactic that occurred in an otherwise open negotiation with one of the senior fund managers of a nationally prominent venture capital firm. In that case, the entrepreneur received a phone call late Friday night from the fund manager saying he could not close the deal on Tuesday unless the entrepreneur agreed to give him significantly more stock if the company did not meet its plan. The deal had been negotiated at length and was ready to be closed. The investor had had numerous opportunities to raise this issue before but waited, instead, to bring it up at the last minute, to couple it with a threat not to fund, and to do so in a manner that made it difficult for the entrepreneur to get his counsel's advice.

The entrepreneur should have called his lawyer at home. Instead, he worried all weekend about his deal dying. On Monday morning, when he called his lawyers, he had convinced himself to make the concession in order "to get the deal done."

The investor's proposal was absurd, particularly in view of the manner in which it was made. It smacked of bad faith. The entrepreneur's lawyers counseled him to reject the proposal in a way that showed how ludicrous it was. The entrepreneur contacted the fund manager and told him he could not go forward with the equity penalty proposed, that it was unfair, and that if an equity penalty was critical, the parties would also have to discuss an equity bonus to management (and corresponding dilution of the investor's interest) if the company met its plan. The investor promptly dropped his demand and closed the next day.
See: Deal Breakers, Financing Agreements, Golden Rule, K.I.S.S., Letters of Intent, Lawyers, Pricing, ROI (Return on Investment), Shopping, Structure.

Networking refers to a method many investors use to identify viable companies and syndicate investments. Networking refers to sharing information and prospects with other investors and persons involved in the venture capital process. Networks can be as informal as loosely knit associations among investors and their consultants or as formal as a trade association or networking organization. Many venture capital clubs provide regular opportunities for investors, and sometimes entrepreneurs, to meet and discuss mutual opportunities. Incubators and technology development centers also provide a base of networking for entrepreneurs.

Networking is important. Many investors will not consider an investment unless it is presented to them by someone they know. Certainly, most investors are more likely to consider a business plan seriously if it is recommended to them by someone they trust. Business plans that come unannounced through the mail have less chance of being read than those that are accompanied and preceded by a call from a friend or acquaintance.

Entrepreneurs should recognize the existence and importance of networking when they solicit funding. Whenever possible, entrepreneurs should use an introduction or an acquaintance to help them get the attention of an investor. Often the best way to become a part of a community's venture network is to join an incubator or attend chamber of commerce or local development authority meetings. Sometimes, the right banker, accountant, or attorney (one who deals regularly with venture capital) can introduce the entrepreneur to the area's network. *See: Deal Flow, Incubators, Shopping, Technology Development Centers, Venture Capital Conferences.*

Noncompete Agreements are contracts that discourage employees from leaving their employer by preventing them from performing a similar job for a competitor. They are used by many companies to encourage key employees to remain with the company and to prevent them from competing with it after they leave. Many venture capitalists require noncompete agreements from top management as a condition to funding for the same reasons. Investors often combine stock vesting agreements and stock bonus plans with noncompete agreements to insure management loyalty. Trade secrecy and confidentiality agreements are also commonly included in noncompete agreements.

To be enforceable, noncompete agreements need to be drafted carefully. Courts dislike noncompete agreements because they interfere with a person's ability to earn a living. As a rule, courts will enforce them only when their provisions are carefully limited. The types of restrictions these agreements must contain to be enforceable vary from state to state. Some states' courts will not enforce any employee noncompete agreement. Others will, but only if they are entered into in connection with the sale or financing of a company. All states require noncompete agreements to be tightly drawn in compliance with the particular requirements of local law.

Although the rules vary from state to state and different states apply similar rules with different emphasis, a few principles of noncompete agreements do have general applicability. All states require noncompete agreements to be in writing and supported by valuable consideration. Most require them to be restricted as to territory and time. That is, an employee cannot be prevented from competing everywhere forever.

Many states require that the competitive behavior that is restricted reflects only the activities the employee undertook for the company. Some states will not enforce a noncompete agreement that is signed after the employee joins the company unless the employee receives something significant from the company at the time. However, most states relax their rules when reviewing a noncompete agreement entered into between management and a company buyer or financier.

It is difficult to draft an enforceable noncompete agreement, especially one that is not entered into in connection with a company financing. Only an attorney who is knowledgeable about his state's noncompete laws can insure that a noncompete agreement is drafted properly. If a noncompete agreement is important to a company or its investors, management should be sure to enlist the aid of an attorney to either draft the agreement or consult with management as to the agreement's scope and enforceability. *See: Confidentiality Agreements, Golden Handcuffs, Incentive Stock Options (ISOs), Options, Think Capital, Vesting Schedules.*

Nonrecourse Debt is an obligation that entitles the holder to collect only against assets pledged to that debt as collateral. A promissory note that permits the holder to take the collateral in payment of the note but not to collect from the maker personally in the event of a default would be nonrecourse debt. Sometimes investors refer to company debt not guaranteed by management as nonrecourse debt in order to point out that the investor cannot look to the personal assets of individual management members to satisfy the loan. *See: Personal Guarantees, Promissory Notes.*

O

Off–Balance Sheet Financing refers to ways companies raise money that do not appear as loans or injections of capital on their financial statements. Joint ventures, R & D partnerships, and leases (rather than purchases of capital equipment) are popular methods of off–balance sheet financing.

Companies usually obtain funds in joint ventures and R & D partnerships by combining their know-how or product with a partner's money. The company may contribute its know-how to a joint venture funded by another party and receive royalties as the venture succeeds. The company may even retain significant control over how the venture operates. The arrangements can also permit the company to purchase the joint venture or the product and know-how at a future date. By using a joint venture instead of funding the project out of its own funds, the company can accomplish an important objective while preserving its cash for other purposes.

R & D partnerships work in much the same way. Generally, the company contributes know-how about a certain product to a limited partnership whose other partners contribute money to fund further development of the product. In this way the company gets its development funded without affecting its balance sheet. If the development succeeds in producing a marketable product, the company may either pay the partnership a royalty or purchase the product for a price that nets the contributing partners a fair return on their investment.

Leases preserve company funds by enabling a company to use equipment or property without having to purchase it. In so doing, the company usually avoids having to come up with a substantial down payment and does not show the leased equipment as an asset on its balance sheet. As with other off–balance sheet financing techniques, leases can benefit a company by permitting it to accomplish a company goal with a minimum of cash.

Off–balance sheet financing often depends on the ability to transfer some tax benefit to an investor or requires a company to part with more control or ownership of its product or know-how than it would ideally like to. Sometimes the trade-off is in the upside potential to the company, with the company having to share more of the potential profit from a project to obtain off–balance sheet financing than it would if it financed the activity in another way. But sometimes off–balance sheet financing is the best or only alternative to keep a company project alive. When this is the case, the ability to keep a project going without depleting a company's other assets can mean more profits for the company and a better deal for the investor. *See: Cash Flow, Licensing, R & D Partnerships.*

Opinion Letters are statements of counsel in correspondence form provided at the request of a party to a transaction. They contain counsel's opinion as to the manner in which the law applies to various aspects of the transaction being closed.

Venture capitalists usually require an opinion letter from the company's lawyer as a condition to funding. Commonly, these letters recite that the company is duly incorporated and qualified to conduct its business, that the company has the authority to enter into and perform its obligations under the financing agreements, that the financing agreements are valid and binding, enforceable against the company, and that the company has no other agreements that conflict with them.

Most of these letters repeat representations the company and management make in the financing agreements. Nonetheless, venture capitalists usually require the opinion of independent counsel as to these and other matters to provide an independent check of the representations of the company and management.

Many company counselors will ask venture capitalists for a legal opinion to provide the company with similar protection. Some venture capitalists, however, object to giving the company their counsel's opinion. When they do, it is usually on the grounds that the opinion is expensive and unnecessary. This is a paradoxical position for an investor to take when he requires an opinion for his protection.

Opinion letters can be expensive, particularly if they involve difficult issues or require extensive due diligence by a lawyer, but they are no more expensive for an investor than they are for a company. They may, however, be more important to the venture capitalist. For one thing, he puts up cash and receives in return only promises and an opportunity to participate in a company's success. As a result, he has good reason to be concerned about the details that insure him that the company's promises are enforceable.

By contrast, the company usually has more than the venture capitalist's promise in hand when the financing agreements are signed. It also has the venture capitalist's cash or, at least, a portion of the cash that has been promised.

This is not to say, however, that management should always forgo the opinion of investor's counsel. Depending upon the way in which the financing is structured, an opinion of investor's counsel on certain matters may be the best or only way management can protect itself from risk or liability. Management's counsel can usually be the best judge of whether an opinion of investor's counsel is needed. Certainly, if a large portion of the company's funding obligation is deferred, management should be more concerned about the enforceability of the investor's promises and more assertive in requesting an opinion of his counsel. *See: Financing Agreements, Structure, Vesting Schedules.*

Options are securities that entitle but do not obligate their holders to purchase company securities in the future for a predetermined price or a price determined by a formula. Because they do not obligate the holder to purchase shares, they cannot be used to ensure future financing for a company.

Venture capitalists often bargain for options when they fund a company. They do so because options enable them to increase the upside potential of their investment without obligating them to purchase additional shares from the company. Options are sometimes used by investors to provide antidilution protection. They do this by giving the investor the right to purchase securities in the future at today's price or another bargain price.

Options are used frequently to attract new employees or to reward existing management personnel. Options provide an attractive incentive for employees because they give them the opportunity to share in the value created by a company's growth. *See: First Refusal Rights, Golden Handcuffs, Incentive Stock Options (ISOs), Warrants.*

P

Packages are business plans that are prepared and marketed for a company by a business consultant. Many entrepreneurs use packages to attract venture capital. They do so in most cases to avoid having to create a business plan and become involved in the funding process.

Business plans that are not prepared with the active involvement of management, however, will stand little chance of attracting investors. Few brokers can present a company's business proposal well without this active involvement. And few investors will invest their money in a company whose management is not involved throughout the funding process.

Why must management participate in preparing the business plan? For one thing, it is rarely possible for a broker to know a client company as well as its management does. For another, regardless of how well informed and connected a broker may be, no savvy investor will invest in a company without dealing directly with management.

There is nothing wrong with seeking professional help in preparing a business plan or even in having a professional prepare parts of the plan as long as management actively participates in the process, understands the entire plan, and agrees with its form and focus. Entrepreneurs should understand that using a broker to help locate funding will not free them from becoming involved in the fund-raising. *See: Brokers, Business Plan, Due Diligence, Negotiation.*

Patents are a limited government monopoly bestowed on inventors who create a sufficiently novel product or process and file the necessary applications. A grant of patent enables the inventor to prohibit others from making his invention in the

United States for seventeen years. Other countries provide similar patent rights.

To obtain a patent, an inventor must file a patent application, which describes the best form of the invention and why it is an improvement on the existing state of the art. The application is made in confidence to the U.S. Patent Office, where it is examined for novelty. If a patent is issued, the invention is made public by the patent office, and the inventor relies upon the patent to prevent others from copying his invention. If a patent is not issued, the patent office makes no public disclosure, and the inventor is left to rely on the trade secrecy of the invention to protect it from being copied.

Only individuals can be inventors, and only inventors and their assignees are entitled to patent protection. As a result, it is important for companies to take steps to insure that they obtain the patent rights to inventions developed by their employees and others hired to conduct research. Employee inventions often become the property of the employer by operation of law, but there are exceptions to this rule that depend on the scope of the employee's job responsibilities and the manner in which the invention is developed. To be certain of acquiring the patent rights to which they are entitled, companies should require their employees and consultants to enter into written agreements that clearly set out the company's rights to inventions. In many cases, these agreements can be included as part of an employment or secrecy contract.

Patents are not always the best way to protect technology for three reasons: (1) They require a high degree of "novelty" before they are even available; (2) they require the inventor to disclose his invention to the public; and (3) their issuance does not guarantee their validity (and thus enforceability) against a challenge by a competitor. The high degree of "novelty" required means that many inventions may not qualify for patent protection even though they may qualify for trade secrets protection. Even for a sufficiently novel invention, the patent disclosure may enable others to reconstruct the invention and help them design around the scope of the claims in the patent. Also, patent disclosures allow others to examine the invention's patent for weaknesses that might enable them to challenge its validity. If they succeed, the inventor's patent protection will be lost, and he will be unable to guard his invention as a trade secret.

There are many situations in which a company might choose to forgo patent protection in favor of trade secrecy protection. For example, if the new product cannot be "reverse engineered" or reinvented (that is, a competitor cannot duplicate it once it appears in the marketplace), trade secrecy protection, which is not limited to seventeen years, might serve the company's interests better.

The formula for Coca-Cola® is one example of a product that was better protected by keeping its ingredients secret than it would have been by applying for patent protection.* If Coca-Cola® had secured patent protection, its formula would now be available to everyone as a matter of law. By keeping it secret instead of securing a patent, Coca-Cola® has managed to retain the exclusive rights to the formulation long after its patent monopoly would have expired.

Sometimes a new product does not warrant the cost or time necessary to secure patent protection for it. A newly invented process that is only one of many cost-effective methods for obtaining a certain result may not give the inventor a sufficient competitive advantage to warrant the expense of preparing and filing for a patent. If the patentable portion of a new product does not add significantly to its commercial value, or the application for the patent would require disclosing other proprietary methods that are valuable but not protectable by patent, reason may suggest that the patent process is better ignored. Sometimes a company simply cannot afford to apply for patent protection in every country in which it needs it and so forgoes it in the United States to avoid disclosing its invention to the world and losing its ability to claim the protection of secrecy elsewhere.

Any inventor who is concerned about protecting an invention should consult with an experienced attorney. An attorney who specializes in patent law can provide a complete explanation of the patent process and the advantages of choosing patents or trade secrecy to protect the invention. There are many pitfalls in the patent process, including strict time limits during which a patent application must be filed in order to qualify. Foreign patents must be timely filed also, or the ability to secure them can be lost. Only an experienced patent attorney can guide an inventor through the process without the inadvertent loss of

* Coca-Cola® is the registered trademark of the Coca Cola Company.

protection. *See: Employment Contracts, Licensing, Trade Secrets.*

P/E is a commonly used abbreviation for the price-earnings ratio. It refers to a multiple applied to a company's earnings (net operating profit after tax) to estimate its value. For example, a company with earnings of $500,000 and a P/E of twelve would have an estimated value of $6 million (or twelve times $500,000). Dividing that value by the number of outstanding shares gives an estimated value for each share of company stock. *See: Price-Earnings Ratio.*

Penny Stock refers to publicly traded corporate shares that trade for $5 or less per share. Often, the phrase *penny stock* is used to indicate shares that actually trade for pennies. Penny stock also refers to an alternative form of venture financing, in which money is raised through a public offering of company stock at prices as low as ten shares for a dollar (or less). Usually, the penny stock offering is underwritten by a professional underwriter who, for a fee, structures the financing and uses his best efforts to sell the shares to the public.

In most cases, the underwriter charges a significant fee up front for undertaking the offering. The underwriter receives additional compensation if he successfully completes the offering. Often, the charges are steep. They reflect the level of risk the underwriter accepts in agreeing to put together the offering. As with all initial public offerings, the other costs associated with completing an offering are high as well. These include the cost of management's involvement in the public offering, the cost of preparing an offering circular and complying with federal and state securities laws, and the costs of engaging independent accountants and lawyers to complete the project.

Entrepreneurs who attempt penny stock offerings often do so in lieu of trying to raise money from private investors. Many do so because they are unable to attract funds from private investors. Others believe they can raise money more cheaply in the public market even after paying the high transaction costs associated with a public offering. Still others enter the penny stock market to increase the liquidity of their shareholdings by creating a public market for shares they may hold personally.

Whatever the reason, managements should consider carefully

the potential ramifications of a penny stock deal before rushing into it. Many professional venture investors view a penny stock offering as an indication of corporate weakness and hesitate to participate in a later round of funding. The large number of shareholders a penny stock offering can create can discourage later investments by venture investors by creating an unsophisticated and unrepresented (by virtue of their inability to elect a representative to the company's board of directors) class of shareholders to whom the directors and controlling shareholders may have fiduciary responsibilities. A sophisticated investor willing to provide significant funding may want a voice in management but not the potential liability that such participation may expose him to with a large class of investors who each hold a very small percentage of the outstanding stock.

Some observers believe that selling penny stock has a depressing effect on the trading value of the company's stock in the long term. These observers contend that investors always will think of the company as a bargain-basement company whose stock price reflects its low value (as compared to companies with higher-priced stocks). Overcoming this market prejudice can be difficult and make it harder for the price of the company's stock to increase significantly.

On the other hand it may be true for a given company that a penny stock offering to the public can command a better price per share than a corresponding offering to private investors because the liquidity of publicly tradable shares adds to their value. If the liquidity adds enough value to offset the high costs of conducting the offering, a penny stock offering may really be the least expensive way to raise money.

When a venture investor cannot be found, a penny stock offering may be a company's only alternative for raising money. When this is the case, comparing the relative advantages of conducting a public offering to private funding is irrelevant. However, in every other case, management should compare the two alternatives carefully before engaging an underwriter and initiating a penny stock offering. In their analysis, management should consider whether the liquidity created by a public offering will create enough extra value to offset the high transaction costs associated with such offering and whether this extra value is worth the extra hassle associated with being a public company. In making the decision, management should also evaluate how likely it is that going public with a penny stock will depress the growth of market value for the stock and, thereby, make future financings more costly to the company than they might otherwise be. *See: Going Public, IPOs (Initial Public Offerings), Mezzanine Financing, Private Placements, Public Offerings, Reg D, Unit Offerings, Appendix A—A Few Words About Tax Reform.*

Personal Guarantees are promises made by an entrepreneur that obligate him personally to repay debts defaulted upon by his corporation.

Entrepreneurs who incorporate their companies to avoid becoming personally liable for company debts are often disappointed when they look for financing. This is because many venture financings include a substantial amount of debt, and most lenders require entrepreneurs to guarantee their companies' loans personally. These guarantees require the entrepreneurs to pay off the loans if their companies default.

Not all guarantees are equal, however. Entrepreneurs should be aware of the concessions lenders sometimes make so that they can negotiate to reduce their personal exposure under their guarantees. For example, when two or more company officers are asked to guarantee a single loan each officer may be liable to repay the entire amount of the loan or just a pro rata portion of it. It depends on how the guarantee is worded.

Also, the availability of company assets to secure part of a loan can often be used to limit a guarantee to a portion of the dollar value of the loan. On long-term loans, sometimes a provision can be obtained that cancels the guarantee upon the happening of some future event, such as the passage of time, the infusion of new equity into the company, or the payment of a portion of the loan.

Personal guarantees are not required in equity financings. Many venture financings, however, are made up of debt and equity. As a result, venture capitalists who fund companies with both debt and equity sometimes ask management to guarantee the debt portion of the financing. A personal guarantee in such a situation, however, may not be appropriate. If the funding is essentially a debt financing with attached stock rights given as a bonus, a guarantee may be unavoidable. When a financing is essentially an investment of equity with a portion recharacterized as debt to "sweeten the deal" for the investor, management is justified in objecting to guaranteeing the "debt" portion of what is really an equity financing. *See: Buy-Sell Agreements, Nonrecourse Debt.*

Phantom Stock Plans are employee benefit plans that give selected employees many of the benefits of stock ownership without actually giving them any company stock. Instead of giving key employees stock or stock options, the company adopts a phantom stock plan and credits each key employee with a number of "units" of phantom stock. Each "unit" increases in value as the company's shares of common stock do and as dividends are declared on it.

When a plan participant retires or his rights in the plan otherwise vest, he receives an amount equal to the appreciation in value of the company's common stock plus the amount of any declared dividends. For example, if the company's common stock is worth $5 a share when the "units" are distributed and worth $10 a share when the employee's right to draw against the plan vests, the employee will receive $5 per "unit" plus any dividends that accrued to those "units" while he held them.

Phantom stock plans have certain advantages over actual stock plans. For one thing, they permit company employees to participate directly in the increased value of the company stock without giving them any voting rights. Also, they do not dilute the ownership percentages of the company's stockholders. Management can design phantom stock certificates that closely approximate actual stock certificates in appearance so that what the employees receive looks very much like the real thing. *See: Compensation and Bonus Plans, Golden Handcuffs, Incentive Stock Options (ISOs).*

Piggyback Rights entitle investors to register and sell their shares of company stock whenever the company conducts a public offering. They usually appear as provisions in a financing or shareholders' agreement. Piggyback rights are common in venture financings. Because they give investors a way to cash out all or a part of their investment, most venture capitalists insist on them.

Piggyback rights should be evidenced in a written agreement to be sure an underwriter will honor them. If management wants piggyback rights, these too should be reflected in an agreement. Except for certain fees required by various state securities law administrators to be shared by all selling shareholders, companies usually bear the cost of investors exercising piggyback rights. *See: Cashing Out (or In), Demand Rights, Exits, Registration Rights.*

Pool refers to a limited partnership venture capital fund. The term comes from the limited partners pooling or commingling their investments to create the fund. *See: Venture Capitalists.*

Preemptive Rights are entitlements that existing shareholders have to purchase new shares of stock issued by a company. In some states, these rights automatically exist unless the company's articles of incorporation specifically waive them. In other states, they do not exist unless they are specifically granted in the company's articles of incorporation.

Preemptive rights complicate fund-raising. By forcing a company to offer its shares to existing shareholders before it offers them to outside investors, these rights can postpone the sale of company shares to outsiders. Because preemptive rights require company shares to be offered pro rata among existing shareholders, they can also delay funding from an existing investor by requiring the company to first offer a percentage of the shares the investor wants to purchase to the other existing shareholders. At best, this requirement will delay the funding. At worst, it will prevent it. If any of the existing shareholders exercise their preemptive rights, the new investor may decide not to provide funding because there are not enough shares left to purchase.

Often, companies with preemptive rights fail to follow the statutory procedures when issuing new shares. This makes it difficult to determine what preemptive rights each shareholder is entitled to. Since the company cannot issue shares that are subject to preemptive rights without first offering them to the existing shareholders according to their rights (at least not without incurring significant liability), not knowing what those rights are can create an imposing barrier to obtaining funding. Untangling such a mess can be costly and time-consuming.

Sometimes preemptive rights are ignored or forgotten until the company is ready to go public. At that time the underwriter will insist on assurances from company counsel that the company can sell its stock to the general public. If existing company shareholders have preemptive rights, company counsel may be unable to give that opinion without first taking expensive and time-consuming steps to cure the problem. In some cases, a practical cure may not be available. *See: Antidilution Provisions, Charter, Dilution (Percentage), First Refusal Rights.*

Preferred Stock is a form of equity ownership in a corporation that has "better" terms than common stock. Usually, it carries no right to vote for directors but does entitle its holders to receive dividends before the holders of common stock do. In a liquidation of the company, preferred stockholders are paid before common stockholders (but after all creditors).

When used in venture capital transactions, preferred stock often includes a convertibility feature. That is, it is exchangeable for common stock at the will of the investor or upon the happening of some event. When preferred stock has this feature it is referred to as convertible preferred stock. *See: Common Stock, Convertible Securities, Debentures, Preferred Stock Umbrellas.*

Preferred Stock Umbrellas are venture financings in which the investors are issued preferred stock while management and founding shareholders hold common stock. The structure is often used when management receives its shares at or about the same time that it issues them to outside investors. The purpose of the umbrella is to establish an argument that the stock purchased by the investors is worth more per share than that held by management. The need to create this argument arises whenever management shareholders pay less per share for their stock than do the outside investors in transactions that are contemporaneous or nearly contemporaneous. When they do, the IRS may treat the difference between the share price paid by outside investors and that paid by management as hidden income to the management shareholders and tax them on the amount of that difference times the number of shares purchased by them at the lower price.*

To try to avoid this result, management can add value to the

* If charged to the management shareholder, this hidden income may be deductible by the company if it withholds taxes from other payments to the shareholders.

shares the outside investors purchase by granting them preference rights over the common stock. Commonly, these preferences include the right to receive dividends before holders of common stock and the right to receive distributions on liquidation of the company before any is made to the holders of common stock. Further preferences and rights can be created to add value to the securities being purchased by the outside investors. To the extent additional value is given to the shares purchased by the outside investor, management can contend that a lower price per share is justified for their common shares. If this argument is successful, management can reduce or eliminate the risk of hidden taxable income.

Another way to reduce the likelihood of hidden taxable income when management receives shares of common stock at a lower price than the outside investors is to have management purchase theirs long before the investors buy theirs. The longer the period of time between the two purchases, the easier it is to argue that the company's stock was worth less when purchased. Neither the preferred stock umbrella nor the passage of time between purchases, however, can guarantee that management shareholders will not be taxed on hidden income—they only reduce the likelihood of being taxed and, then, only to the extent they create distinctions that reflect real differences in value.

Structuring a financing so that outsiders receive preferred stock while insiders receive common stock can sometimes make it easier for management to use the latter to attract and retain key personnel. This is because shares issued to employees must be issued at their fair market value, or the IRS may claim that the recipient must pay taxes on the difference between the fair market value of the stock and the purchase price. If only one class of stock has been issued, that fair market value will be equal to or more than the price per share paid by the outside investors (unless the company's per share value has decreased since the financing). If little time has transpired since the venture capital financing or the company is growing or becoming more profitable, a lower valuation is unlikely. In other words, the issue price of the shares used to attract a new key employee will probably have to be as high or higher than the price paid by the venture investors.

If, by contrast, the outside investors were issued preferred stock, the company might be justified in issuing common stock to the new employee at a price that is lower than that paid by the venture investor because the common shares issued to the employee have fewer rights than the preferred shares. This, in turn, can make it easier for the new employee to purchase the shares and make the purchase more attractive. The justification, of course, depends on a real difference between the value of the preferred shares and the common shares.

Company financings should not be structured with preferred stock umbrellas without carefully weighing the cost to the company. This cost is the increased value given to the outside investors for their investment in order to improve management's argument that its shares were purchased at fair market value. The benefit to management in avoiding being taxed on hidden income or in being able to issue cheaper stock to new employees may or may not be real, depending on the findings of the IRS. (Other methods, such as earnups, puts, incentive stock options, stage financings, and unit offerings can be used to avoid potential hidden income problems. Often, these techniques can be used more effectively than a preferred stock umbrella.)

Whenever a preferred stock umbrella is used, management should be careful to balance the need to create real value with the desire to put the outside investors' rights on as near an equal footing with the insiders as possible. For example, if a liquidation or dividend preference is given, should it continue forever or expire within a few years? Should it expire in the event of a public offering or sale of the company? If each share of preferred stock is convertible into two shares of common stock, should the company be entitled to force a conversion of one share of preferred into one share of common if it accomplishes certain goals? Other restrictions can also be structured into the preferred stock.

In light of the complex issues raised by issuing preferred stock and the fact that the issuance generally only creates an argument that there is no taxable income hidden in the issuance of common stock to management at a lower price, management shareholders should review their situation carefully before deciding to structure their company's financing as a preferred stock umbrella. Whenever possible, experienced counsel should be consulted to help management determine whether the structure is warranted and, if so, what preferences to give to the preferred stock. *See: Convertible Securities, Incentive Stock Options (ISOs), K.I.S.S., Preferred Stock, Pricing, Unit Offerings.*

Price-Earnings Ratio is the relationship of the market value of a company's stock to its earnings expressed as a fraction with the current share price as the numerator and the current per-share after-tax earnings as the denominator. For example, if a company's stock sells for $10 a share and its per-share earnings for the year is $1, the company's price-earnings (or P/E) ratio is ten to one, or ten. Companies in industries that boast high price-earnings ratios make attractive investments for venture capitalists because they require fewer dollars of earnings to support a high company valuation and stock price. *See: Emerging Growth Companies, P/E, Pricing.*

P/Es BY INDUSTRY

	2nd Quarter 1986 Ratio	
	High	*Low*
Computer and Business Equipment	16.9	16.1
Computer Services	23.9	21.4
Electronics (Instrumentation)	31.1	28.0
Entertainment	32.1	27.6
Hospital Management	15.4	13.5
Hospital Supplies	31.7	25.3
Publishing Newspapers	24.5	20.6
Retail Stores—Department Store	14.9	12.6
Retail Stores—Drug Stores	25.3	21.5
Restaurants	21.8	20.0

—Excerpted from the *Analyst's Handbook* by Standard & Poor's Corporation

Pricing refers to the methods investors use to determine the percentage of total equity they will require in return for providing a company with funding.

How much equity must a company sell to attract an investor? Unfortunately, there is no easy answer.

Venture capitalists weigh many factors when deciding how much equity they want in return for their investment. The amount of equity (or price) they want for their money depends on when they think the company can "go public" or attract a buyout, what they expect the total valuation of the company to be at that time, and how likely the company is to reach that goal on schedule. Also, they consider how much of its own money management has invested in the company, how much more money the company will need before it can support a public offering, how likely the company is to fail, and how much of the investment the venture capitalist will recoup if the company does fail.

Still other factors affect pricing as well. For instance, if a venture capitalist invests all of his money in common stock, he will probably expect a higher percentage of equity than if he puts part of his money into common stock and the rest into a senior security or debenture. An investor who puts his money into the company in stages instead of all at once can afford to take less equity since a portion of his money is invested only after the company has met goals that reduce the risk of later investments. The availability of collateral can also reduce a company's cost of funding by reducing the downside risk of the investor.

The stock market affects pricing too. If the IPO market is supporting high P/E ratios for businesses in the company's industry, investors are more likely to be enthusiastic and use a higher P/E when evaluating the company. This higher P/E means the company can raise its funding with fewer shares of stock. By contrast, if the market is doing poorly, investors will tend to think in terms of lower P/Es and require more shares to do the same funding.

Notwithstanding all these variables, venture capitalists do make concrete funding proposals to companies that are specific about price. How do they do it? Most often, the process goes something like this: After reviewing the company and its business, the venture capitalist determines what rate of return he thinks he needs to "justify" the investment. He knows what he normally requires in similar-stage investments, but in making this one he will determine whether the risks are greater than normal. If he usually requires a 40 percent compounded annual rate of return and this investment is riskier, he may require a higher rate. If the company's success is more certain, he may take less.

Having arrived at an appropriate rate of return, the investor next analyzes the company's projections to determine when he thinks the company will be ready for a public offering (or other profitable exit) and how the company should be performing by then. The sooner the venture capitalist thinks the company will be ready for a public offering, and the greater he believes its after-tax earnings will be, the lower his price for providing the funding.

After this, the investor investigates the price-earnings ratios of publicly traded businesses in the same industry as the company. Usually, this means that the venture capitalist compares the P/Es of several of the company's competitors in the present market. If there have been any recent initial public offerings by competitors, he will be most interested in the price-earnings ratios of those offerings. Although the investor is really interested in the approximate P/E when the company is ready to go public, the present P/Es of the company's competitors usually make the greatest impression on the investor. If the stocks of the industry leaders are selling at twenty times earnings, and smaller competitors are selling at between fifteen and ten times earnings, the venture capitalist will probably pick a number between fifteen and ten depending on what he expects the size of the company to be when it is ready to go public.

Once these decisions are made, the venture investor computes what percentage of the company's stock he needs to acquire in order to give him his rate of return based on his assumptions of value, timing, and price-earnings ratios. After this, he may adjust his percentage up or down depending on whether he feels he has adequately considered his downside risk or the likelihood that the company will not make its projections.

For example, an investor may determine that: He needs a 38 percent annual rate of return; the company will be ready for its initial public offering in five years; and sales at that time will be $8 million with earnings of $800,000. A company of that size with those earnings, he believes, should support a P/E of fifteen. If the investor is asked to invest $600,000, and this amount will be sufficient to carry the company to a public offering without the need of additional equity financing, the investor would compute his price proposal by multiplying the company's projected earnings of $800,000 by the P/E of fifteen to project a value for the company of $12 million in five years. In order to obtain a 38 percent rate of return in the fifth year, the investor must receive five times the amount of his $600,000 investment, or $3 million. To do this, the investor must own 25 percent of the company's equity when it goes public in five years with a $12 million valuation.

This is a simplistic example of pricing, and it is only one way of arriving at a valuation. The actual process can be less analytical or more so. The investor can employ a number of different techniques that evaluate not only the prospect of success but also the probable value of his equity if the company is only moderately successful or unsuccessful. Factors such as the need for additional funding and the structure of the funding can complicate the pricing analysis. Nonetheless, this example portrays the fundamentals of venture capital pricing and provides management with a yardstick it can use to evaluate a venture capitalist's funding proposal.

How does management evaluate a funding proposal and negotiate a better price (that is, reduce the percentage of equity the company must sell)? First, ask the investor how he arrived at his price. Sometimes the investor will give a detailed explanation of his assumptions and method of pricing so that management can evaluate its fairness. Even if the investor is vague, often he will explain when he thinks the company will grow to a size large enough to support a public offering and what size and how profitable he thinks it will be then. He might also tell management what he thinks will be an appropriate price-earnings ratio for the company.

Even without this information, management can still analyze a funding offer and respond with intelligent arguments for reducing the company's cost of capital. Consider the following scenario: Zappy Computer Co. develops and markets specialty computer software. It has current sales of $500,000 and is looking for $700,000 to fund expanded activities, which management asserts will position the company to conduct its public offering in three years. At that time, management forecasts sales of $5 million and earnings of $500,000. At present, the stock market is sluggish, and Zappy's publicly held competitors support price-earnings ratios of between five to twenty times earnings. Publicly held competitors with sales and earnings similar to Zappy's projected sales in three years are supporting P/Es of between ten and fifteen. Six months ago, when the market was bullish, similar companies were supporting P/Es of between twenty and thirty.

The venture capitalist says he thinks the company's projections are unrealistic and that it will probably not be able to support a public offering until its fourth year. At that time he thinks the company may have reached $5 million in sales and $500,000 in earnings. He offers to fund the $700,000 needed in return for 56 percent of the company's outstanding common stock.

Is the offer fair? What assumptions is the investor making? To answer these questions, management needs to conduct its own analysis of pricing.

The first thing for Zappy's management to do is pick a P/E for the purpose of estimating company value. The price-earnings ratio for similar companies ranges from a high of thirty in the best markets to a low of ten in sluggish ones. Assuming a P/E of ten in the worst case, the investor is asking for 56% of ten times the $500,000 earnings he projects the company will make in its fourth year. In other words, the venture capitalist expects a return equal to 56 percent of $5 million in four years. Assuming the lowest P/E, this means that in four years the investor expects to hold $2.8 million worth of company stock in return for making a $700,000 investment today. Stated another way, he expects to receive a return of $4 for each $1 he invested four years earlier. In percentages, this is a compounded annual rate of return of 41 percent.

Assuming a P/E of twenty makes the investor's return much higher. At this rate, the company's $500,000 earnings will be worth twenty times $500,000, or $10 million, and the venture capitalist's 56 percent will be worth $5.6 million, or eight times his original investment just four years later.

Now management should evaluate the company based on its own projections and a fair but conservative price-earnings ratio. The projections assume the company will generate $500,000 of profits in its third year. If management splits the difference between the best and worst possible P/Es and uses twenty, then Zappy could be worth $10 million in three years. To give the investor a 44 percent compounded annual return on his investment would triple his money in three years. In other words, the investor's stock should then be worth three times $700,000, or $2.1 million. The percentage of stock necessary to generate this value would be 21 percent. This is much less than the 56 percent originally proposed.

Despite all the computations of management and investors, the price the venture capitalist will receive for his investment will be the one the parties agree on. The foregoing illustration, however, does give management some clues as to how it can negotiate to reduce the percentage of equity the venture capitalist will be willing to take and still do the deal. To reduce the price, management must convince the investor that some of his assumptions are unrealistically conservative or that his return on investment is too high. (The latter may be close to impossible to accomplish.)

This can best be done by discussing those assumptions with the investor. Several pricing assumptions are always open to further analysis and refinement. These include:

- *The price-earnings ratio employed by the investor.* A higher ratio would reduce the cost of the company's funding. How did the investor arrive at the ratio he chose? Have higher P/Es dominated the industry? Is his P/E based on current P/Es in a sluggish market? Does the investor really believe the low P/E he chose will prevail when the company is ready to sell its stock to the public?
- *The return on investment the venture capitalist expects to make.* Does the return his pricing proposal generates reflect the rate of return he usually requires, or is it significantly higher? Is the return on investment in line with those commonly quoted within the venture capital industry? If not, why not?
- *The future valuation of the company assumed by the investor.* How does it compare with the company's projections? Certainly, it will be less optimistic. But should not the valuation be a higher number that is closer to that projected by the company?
- *When the investor expects to be able to cash out.* Most likely this will be later than when the company projects. After all, things never go according to plan. But if the company's projections were well done, they should have provided for some of the unexpected contingencies. If they have, perhaps the investor should move his projected exit date forward.
- *What the investor thinks his downside risk is.* This may be difficult to quantify but plays an important role in the investor's pricing. Is his analysis of the downside realistic? Does

he think company failure is more likely than it is? (Certainly, he will think it is more likely than management does.) What does he think his likely loss will be if the company fails? Should his expectations be mitigated by factors he did not adequately consider?

The price of a deal can also be reduced by changing its terms to reduce the investor's risk. For instance, if collateral can be given, the venture capitalist's downside risk will be reduced. Issuing senior securities to the investor can give him priorities in the case of liquidation and thereby reduce his risk. Recasting some of the investment as debt that will be repaid even if the company is not successful enough to support a public offering at a high P/E also reduces risk. Raising more of the needed money from other sources does the same, especially if the source is management. *See: Convertible Securities, Debentures, Negotiation, P/E, Preferred Stock Umbrellas, Price-Earnings Ratio, ROI (Return on Investment).*

Private Placements are sales of company securities that do not involve a public offering and that are not required to be registered with the federal and state securities commissions. "Private placement" refers to offerings that comply with the requirements of an exemption to the registration requirements of the securities laws. In most cases, the exemption calls for the preparation of an offering memorandum that describes the company and the risks associated with investing in it. Sometimes the exemption permits a sale of a limited number of securities to certain qualified investors without a formal offering memo.

Failure to register the sale of securities or to comply with the requirements for an exemption from registration can impose serious liabilities on a company and its management. Experienced counsel should be consulted before any offering of company securities is made, including an offer to a professional venture capitalist.

Whether an offering is a private placement depends upon a number of factors, including requirements and limitations relating to:

- the number of offerees (not purchasers)
- the experience and knowledge of the offerees in making investments

- the ability of the offerees to bear the economic risk of the investment
- the number of securities offered
- the size (in dollars) of the offering
- the manner in which the offering is conducted

The company issuing securities also bears the burden of establishing that each offeree in a private placement has had appropriate access to sufficient information about the company and is capable of fending for himself in analyzing such information to reach an investment decision. The fulfill this burden the issuing company must document the identity of each offeree, the characteristics that make him an appropriate sophisticated purchaser, and the nature of his access to company information.

This "sophistication" requirement can be hard to meet with any certainty. This is because it requires the issuing company to make judgments about the nature of the offerees. While this may be relatively easy to do with institutional investors (such as established venture capital funds), which are clearly sophisticated and able to fend for themselves (based on the fact that they have made many other investments), judging the qualifications of individual investors is more difficult. As a general rule, individuals who are officers of the issuer or who have made similar investments before and are familiar with the issuer's operations will be easier to qualify than individuals who are not involved in the company's ongoing operations or who have not made investments in similar ventures.

Companies must also be sure that the purchasers of their securities are acquiring shares for investment and not for the purpose of redistributing them. If those purchasers, in turn, transfer the securities to others, the company may be deemed to have engaged in a public offering from the outset and to have violated the registration requirements.

In order to prevent such transfers, companies should require each purchaser in a private placement to state in writing that he is purchasing the securities for his own account and without a view to their subsequent distribution. In addition, the company should place a restrictive legend on the certificate of the securities that is delivered to the purchaser stating that the securities represented by the certificate may not be transferred unless pursuant to an effective registration statement or an exemption from the registration requirements which is satisfactory to the company's counsel. The company should also instruct its transfer agent not to transfer any of the securities (containing the legend or not) without counsel's written approval.

It is not difficult to see that the general exemption for private placements (Section 4 [2] of the 33 Act and corresponding state laws) contains subjective requirements that can be difficult for a company to fulfill with any certainty. Because of this, the Securities and Exchange Commission and the state securities commissions have identified a number of more clearly delineated "safe harbor" exemptions that companies can use to avoid the registration requirements of the securities laws. These safe harbors set out very specific objective requirements which must be followed in order for them to apply. Because of this specificity, companies find them easier and safer to use than the general 4(2) exemption.

The federal safe harbor exemptions include the Rule 504, 505, and 506 exemptions of Regulation D (which are discussed in detail in the *Reg D* entry), the federal intrastate exemption, and the Regulation A exemption. In general, these exemptions provide for three types of offerings with different requirements for disclosure, investor sophistication, and maximum number of investors. One exemption permits offerings of up to $500,000, another allows offerings of up to $5 million, while the third contains no dollar limitation but imposes sophistication requirements on "unaccredited" investors.

The federal intrastate safe harbor provides a registration exemption for local offerings by local companies that are conducted entirely in one state. It provides objective standards companies can follow to be sure of obtaining the more general intrastate exemption contained in Section 3(a) (11) of the 33 Act. The standards are contained in Rule 147. In general, they permit sales only in the state of residence of the issuing company and only to residents of that state. They require that the issuing company derive at least 80 percent of its revenues from the state and limit resales of securities purchased in the offering. Under the rule, resales may be made only to residents of the state for a period of nine months after the offering. If any resales are made outside the state during the period, the exemption for the entire offering can be disqualified. Because of this resale requirement and the restriction of the exemption to local companies, other exemptions are more commonly used than the intrastate exemption.

The SEC's Reg A exemption permits offerings of up to $1.5 million. To meet this exemption's requirements, companies must prepare an offering circular (unless the offering is for less than $100,000) that includes two years of financial statements. The offering circular is reviewed by the Securities and Exchange Commission much like a public offering circular. Also, as in a public offering, there is no limitation on the number of persons the shares may be offered or sold to and no special investor qualification requirements. Nonetheless, the Reg A exemption is seldom used because of the restrictions on the amount of money that can be raised and the expense generated by preparing the offering circular and completing the Securities and Exchange Commission review. *See: Blue Sky Laws, Investors, Public Offerings, Reg D, Restricted Securities, SEC (Securities and Exchange Commission), Safe Harbors, 10b5, 33 Act.*

Procrastination can sometimes help management retain more of its company's equity. As a general rule, the longer a company avoids selling stock to outsiders the less stock it will have to sell in order to raise needed funding, and the less management's stockholdings will be diluted. Put another way, the more management can accomplish without using outside equity, the better bargaining position it will be in when it eventually does look for venture capital.

There are two reasons for this. First, delaying the company's need for additional investment shows prospective investors that management can make things happen and manage cash flow wisely. Second, and more important, the more the company can achieve without outside help, the less risk an investor must take when he invests in the company. *See: Cash Flow, Dilution (Percentage), Stage Financing.*

Projections are management's best estimates of how its company will progress. The word is usually used to refer to the financial estimates contained in a business plan. They are where all the narrative analysis and market research of the plan is translated into language investors understand best: dollars and cents. In a way, they are the heart of the business plan.

Usually, projections are given in substantial detail, in the format of financial statements, and include *pro forma* cash flow and income statements broken out on a quarterly or monthly basis. Projections usually appear immediately after the company's historical financial data in the business plan. Most venture capitalists like to see projections carried three to five years forward.

Investors scrutinize projections. If the numbers interest them, they will question management thoroughly about the assumptions underlying the projections. The more rigorous, considered, and realistic the projections, the more likely they are to be achieved, and the more likely they are to withstand an investor's scrutiny.

Projections provide investors with a basis for determining how much equity they will require in return for funding a company. Unrealistic projections that fail to provide for foreseeable contingencies are not likely to attract funding. If a venture capitalist does offer to fund a company with unrealistic projections, it will usually be at a substantially higher price than management anticipated. By contrast, realistic projections not only help attract funding but also help management to forecast how much equity the company will have to sell to obtain funding.

Some entrepreneurs believe that having a large accounting firm review their projections will help them raise money. The theory is that such projections are more believable and, therefore, more likely to convince prospective investors to invest in the company. The fact is, however, that accountants cannot guarantee the accuracy of the assumptions underlying the projections, and investors know this. As a result, an accountant's signature near a company's projections may make an investor more comfortable with the accuracy of the arithmetic in the projections but will probably not make him more likely to invest. *See: Benchmarks, Business Plan Format, Pricing.*

Promissory Notes are written promises to repay money borrowed plus interest. They typically describe the amount borrowed, the interest charged, and the method for repaying the lender.

Promissory notes can be secured or unsecured. If they are secured, property (collateral) is pledged to back up the company's promise to pay. If the note is not paid on time, the lender can foreclose on the collateral and apply the proceeds to pay down the note.

Unless they specify otherwise, promissory notes are assumed to be with recourse. That is, the holder of the note can collect it against the maker directly if it is not paid. If the note specifies, however, its holder can be limited to proceeding only against the collateral that secures the note.

Promisory notes can be, and often are, backed up by personal guarantees of key management members. Guarantees are commonly required by banks and lending institutions that lend to entrepreneurial companies. Promissory notes that are not secured or guaranteed are backed only by the company's promise to pay.

In young companies, unsecured promissory notes are used frequently when money is raised from family, friends, and relatives. These notes sometimes contain simple terms and are often drawn without adequate counsel for either party. Nonetheless, they create enforceable obligations against companies and should not be entered into lightly.

Professional venture investors often require more sophisticated debt instruments, such as debentures or convertible preferred stock. When they use notes, they generally require management to execute guarantees. *See: Angels, Collateral, Debentures, Factoring, Inventory Financing, Nonrecourse Debt, Receivables Financing.*

Public Offering refers to a sale of company securities that is registered with the federal Securities and Exchange Commission and state blue sky commissions. It is an offering and subsequent sale of company securities that does not rely on an exemption from the 33 Act's registration requirements. Shares issued in a public offering are freely tradable (unless they are otherwise restricted because the holder is an insider).

Public offerings generate needed cash but are expensive and time-consuming to conduct. They also subject the company to reporting and disclosure requirements with the SEC. At the same time, however, they create a market of freely tradable company securities that the company can use to raise capital in the future and that management or employee shareholders can use to convert their holdings into cash. Having publicly traded stock makes company shares in employee incentive plans more attractive because the shares are easier to convert into cash.

An active market for company shares makes it easier for a

company to expand its activities through the acquisition of other businesses. Because they are readily convertible into cash, registered company shares can often be used instead of cash to acquire a company. With the proper deal structure, registered company shares can also be used to ease the immediate tax burden of a seller caused by his company's sale and make the acquisition easier to close. *See: Going Public, IPOs (Initial Public Offerings), Appendix A—A Few Words About Tax Reform.*

Puts are an investor's right to force a company or another shareholder to purchase his shares for an agreed-upon price. Puts usually appear in a written agreement such as a financing or shareholders' agreement. Puts provide investors with wanted liquidity but at a significant cost to the company. Because they are exercisable at the will of the shareholder (although sometimes only after a certain event has occurred), they can be exercised at a time that is inconvenient for the company, forcing it to devote its resources to paying off the investor when it needs to devote them to its operations. For example, an investor may exercise a put of a hundred thousand shares of common stock when the formula put price entitles him to receive $500,000 for those shares. Without the put, management might have used that $500,000 to purchase needed equipment or to expand inventory to meet the demands of growing sales. The exercise of the put forces the company to delay its plans and to search for funds to replace the $500,000 withdrawn from the company. *See: Calls, Cash Flow, Liquidity Agreements.*

R

R & D Partnerships refer to research and development limited partnerships, which are used to obtain financing for a specific company project. Properly structured, R & D partnerships can give investors sizable write-offs against taxes and, thereby, make an investment in a company project more attractive.* By structuring the investment as an R & D partnership, investors are able to deduct certain types of expenses incurred by the partnership against their personal income.

In this type of arrangement, the company usually sells its rights to its product to a "limited partnership" of which it is the general or "managing" partner. The funding is used to complete development of the product. The investors expense the portion of the funding used to complete product development and use that expense to reduce their taxable income. The company retains a right to license or repurchase the product or the technology when the development work is successful.

Obtaining these tax write-offs for investors requires careful attention to a variety of complex and interrelated tax laws. Failure to structure the partnership and the funding correctly will lose the advantages of the R & D partnership. A qualified tax professional should be consulted before undertaking to structure any R & D partnership investment. *See: K.I.S.S., Lawyers, Limited Partnerships, S Corporations, Structure, Appendix A—A Few Words About Tax Reform.*

* The utility of this device may be limited by new "passive loss" rules contained in the 1986 Tax Reform Act. See *Appendix A—A Few Words About Tax Reform* for more information.

Ratchets are a particularly powerful form of antidilution provision. In a ratchet, an investor is given the right to obtain additional shares of stock *for free* if the company sells any of its shares to outsiders at a lower price. For example, if an investor who has negotiated a ratchet purchases one hundred thousand shares of company stock for $200,000, or $2 a share, and the company later sells another investor *one share* for $1, the first investor would be entitled to get another hundred thousand shares for free. If the ratchet was tied to an option instead of an outright purchase of shares, the first investor would become entitled to receive enough extra shares (one hundred thousand) when he exercised his option so that his average purchase price per share would be only $1. Other types of antidilution provisions that employ weighted averages or some other fairness mechanism would require a much larger purchase by the second investor before a significant number of additional shares would be given to the first. *See: Antidilution Provisions, Dilution (Percentage).*

Receivables Financing refer to any borrowing that is secured by a company's accounts receivable. *See: Factoring, Inventory Financing.*

Reg D refers to Regulation D of the federal Securities and Exchange Commission, which sets out certain "safe harbor" exemptions to the 33 Act's registration requirements. These safe harbors have clearly delineated requirements that enable companies to safely sell their shares in private or limited placements without conducting public offerings. Because of their specificity, Reg D exemptions are easier to rely on than the general private placement exemption contained in Section 4(2) of the 33 Act. Whenever possible, one or more of the exemptions spelled out in Reg D should be followed.

The provisions of Reg D are set forth in six rules, the last three of which contain the exemptions. Because of their importance, each of the rules is summarized below.

Rule 501. Rule 501 provides the method of calculating the number of purchasers who can be involved in sales conducted under the exemptions in Rules 505 and 506 and defines the term *accredited investor* as it is used in Reg D. Under certain circumstances spelled out in Reg D, sales to these accredited investors can be made without counting them toward the maximum number of allowable investors under the exemption. The accredited investor category consists of persons who come within, or who the issuing company reasonably believes come within, one of the categories summarized below:

- a qualified bank, insurance company, investment company, or employee benefit plan
- a business development company that is subject to the Investment Advisers Act of 1940
- a 501(c)(3) charitable organization with at least $5 million in assets
- a director, executive officer, or general partner of the issuing company
- an individual who purchases $150,000 or more of the securities if such purchase does not exceed 20 percent of his net worth
- a natural person whose net worth (individual or jointly with his spouse) exceeds $1 million counting all assets
- a person who has had individual income of over $200,000 during each of the last two years
- an entity in which all of the equity owners are accredited investors under one or more of the foregoing categories (except the fifth)

Rule 502. Rule 502 describes general conditions that must be met to secure a Reg D exemption. The rule deals with integration, information disclosure, the manner of conducting offerings, and resale limitations.

Integration

Under Rule 502(a) the Securities and Exchange Commission will not integrate (or combine) sales made more than six months prior to or after a Reg D offering so long as within such period the issuing company makes no offers or sales of a same or similar class of securities (other than under certain employee benefit plans).

Information Required

Rule 502(b) provides that no prescribed information need be furnished for offers and sales of up to $500,000 under its rule 504 exemption or where such sales are made only to accredited investors under the Rule 505 and 506 exemptions. For offers above $500,000 that include nonaccredited investors, the type and degree of disclosure is linked to the size and nature of the offering under Rule 505 and 506. For offerings up to $5 million, the issuing company must provide the kind of information required in Part I of Registration Form S-18. If Form S-18 is unavailable to the issuer (e.g., if the company is a reporting company), the issuing company must supply the same kind of information "as would be required in Part I of a registration statement filed under the [33] Act on the form the issuer would be entitled to use." (For most companies this will be Registration Form S-1.) Offerings over $5 million also require disclosure of the type required in Part I of a registration statement. If a Rule 505 or 506 offering involves both accredited and nonaccredited investors, the issuing company must distribute the information to all investors.

Manner of Offering Limitations

Rule 502(c) provides that, with the exception of state-registered offerings under Rule 504, the issuing company or anyone acting on its behalf may not publicly solicit or generally advertise in connection with any offer.

Resale Limitations

Rule 502(d) requires issuers to exercise reasonable care in determining that purchasers of their securities are not engaging in illegal private resales. The reasonable care required by the rule includes (but is not limited to):

- making a reasonable inquiry into whether the purchaser is acquiring the securities for himself or another
- providing written disclosure to each purchaser prior to sale that the securities are not registered under the 33 Act and cannot be resold unless registered or exempted

- placing a legend on the stock certificate stating that it has not been registered under the 33 Act and setting forth the restrictions imposed on the transferability of the underlying security

Rule 503. This rule requires a written notice of sale to be filed on Form D. The issuing company must file five copies of the form within fifteen days after the first sale, every six months after the first sale, and thirty days after the last sale in order to receive a Reg D exemption. (Some states require filing before the first sale.)

Rule 504. Rule 504 provides an exemption for issuing companies that are not reporting companies or investment companies. The exemption applies to sales of up to $500,000 in securities made during a twelve-month period. It prohibits the issuer from making any general advertisement or solicitation in connection with the offering and requires the filing of a timely notice on Form D. The ceiling of $500,000 is reduced by the aggregate of all sales in the twelve months preceding and during the 504 offering that are made in reliance on any exemption under Section 3(b) of the 33 Act or are in violation of the registration requirements of Section 5(a).

Rule 505. Rule 505 allows an exemption for offers and sales of securities up to $5 million, subject to offsets for certain types of sales occurring within the past twelve months and throughout the Rule 505 offering. The issuing company, which cannot be a reporting company or an investment company, must meet the disclosure requirements set forth in Rule 502, as well as the offer and resale provisions in rules 502(c) and (d). Although there may be an unlimited number of accredited investors, Rule 505 requires that the issuer reasonably believe that it has sold securities to no more than 35 nonaccredited purchasers.

Rule 506. This rule provides an exemption for limited offers and sales of securities without regard to the dollar amount of the offering. Like Rule 505, it limits the number of nonaccredited purchasers to thirty-five. Unlike Rule 505, however, Rule 506 is available to reporting companies and requires that nonaccredited investors be "sophisticated" before they can purchase company securities. The language of the sophistication requirement reads as follows:

> The issuer shall reasonably believe immediately prior to making any sale that each purchaser who is not an accredited investor either alone or with his purchaser representative(s) has such knowledge and experience in financial and business matters that he is capable of evaluating the merits and risks of the prospective investment.

Summary of Reg D. The safe harbor exemptions contained in Reg D are nonexclusive. That is, companies that rely on them need not rely on them exclusively. They may also rely on other exemptions, such as the general 4(2) private placement exemption, to avoid the 33 Act's registration requirements. Nonetheless, because their detailed requirements make them the safest way for companies to obtain a registration exemption, they should be used whenever possible, even in financings to a single venture capitalist.

The Reg D exemptions do not relieve a company or its management from the need to comply with the provisions of the securities laws in the states in which they offer or sell securities. Also, they do not exempt a company from the federal and state antifraud provisions, such as the 33 Act's Rule 10b5. The antifraud provisions make it necessary for issuing companies to disclose or make available to offerees material information about the issuing company and the offering even in offerings conducted under exemptions that do not require the disclosure of any prescribed information. Failure to comply with state blue sky laws or the antifraud provisions of the federal and state securities laws can impose serious liabilities on a company and its management. It can even impair a company's ability to raise money in the future.

Because of the complexity of the federal and state securities laws and the severity of the penalties for failure to comply with those laws, companies should consult experienced counsel before offering or selling any of its securities. Only a qualified professional can assure management that the company's security offering has been conducted in a manner that will not create significant liabilities for the company and its management. *See: Blue Sky Laws, Going Public, Integration, Investment Reps, Investors, IPOs (Initial Public Offerings), Private Placements, Restricted Securities, 10b5, 33 Act.*

Registration Rights entitle investors to force a company to register their shares of company stock with the Securities and Exchange Commission and state securities commissions. This registration, in turn, enables the investors to sell their shares to the public. Registration rights give investors liquidity by enabling them to free their shares from the transfer restrictions imposed on unregistered securities by the federal and state securities laws. Venture capitalists invariably require them as a condition to funding.

Registration rights come in two varieties: demand rights, which enable investors to require a company to register their shares for sale in a public offering any time the investor demands; and piggyback rights, which allow investors to include (or "piggyback") their shares in a public offering the company is already conducting.

Entrepreneurs often treat registration rights as a necessary evil and pay only cursory attention to the details of these agreements. This attitude can prove costly later on. Management should negotiate the registration rights agreement as it would any other important part of its financing arrangements. Some important issues management should address are:

- the number of demand registrations the investor can require (generally, one is enough)
- when the investor can make demand (try to get him to refrain from making a demand for at least a year and to give up the demand right after three or four years)
- who pays for the demand registration (registrations are expensive; the investor should pay for it if he requires it)
- the minimum and maximum dollar size of a demand registration (the larger the minimum and smaller the maximum the better)
- whether management shareholders can participate with the investor in demand and piggyback registrations (if they can, put it in writing)
- how often the investor can participate in a piggyback registration and how many shares he can sell

Most companies have no trouble giving an investor piggyback registration rights as long as his rights are subject to the veto of the company's underwriter. Giving such rights does little to disrupt a company's plans and does not require the special effort of demand registrations.

Demand registrations, however, do nothing for a company after the initial funding but do require it to undertake the expensive and time-consuming effort of conducting a public offering whenever the investor demands. These offerings require significant efforts from management, diverting them from the business of running the company. They can even depress the market price of the company's stock if the offering is poorly timed. For these reasons, it pays to limit the demand registration rights as strictly as possible. *See: Demand Rights, Liquidity Agreements, Piggyback Rights.*

Reports and Records refer to the monthly balance sheets, income statements, and cash flow statements that most venture capitalists require of the companies in which they invest. Investors expect these reports to be provided promptly and regularly after a funding is completed.

Well-kept records tell them what the company has done and how it is proceeding toward accomplishing its goals. The types of records a company generates (beyond balance sheets and income statements) tell investors a lot about how much control management exercises over the company and how well informed management is about its company's performance. In short, a well-maintained set of books with appropriate reporting mechanisms to management is essential to attract investors. Without these fundamental reports investors cannot evaluate the history of a company or the prospects for its success. *See: Audits, CPAs (Certified Public Accountants).*

Reps and Warranties refer to the statements of facts, opinions, and estimates investors ask companies and managements to put into writing as a condition to funding. These representations (reps) and warranties usually appear in the financing agreement. Some of the more common ones are:

- *Organization and corporate power.* The company is duly organized, in good standing, and is qualified to conduct business in the manner and at the locations it is conducting business.

- *Authorization.* The company has the power and authority to enter into the financing agreements and to perform its obligations under them. The agreements have been duly authorized by the company's board of directors and by all other necessary corporate action.
- *Capitalization.* The company's outstanding shares of capital stock consist of only those disclosed in the representation. No person has any rights to acquire any capital stock in the company except those that management has described. If the company owns shares in any other companies, that ownership is disclosed too.
- *Financial statements.* The financial statements delivered by the company to the investor are accurate and complete and prepared in accordance with "generally accepted accounting principles."
- *Undisclosed liabilities.* The company is not subject to any material claims or liabilities that are not disclosed on its most recent balance sheet.
- *Absence of changes.* There have been no material adverse changes in the company or its operations since the date of the last balance sheet delivered to the investor.
- *An accurate business plan.* To the best of management's knowledge, neither the company's business plan nor any other information delivered to the investor contains any untrue or misleading statements. The business plan projections were prepared based upon the assumptions disclosed therein, which assumptions management believes to be reasonable.
- *Properties.* The company has good and marketable title to all of its properties.
- *Compliance with laws.* The company has complied with all laws and regulations that apply to its business.
- *Taxes.* The company has filed all of its tax returns on time and has paid its taxes.
- *Contracts and laws.* All of the company's material contracts have been disclosed to the investor. The company is not in default under any of its agreements. The financing agreements do not conflict with or cause a default under any of the company's other agreements, its charter, or any laws.
- *Intellectual property.* The company has sufficient title to its patents, trademarks, and copyrights to conduct its business.

To management's knowledge, the company's business does not infringe upon any patents or intellectual property rights of others.

- *Litigation*. Except as has been disclosed to the investor, there is no litigation or other claim pending or threatened against the company.

Other reps regarding cost estimates, market research conclusions, and revenue projections may also be requested.

Reps and warranties should be made carefully. If they are inaccurate, they should be corrected. If they are overbroad, they should be narrowed. Otherwise, they may create a default that releases the investor from his obligations and subjects management and the company to liability. *See: Boilerplate, Investment Reps, Opinion Letters.*

Restricted Securities refer to shares of company stock that were not registered in a public offering and consequently cannot be resold or transferred until certain events occur that exempt the resale from registration or fulfill the registration requirements. Usually, the certificates for restricted securities bear legends identifying the limitations on their transferability. When issuing restricted securities, prudent managements require investors to represent in writing that they are purchasing the shares for investment purposes only and do not intend to resell them.

The shares of stock a venture capitalist buys from a start-up company are usually restricted securities. The reason for this is that most start-up companies rely upon exemptions from the 33 Act registration requirements when selling their shares and thus do not register them. As a result, the venture investor cannot resell them without first causing the company to either register the shares with the SEC and state securities commissions or complying with an exemption to those registration requirements. It is for this reason that venture investors look to other devices, or exits, to enable them to liquidate, or cash out.

The shares held by management and other company shareholders are usually restricted too. Unless these shareholders negotiate rights to participate with the company's venture investor in some of its exits, they must register their shares or rely upon an exemption from registration before they can sell them. Absent a public offering in which they can register their shares, this usually means selling them under the provisions of Security and Exchange Commission's Rule 144. This rule identifies circumstances in which restricted securities may be sold. In general, it allows holders of restricted securities who have held their securities for two years after they have paid for them to sell in any three-month period a number of their shares no greater than the larger of:

> one percent of the total number of shares of their class of stock then outstanding or, if the security is listed on a national exchange or quoted on NASDAQ, the average weekly trading volume of their class of stock.

After three years, most resale restrictions lapse for persons who are not significant shareholders or members of company management. State securities laws and other rules relating to insider trading and certain Securities and Exchange Commission reporting requirements must, however, be complied with before any restricted security is sold. Because of the complexity of these laws, any holder of restricted securities should consult an attorney before transferring ownership of his stock. *See: Exits, Going Public, Investment Reps, IPOs (Initial Public Offerings), Legend Stock, Liquidity Agreements, Private Placements, Reg D, Registration Rights.*

Revenue Participations refer to financing structures that give an investor the right to receive a percentage of company sales or revenues. Revenue participations work like royalties: The company pays the investor an agreed-upon percentage of sales and deducts the payments as a business expense. The investor shows the payment as ordinary income. Unlike royalties, however, revenue participations usually grant a percentage of all sales instead of just those on a particular product. Revenue participations can be reflected in a written agreement or in a certificate, sometimes referred to as an RPC.

Sharing a percentage of revenue with an investor can accomplish some interesting results. First, the investor may become less concerned with the company maximizing earnings (profits) because he is paid based on sales. Second, management's attention may be focused on maximizing profits by minimizing expenses, so that its projected profit margin can be realized after the participation payment is made. Third, the investor may be less concerned with controlling or participating in company affairs. He may not even require a seat on the board or audited financial statements, at least as long as he is being paid and things are running smoothly. He will, of course, expect regular payments and regular statements of sales. Fourth, the entrepreneur gives up no equity.

The terms of a revenue participation should be negotiated carefully so that it will not create a cash flow crisis. Payments should not "kick in," or be triggered, until agreed-upon levels of sales revenue are accomplished in order to ensure that the company can handle the drain on cash flow caused by the revenue participations. RPCs can also be made convertible or be ratcheted, so that the investor's percentage increases or decreases according to predetermined sales levels. In all events, revenue participations should be capped so that the company's obligations expire once the investor has obtained the return he bargained for.

Revenue participations are not too common, but they do have their advocates among investors. According to Arthur Lipper III, a venture capitalist and chairman of *Venture*,

> One of the reasons I like to use the revenue-participation certificate method of investing in private companies is that matters of management perks are then of no concern to me. The entrepreneur should be free to live well "on the company" and spend as he feels justified without fear of shareholder or profit-interest holder criticism. That's fine as long as every week, month, or quarter I receive the agreed-upon share of revenues. I fly economy class, and I expect others spending my money to do so also if my interest (and reason for my assuming financial risk) in their activities is profit-related.

Revenue participations may become more common in the future. One reason many venture capital funds have historically invested in equity was to take advantage of lower capital gains rates on the profits they obtain from their investments (which result from the appreciation in value of the fund's portfolio companies). The ability to obtain lower rates was a powerful incentive to purchase equity instead of revenue participation rights because RPCs were taxed at higher ordinary income rates. With the differential between ordinary income rates and capital gains tax rates being phased out by 1986 tax reform, this incentive to purchase equity may disappear, making RPCs more common in venture financings. *See: Equity, Structure, Appendix A—A Few Words About Tax Reform.*

Risk Capital is what venture capitalists provide to entrepreneurs. These investments of capital are risky because of the early stage of the companies, the lack of collateral to secure the investment, and its illiquid nature. This is why venture capitalists require annual rates of return in excess of 35 percent and a measure of control over company management. Most studies of venture capital investment reveal that as many as seven out of ten venture investments fail to meet their projections, thus justifying the rate of return venture firms require and the suspicion with which business plans are greeted by investors. *See: Pricing, ROI (Return on Investment), Venture Capital.*

ROI (Return on Investment) is the premium an investor receives for investing in a company when he liquidates his holdings. Venture capitalists expect high returns from their investments.

Venture investors express the return they want to make from an investment in terms of percentages, much the same way lenders price loans. By determining what compounded annual rate of return he wants from a given investment, a venture capitalist can then work with his projections for the company's growth to arrive at the percentage of the company's stock he needs to receive in order to do a funding.

What ROIs do most venture capitalists require to fund a company? It varies from company to company. The following chart give some general ranges, based on an economy supporting prime interest rates at or near 10 percent.

Company Stage	*Compounded Annual ROI*
Seed or Startup	40% and up
First and Second Stage	30% to 50%
Third Stage and Mezzanine	20% to 30%

How these rates of return translate into cost to a company depends in large part on how long it takes the investor to exit. The following table illustrates this fact:

Payoff	*Compounded Annual ROI*
three times investment in three years	44%
five times investment in three years	71%
seven times investment in three years	91%
four times investment in four years	41%
three times investment in five years	25%
five times investment in five years	38%
seven times investment in five years	48%
ten times investment in five years	58%

As these tables show, venture capital money is expensive. The longer management can delay its need for funding and the earlier it can provide an investor with an exit the less expensive the money will be. *See: Pricing, Procrastination, Projections.*

S

Safe Harbors refer to exemptions from the registration requirements of federal and state securities laws that are so explicit in their requirements that they enable a company to offer and issue securities privately without fear of running afoul of the securities laws registration requirements. The Reg D private placement exemptions and integration rules are examples of safe harbors. Whenever possible, companies should structure their offerings to fall within a safe harbor. By doing so, they reduce the risk that their offering will be recharacterized as an unregistered public offering. Any such recharacterization could have disastrous effects upon the company's ability to raise money and could subject it and management to serious liabilities. *See: Integration, Private Placements, Reg D, 33 Act.*

SBA (Small Business Administration) refers to an agency of the U.S. government that lends and guarantees loans to small companies. Because of funding cutbacks, however, the SBA's present activities are limited primarily to guaranteeing loans made to small companies by banks and other financial institutions.

These loan guarantees are administered under the SBA's "7(a) Loan Guarantee Program." Under the program, participating banks, business development corporations, and other institutional lenders evaluate borrowers, set the borrowing terms, and prepare the lending paperwork. They also set the interest rate (but are prohibited from charging more than 2.75 percent over prime). The SBA then guarantees up to 80 percent of qualifying loans, which decreases the lender's risk and makes it more feasible for small companies to borrow.

The SBA relies heavily on its participating lenders to evaluate and service the guaranteed loans. Two of its programs demonstrate this reliance. Under the Certified Lenders Program, qualifying lenders are certified by the SBA and promised three-day turnaround on loan applications they submit to the SBA. "Preferred Lenders" are actually delegated authority to extend SBA guarantees on loans that meet SBA guidelines.

Whichever type of SBA lender a company approaches, management should be prepared to meet a slew of requirements. Each lender evaluates loan applications against its own and the SBA's requirements. Borrowers should expect questions relating to the company's capitalization, its ability to repay the loan, and the personal resources of its principals. To meet the SBA's requirements alone, management must show, among other things, that it owns a for-profit business that is not dominant in its industry (usually not too hard) and that it does not discriminate in employment practices.

The documentation for SBA guarantees is usually extensive, containing protective provisions that limit the manner in which the company can use the money loaned, require extensive personal guarantees from management, and require regular and extensive reporting to the lender. SBA guaranteed loans are usually collateralized by "everything in sight," including the company's real property, receivables, inventory, equipment, stock, and even the personal assets of management.

The guarantee of a loan by the SBA makes money available to companies that might not otherwise be able to borrow it at commercially reasonable rates. The SBA guarantee does not, however, reduce the lender's desire for company collateral or for the personal guarantees and property pledges of management. Nor does it reduce the requirements for covenants and restrictions in the loan documentation. This is because lenders still look to the borrowing company and its management as the parties primarily responsible for the loan. SBA lenders will foreclose against the assets of a company and its management. They will do everything in their power to avoid calling on the SBA guarantee, because in doing so they jeopardize their relationship with the SBA. *See: BDCs (Business Development Corporations), MESBICs (Minority Enterprise Small Business Companies), Promissory Notes, SBICs (Small Business Investment Companies).*

SBICs (Small Business Investment Companies) are lending and investment firms that are licensed by the federal government. The licensing enables them to borrow from the federal government to supplement the private funds of their investors. Some of these funds engage only in making loans to small businesses or to invest only in specific industries. The majority, however, are organized to make venture capital investments in a wide variety of businesses.

SBICs usually have at least $500,000 in private capital. Some have as much as $10 million. By using their special access to government loans, SBICs can leverage their private capital by as much as four to one. That is, if an SBIC invests $100,000 of its own money in a company, it can borrow another $300,000 from the federal government and invest that as well.

In practice, this means that SBICs almost always require a large part of their investment in a company be in the form of loans or income-producing securities. This is because the majority of the funds they invest are borrowed money on which they have to pay interest and repay principal.

Other venture capital funds often require that part of their investment be in the form of a loan as well, but there is an important distinction between SBICs and other venture capital funds. SBICs, because they must immediately begin servicing the interest on their government loans, usually require a company to start making some payments to them on their investment earlier than a private venture capital fund will.

As a group, SBICs also tend to avoid the earliest stage investments when the risks are greatest. They do, however, represent a good source of funds for later stage companies whose prospects are more secure. If the prospects are secure enough, an SBIC will invest in a company that offers a more moderate potential for growth than might be required to attract a traditional or private venture capital firm. *See: CDCs (Community Development Corporations), MESBICs (Minority Enterprise Small Business Investment Companies), Venture Capitalists.*

S Corporations are a special kind of corporation recognized by the Internal Revenue Code that are taxed differently from the more customary C corporations most people think of when they think of corporations.

S corporations differ from C corporations in one important particular: They are not taxed by the Internal Revenue Service as entities separate and distinct from their shareholders. In S corporations, the income and losses of the company pass directly to their shareholders. If the company earns $100,000 in profits during the year, its 50 percent shareholder would be responsible for showing 50 percent of the profit, or $50,000, on his tax return as income. If the company lost money during the year, each of its shareholders would be entitled to claim a portion of the company's losses on his individual tax return as a loss.

These profits and losses pass directly to the shareholders without regard to whether or how much money the company distributes to them. If the company makes a profit and needs it to fund operations, the shareholders will have to show that profit on their individual tax returns and pay taxes on it even though they receive no cash. Agreements can be made among shareholders and management to require cash payments that are sufficient to pay taxes.

In the past, when maximum individual tax rates exceeded corporate maximum tax rates, S corporations were used primarily during the early stages of company development while losses exceeded profits. With individual tax rates falling below corporate tax rates under 1986 tax reform, S corporations can now be used in many cases to actually reduce federal taxes paid on corporate earnings by effectively giving the company the benefits of its shareholders' lower maximum tax rates.

The S form can reduce the cost to the shareholders of their investments in a company that is losing money by allocating back to those shareholders the company's losses in its first years. These losses can be used by the shareholders to reduce their income tax obligations and thereby effectively reduce their after-tax cost of investment. At the same time, however, the company loses the ability to use these losses to shelter future income from taxes and thereby increases the likelihood that it will need additional funding in the future.

S corporations are not particularly effective at attracting outside investors with the promise of allocating company losses to them to use to reduce their taxes. This is because losses and profits are allocated to S company shareholders on the basis of the number of shares held. In other words, an outside investor will only receive a portion of the company's losses equal to his percentage ownership. If he puts in $1 million and gets 40 percent of the stock, he will get only 40 percent of losses generated by the company's use of his money. If the company loses all of his $1 million, he will only get $400,000 of it.

Other devices, such as limited partnerships, permit more flexibility in the allocation of losses and profits and consequently are used more often than S corporations to attract venture capitalists who want to reduce the after-tax cost of their investment. Limited partnerships can be structured so that almost all of the company's losses are allocated to the outside investor. This means an investor who purchases a 40 percent interest in a limited partnership could, nonetheless, receive almost all of the losses attributable to the use of his $1 million even though he may only be entitled to receive 40 percent of the profit.

Establishing an S corporation requires strict compliance with a number of IRS requirements, including rules relating to the nature of the company's shareholders and its outstanding securities, and may not be available to all entrepreneurial companies. For example, S corporations are available only to companies organized under the laws of a state. Foreign corporations, even if they have assets or do business in the United States, cannot qualify. Even some domestic companies defined by the IRS as "ineligible corporations" (e.g., insurance companies, certain financial institutions, and other enumerated companies) cannot qualify. S corporations can have no more than thirty-five shareholders, all of whom must be individuals, estates, or certain qualifying trusts. And only one class of stock can be issued without jeopardizing the S corporation's tax status (although that class can be divided into subclasses with different voting rights). Certain consent and timing requirements must also be met to secure S corporation status.

As you might imagine, the flow-through of profits and losses is not without its complications. For one thing, losses can be used by a shareholder only to the extent of his "basis" in his stock. Initially, this basis equals the individual's purchase price for his stock plus his basis in any loans he makes to the company. As the company operates, this basis can fluctuate, however, generally increasing with company income and gains and decreasing with company losses.

Because of the complexity of S corporations and the peculiarities of the manner in which they and their shareholders are taxed, entrepreneurs should always consult with their accountants and legal advisers before organizing one. Failure to do so could result in unwanted surprises for the company and its shareholders. *See: Limited Partnerships, R & D Partnerships, Structure, Appendix A—A Few Words About Tax Reform.*

SEC (Securities and Exchange Commission) is the government agency that administers the 33 Act and other federal securities laws. It reviews public offering documents and promulgates rules and regulations interpreting the federal securities acts and establishing safe harbors from the registration requirements of the 33 Act. *See: Going Public, IPOs (Initial Public Offerings), Private Placements, Reg D, Restricted Securities, Safe Harbors, 10b5, 33 Act.*

Secrecy Agreements *See: Confidentiality Agreements.*

Seed Capital refers to financing obtained by a company before it has completed developing a prototype of its product. Sometimes it refers to capital raised after a company has developed a prototype of its product but before it has manufactured any production units of it. This is the most difficult and expensive money to raise because it is sought and needed before management can prove that the product will sell and be produced and distributed at a competitive price. The entrepreneur's family, friends, and relatives and his personal savings are the primary source of seed capital. *See: CDCs (Community Development Corporations), Stage Financing.*

Shareholders' Agreements are contracts entered into between company shareholders, usually at the insistence of a minority shareholder. A venture capitalist who does not acquire control with his purchases of company stock will usually require a shareholders' agreement as a condition of funding. Managements that sell a controlling interest in their company's common stock normally insist upon a shareholders' agreement to insure their continued ability to run the company.

Shareholders' agreements can take a variety of forms and can serve a variety of purposes. They are usually in writing and signed by persons who together own at least a majority of the outstanding shares of the company's voting stock.

Shareholders' agreements enable a minority shareholder to exercise more control over a company than he would have otherwise. (By voting his minority interest in the company's shares, he would have no control.) A venture capitalist who invests a substantial sum of money in a company, for example, will almost always insist that management agree to vote its shares so that he will be insured a seat on the company's board of directors. Sometimes an investor will ask for other types of control as well, such as the right to veto certain important financial decisions made by the directors.

Management should be careful when negotiating a shareholders' agreement to grant the investor only those rights for which he bargains. Shareholders' agreements should have a limited term and, in most cases, should terminate in the event of a public offering of the company's stock or sale of the company. *See: Benchmarks, Common Stock, Control, Cumulative Voting.*

Shark Repellents are provisions in a company's charter and bylaws that make it more difficult for an outsider to gain operating control of a company. (The shark being repelled is the outsider who would change management if he gained control of the company.) Shark repellents are commonly used by managements of public companies in which outsiders have an opportunity to acquire control of the company by purchasing shares in the public market.

Common shark repellents include "super-majority" voting requirements (for example, 67 percent of shareholders) to approve a sale of the company, the staggered election of company directors, and the use of classes of voting stock, so that holders of publicly traded shares are entitled to elect only a minority of the board of directors. *See: Control, Going Public.*

Shopping refers to the practice of presenting a company's business plan to several investors simultaneously (a.k.a. "shopping the deal"). Many people advise companies against presenting their business proposal to several potential investors at the same time. It is bad form, they say, and makes the venture capitalist think the company is not serious about working with him.

The fact is, however, that few entrepreneurs have the time to let only one venture capitalist look at their investment proposal.

Most venture capitalists take at least six to eight weeks to conduct their investigation and make an investment decision. At that rate, one or two rejections can cripple a promising company if it pursues only one investor at a time.

The better practice is to present the company's proposal to two to four carefully selected venture capitalists simultaneously, explaining to each that the company is doing this because it recognizes that most venture capital firms prefer to invest with other firms and that time pressures require the company to speak with a few select firms at the same time. Often, if an entrepreneur asks, investors will suggest other investors to whom the company can present its business plan.

Another good practice is to send an inquiry letter to a larger number of venture investors. The letter should identify the company, its business, the amount of money needed, and the way in which the money will be used. After providing this information, the letter can offer to send business plans to interested investors. Used in a mailing to venture firms that have invested in the company's industry and stage of investment before, this process can help management identify those investors who are currently funding companies like theirs. This, in turn, allows management to concentrate its efforts on investors who are interested and more likely to fund.

The following is the body of an inquiry letter that was sent to a number of investors around the country. The investors were selected based on their history of funding companies in the company's industry. The letter generated significant interest and led to serious funding negotiations.

> Dear Sirs:
>
> We are seeking first-stage investment capital for our operating subsidiaries and holding company. Minimum investment requirements are $500,000 with a comprehensive package totaling $2.5 to 3 million. We have been in business for one year and can demonstrate rapid growth and achievement and potential. All of our operating subsidiaries are involved with musical merchandise and high-tech electronic application to this field.
>
> We are interested in taking our companies public. Our management team is very experienced and already in place. I have enclosed an issue of *Musical Merchandise Review* (the trade publication) that features our company. This will provide you with some background information. We have made a significant

impact on our industry with our merchandising ability as well as our rapid success.

Please contact me personally if you are interested in investment with our firm.

Sincerely,

Entrepreneurs should be flexible in their search for funding and speak with lenders, individuals, family, friends, relatives, and other money sources in addition to venture firms. A common mistake many entrepreneurs make when raising capital is limiting their search to one type of investor. Many believe (mistakenly) that if they need capital, they must always get their money from a venture capital fund.

Another common mistake is to assume that one investor will provide all of the debt and equity financing the company needs. In fact, most venture capital financings involve more than one investor. Many involve a separate lender who receives no equity for lending.

To improve the odds of being funded, managements can separate their funding needs into debt and equity requirements and approach lenders and equity investors at the same time, asking each to commit to fund a portion of the company's total financing needs. Getting a commitment for part of a funding is often easier than getting one for all of it. This is particularly true when each investor's commitment is contingent upon the company securing the rest of the financing because each investor knows that his money will not be committed until another investor agrees enough with his positive assessment of the company to put his money down as well. Once a company gets its first commitment using this approach, other investors become easier to find and more inclined to join in. *See: Networking, Syndication, Venture Books, Venture Capitalists.*

Software Protection refers to the fact that both copyrights and trade secrets protection can be used to prevent others from misappropriating valuable company software. Often, this software is essential to the success of the company, and protecting it adequately is not only prudent but necessary to convince an outsider to invest his money in the company. Venture investors expect companies to take reasonable steps to protect their proprietary software and other valuable secrets from being misappropriated by their competitors.

Copyright and trade secrets protection each protects a different aspect of computer software, and both require the company to take certain actions to secure their protections. Copyrights protect the expression of ideas rather than the ideas themselves. That is, copyrights can prevent someone from using (copying) a program but not from using the ideas (algorithms) in the program to produce a new program that does the same thing.

Copyright protection is governed by federal statute and protects both published and unpublished works. To secure copyright protection, a company must attach the statutory notice to the program and file with the Federal Copyright Office within five years after the program is developed. Filings with the Copyright Office can be done in object code or source code, and there is a procedure that permits companies to file the first twenty-five and last twenty-five pages of a program printout. This procedure can help a company preserve its trade secrets in a program while obtaining copyright protection as well.

By contrast, trade secret protection protects ideas themselves rather than the expression of them. Trade secrets protection is governed by state law and protects only ideas that are kept secret. Protecting a trade secret through litigation involves proving that the trade secret exists, that it was disclosed only in confidence, and that the use or disclosure of the information complained about was obtained in violation of a confidence and to the injury of the company.

The existence of a trade secret is a matter of fact. The factors courts generally consider in determining whether a trade secret exists include the extent to which the information is known outside the company's business, the extent the information is known to employees and others involved in the business, the value of the information to the company and its competitors, the amount of money and effort expended to develop the information, and the ease or difficulty with which the information can be properly acquired by competitors. In other words, the more valuable the information and the more safeguards the company takes to protect that information, the easier it will be to prove a trade secrets case in court. Both trade secrets and copyright protection can provide a company with rights to money damages and to enjoin a competitor from using its misappropriated software.

The difference between copyright protection and trade secrets protection are not well understood by many software entrepreneurs. Many, particularly those whose software is a big-ticket item that is licensed to a relatively small number of licensees under contract, forgo copyright protection and rely solely on trade secrets protection to guard their rights in their programs.

This course of action can be dangerous, however, because it ignores some of the substantial advantages copyrights offer for protecting software. A better strategy is usually to claim the protection of both trade secrecy and the copyright laws. Securing both gives a company more ways to stop infringers from stealing its software and gives it access to the federal courts to pursue its claims. In many situations, copyright infringement cases are easier to prove in court than trade secret infringement cases, giving the company that obtains copyright protection a significant advantage over one that relies solely on trade secrecy.

Care must be taken, however, whenever both copyright and trade secrecy protection are sought, to preserve the confidentiality of the software during the copyrighting process. The careless filing of materials with the copyright office or overreliance on copyright protection in the wrong situation can lead to the loss of important trade secrecy rights in a computer program. A qualified attorney can advise management on the best strategy to follow to obtain the most protection available under both laws. *See: Copyrights, Trade Secrets.*

Specialty Funds are venture capital firms that invest their money only in companies or products that fall within an identified industry or field of endeavor. Utech Venture Capital Fund, headquartered in Baltimore and Atlanta, is one such focused fund. It invests "in ventures which offer a product or service directly, and not necessarily exclusively, related to the needs of the electric and gas utility industry." Other funds exist in other industries.

Specialty funds use their industry focus to help attract investors and give them an edge in identifying promising companies in their chosen industries. By specializing, they are able to develop industry-specific expertise that can not only help them understand and identify the potential of a new company in the industry, but that can also help them assist that company after they have made their investment.

Spending time to identify specialty funds in his company's

industry can often help an entrepreneur raise capital. Even funds that are not specialty funds tend to specialize in industries or stages of financings. Identifying the tendencies of investors can help a company focus its fund-raising activities and increase its chances for success. *See: Venture Capitalists* for several sources containing listings of investors. *See also: Corporate Venture Capital, Shopping, Value Added.*

Stage Financing refers to a method many investors use to reduce their risk when funding companies. Funding a company in "stages" means providing the money that has been committed in pieces as the company meets certain preestablished goals. Customarily, the company doles out the shares to the investor as the money is received. For example, an investor might agree to provide $800,000 to a company by paying $400,000 down, $200,000 when the company gets its first order, and $200,000 when it receives its first payment from an order. The stock sold to the investor might be issued in five thousand shares up front, fifteen hundred shares when the first $200,000 payment is made, and one thousand when the last $200,000 is put in. (The earlier dollars buy more shares because there is more risk at the beginning.) Often, these goals are tied in some fashion to the financial projections contained in the company's business plan.

While the commitment is to fund the entire amount, the later stages of funding are contingent on the company attaining its goals. If the company fails, the investor is relieved of his obligation to fund any further. In this way, the investor can cut his losses when a company does not meet expectations. At the same time, the company gets a commitment for its full funding, which it can obtain by meeting its goals.

Stage financing also refers to the fact that most growing companies need funding at various points in their development. At each point, or stage, the company solicits new investors to fund the next phase of company growth.

Usually, a company goes through two or three venture "rounds" of financing before it is large and healthy enough to sell its stock on the public market. Each stage of financing can reduce management's percentage ownership in the company. As the company progresses, however, its stock should command a higher price in each successive stage. The reason for this is that the investor's risk decreases as the company succeeds and meets its goals. As a result, if management gave up 30 percent of its company's stock to attract $500,000 in venture capital the first time around, it may only cost an additional 15 percent of the company's stock to raise $1 million in the second round of financing.

The first stage of financing is commonly called "seed financing." This is money raised to make an idea for a product into a working prototype. Quite often, this money is invested by an individual or by the entrepreneur and his management team.

Seed money is the hardest to find, and the most expensive (in terms of equity). Because it is so expensive, many entrepreneurs try to forestall asking for equity investments from outsiders as long as possible. Investing his own savings is one way for an entrepreneur to delay or avoid this stage of financing. Borrowing against the equity in his house is another.

Start-up capital usually refers to money raised to modify a working or almost-working prototype product into a product that can be manufactured at a cost that allows the company to make a profit. It can be the first or second stage of a company's financing. Start-up capital is used to test-market products and prepare companies for their first round of product sales. This money is more readily available than seed capital.

Second- and third-tier financings come next (if they are needed). These are traditionally used to finance inventory and company expansions. If a second- or third-tier financing is used to fund a company expansion that enables the company to later conduct a public offering, it is referred to as a mezzanine financing.

In the dynamic world of venture capital and start-up companies, no two companies have the same capital needs or grow in the same way. If management delays the need to acquire seed money until its prototype is almost ready, one venture capitalist might consider the proposed investment a seed investment while another might consider it an early start-up financing. There is no magic to the labels. They are conventions that are casually observed in the industry to describe financings. *See: Benchmarks, Mezzanine Financing, Pricing, Procrastination, ROI (Return on Investment), Seed Capital, Start-Up Capital.*

Start-up Capital refers to money raised to enable a company to get its working prototype product into production and to make initial marketing efforts. This money costs companies less equity per dollar of funding than seed capital does but more than later-stage financings. *See: Stage Financing.*

Stock Committee refers to a group of company officers and/or directors designated by a company's board of directors, with the mandate of determining when and how additional shares of the company's stock should be issued to employees or others. These committees are used to allocate a pool of shares to employees as part of an incentive plan, for example.

Venture capitalists will usually consent to the reservation of a small pool of shares to be issued to employees after closing of a funding even though the issuance of those shares will dilute the percentage interest of the investor. Often, however, the investor will want to participate in the allocation of these shares. One way for an investor to do this is to require that they be issued by a stock committee of which he is a member. *See: Board Committees, Incentive Stock Options (ISOs).*

Structure refers to the combination of debt and equity an investor receives for funding a company. Sometimes called "deal structure," it covers the timing of his funding and the protections and exits he receives. For example, one structure may call for $500,000 to be invested in a company in return for 20 percent of the company's outstanding stock. The deal might require all of the money to be invested at once and might include piggyback registration rights and a right of first refusal. Another structure might call for the money to be invested in stages as the company meets certain benchmarks and might require preferred stock or convertible debentures to be issued to the investor. That investor might also receive demand and piggyback registration rights, rights of first refusal, puts, and options to purchase additional shares. Both might require antidilution rights, but the amount of antidilution protection they require may be very different.

Most of the negotiations in a venture financing revolve around the price and structure of the proposed deal. Revising a structure can turn a bad deal into a good one, or vice versa. To negotiate effectively, management and its advisers must understand the ramifications of the various deal structuring devices employed by investors and the concerns of investors those devices are designed to address. Those devices and concerns are addressed elsewhere in this book. *See: Antidilution Provisions, Benchmarks, Buy-Sell Agreements, Convertible Securities, Co-Sale Agreements, Debentures, Earnouts, Earnups, Equity Penalties, Exits, First Refusal Rights, Leverage, Leveraged Buyout (LBO), Liquidity Agreements, Negotiation, Personal Guarantees, Pricing, Projections, Puts, Registration Rights, Revenue Participations, Stage Financing.*

Subordinated Debt is borrowed money that stands to be repaid after other debts but before company shareholders receive consideration in the event the company is liquidated. Subordinated debt is frequently used in venture financings to provide investors with a way to increase their return on investment or to withdraw a portion of it as debt repayment without unduly prejudicing the company's ability to obtain other borrowings.

Since it stands behind other debt if the company liquidates, subordinated debt is often treated as equity by other lenders. That is, lenders are willing to extend additional credit to the company as if the debt did not exist, as long as their debt matures and is repaid before the subordinated debt. This usually means that the subordinated debt agreement not only contains specific language subordinating it to other debt but that its maturity date occurs after that of the company's other debt. Therefore, the later the payback on subordinated debt, the easier it is for a company to borrow additional funds.

Subordinated debt provides a company with cash, usually with a long-term payback, and gives the investor a way to withdraw a portion of his investment without adverse tax consequences. Sometimes subordinated debt contains a convertibility feature that allows the investor to convert it into shares of stock. This gives the investor the flexibility to withdraw his funds as debt repayment or to convert to share ownership if the company's stock is selling for a good price. *See: Cash Flow, Convertible Securities, Debentures, Structure.*

Summary refers to a synopsis of the key points of a business plan. Sometimes referred to as an executive summary, it appears at the beginning of a business plan and highlights certain aspects of the company's proposal that are particularly important to prospective investors. It is one of the most important parts of a business plan.

The importance of the summary can be illustrated by a simple fact: Few venture capitalists will spend more than five or ten minutes on a business plan before deciding whether they are interested enough to study it seriously. The two portions of the business plan most venture capitalists focus on during this critical first reading are the summary and the financial information (projections). If the summary does not heighten their interest, few investors will turn to the financials or consider the company further.

Because of its importance in getting investors to investigate further, the summary should be prepared with particular care. It should be short (two to four pages is ideal), concise, descriptive, well organized, *and enticing.*

A lot to ask of a summary? Maybe, but while no professional investor is likely to invest in a company on the basis of two pages of reading, many will decide against investing just that quickly. To insure that the potential investor does not discard the company's business plan after reading only the summary, the plan writer should be sure it provides the investor with the right information about the company.

A good summary should cover the following information:

- *Company identity and contact.* Give the name, address, and telephone number of the company. The name of the person the investor should contact and how he or she may be reached should be prominently displayed.
- *Business of the company.* A short description of the company's business should be given here. How did it get started? What is its market niche, and why will it succeed?
- *Management.* What are the strengths of the company's key management personnel? A short itemization of the relevant accomplishments of key management members should be given.
- *The product.* This paragraph should contain a short description of the company's product and what makes it unique. A brief analysis of the company's competition and why management believes its product will succeed in the marketplace should also be included.

- *Funds required.* How much money does the company need? Does management have any preference as to equity versus debt? If the funds are requested on a staged basis, this should also be set forth. If there is collateral available, it should be described.
- *Use of funds.* How the company plans to use the funds should be detailed here.
- *Financial history.* A short financial history of the company should be provided here. This can be done in a narrative or in a chart listing four or five key figures such as revenues, income or loss, assets, liabilities, and net worth for each year of the company's operation.
- *Projections.* This section should contain a short summarization of the key elements of the company's projections for the next three to five years.
- *Exits.* Any plans the company has to go public or to provide the investor with other exits in the next three to five years should be spelled out. The investor wants to know how he will get his money out.

See: Business Plan, Business Plan Format, Negotiation, Three Questions.

Sweat Equity is the hard work, long hours, worry, and fatigue that a founding entrepreneur suffers to make his company succeed. The founder's stock initially issued to the entrepreneur usually costs a great deal less money than does stock later sold to investors who take less risk. This difference between the higher price paid for shares of the company's stock by investors and the price paid by the company's founders is the value of sweat equity. *See: Bargain Stock.*

Syndications are venture investments that are shared between several investors, with each providing part of the total funding to the company. Syndications are popular among venture investors because they allow them to spread their money over more deals and diversify their risks. They also allow them to share information with other investors as well as the cost of closing the funding.

Sometimes an investor who is willing to invest part of the money is not willing to put together the syndicate necessary to provide the rest. Such an investor is much less attractive to a company than one who is willing to help find all the capital a company needs. A good question to ask any interested venture capitalist is whether he is able to provide all the funding needed by the company. If not, ask if he will syndicate the investment. Most established funds will do so.

A problem that sometimes accompanies a syndicated funding is the desire of each investor to have a seat on the company's board of directors. As a rule, management should try to limit its outside investor group to the same number of board seats management would have given one investor had he provided all of the funding. Usually, this means one board seat for the investor group with the investors choosing among themselves who will represent them on the board. Others may attend board meetings and consult with management, but only one will be entitled to vote.

This encourages the syndication's members to cooperate among themselves so that management is not distracted by disagreements among its investors. At the same time, it preserves a small working board of directors and gives management the ability to tap into the expertise and contacts of each investor. *See: Lead Investor, Shopping, Underwriters.*

T

Technology Development Centers are facilities designed to assist entrepreneurs in creating viable businesses from their innovations. Many state governments and universities are now sponsoring programs to promote the development of new high-tech companies in their areas. These programs locate several services in one facility, sometimes called technology development centers, or technology incubators. If one exists nearby, management may be well advised to explore the services the center can provide.

Some centers provide "incubator assistance" by giving entrepreneurs inexpensive space, access to university research facilities, and consulting services on a reduced-fee basis. Others assist in company promotion and in obtaining government permits and licenses. If the program is an established one, it may also provide assistance in obtaining funding. *See: Incubators.*

HOW MUCH FOR A SECURITY BLANKET?

Polar Materials Inc. (PMI) was just three days old when founder H. Ronald Thomas met with Michael G. Bolton over breakfast in January, 1984. Thomas knew he had a good idea: Using plasma technology, he would create superior protective coatings for metals and fabrics. Only a few minor details stood in his way. He didn't have lab space, financing, or a business plan. He and partners Craig Passe and George Walpert had almost no inkling of how to run a business, either. "I was certainly a novice as a businessman," admits Thomas, 43.

That was pretty much what his companion had expected. By the end of breakfast, though, Bolton, executive director of Pennsylvania's North East Tier Ben Franklin Advanced Technology

Center at Lehigh University in Bethlehem, had offered Thomas lab and office space at $3 a square foot (about one-third the local going rate) inside the center. But space wasn't all he offered. With access to Lehigh's labs, Thomas hired six graduate students, under the tutelage of faculty advisers, and two post-doctoral researchers. PMI received a $208,000 grant from Pennsylvania's Ben Franklin program, which funds high-technology initiatives. And Bolton introduced Thomas to George W. Miller, a banker, who worked without pay as PMI's unofficial chief financial officer. Miller revised Thomas' business plan, and helped PMI raise $600,000 from private investors. Today, PMI has completed its first line of plasma coatings, and Thomas expects to earn $100,000 on $1.5 million in sales in the 12 months ending June 30, 1986.

Thomas collected his bundle of management help and financial support from an innovation center, one of an increasingly large group of organizations devoted to developing technology-based businesses. Run by state agencies, universities, and a slew of private, not-for-profit and for-profit organizations, innovation centers blend into new business incubators at one end of the spectrum and the old-fashioned research park on the other. Like the new business incubator, the innovation center rents space, often at below market rates, and—unlike the research park—offers shared services, such as copying machines and word processors, along with management help. Like the research park and unlike most incubators, the innovation center concentrates on technology-intensive businesses and provides some kind of access to scientific facilities and talent. Some, such as Pennsylvania's Advanced Technology Centers, have direct links to funding sources and operate in conjunction with large universities. Others provide no facilities at all and offer only technical and management assistance. All aim to hasten the transfer of ideas from the laboratory or workshop into the marketplace.

Of course none of this help is exactly free. In fact, some innovation centers seem downright expensive. And what you get doesn't really determine what you pay. For example, the Business Technology Center, Columbus, Ohio, charges $5 a square foot for space in its center. That fee includes the shared use of a receptionist and telephone answering service, a conference room, a microcomputer, a copying machine, a business library, and consultation with members of the center's board. A similar setup at Philadelphia's University City Science Center runs $12 to $18 a square foot. With its larger staff—150 in Philadelphia compared with one full-timer in Columbus—and connection with 28 Philadelphia-area universities, the Science Center offers a great deal of technical and managerial help that may justify its cost.

Many innovation centers also take an equity stake in new companies, often in lieu of fees. The Minnesota Cooperation Office, Minneapolis, which doesn't rent space to companies, takes 2% to 4% of equity in return for its management advice. The Milwaukee Innovation Center, also without a physical incubator, takes 5% to 20% shares. The Utah Innovation Center, Salt Lake City, which operates a 157,000-sq.-ft. center through a limited partnership, will take up to 35% of a startup company. Entrepreneurs, searching desperately for help, don't always recognize what they are giving up.

—From an article by Edmund L. Andrews
that appeared in the February 1986 issue of *Venture*

10b5 is the common nomenclature for a provision in the federal securities laws that prohibits fraudulent and misleading activities in securities transactions. The provision is mirrored in the states' securities acts as well. Provision 10b5 (and corresponding state laws) make fraudulent practices in the sale of securities unlawful and prescribe severe penalties for violators. As a result, the use of fraudulent material, the making of misstatements, or the existence of material omissions in dealing with potential investors or in descriptions of an offering or company can have serious consequences to a company and its management. The text of the 10b5 provision reads as follows:

> It shall be unlawful for any person, directly or indirectly, by the use of any means or instrumentality of interstate commerce, or of the mails, or of any facility of any national securities exchange,
>
> 1. to employ any device, scheme, or artifice to defraud,
> 2. to make any untrue statement of a material fact or omit to state a material fact necessary in order to make the statements made, in the light of the circumstances under which they were made, not misleading, or
> 3. to engage in any act, practice, or course of business which operates or would operate as fraud or deceit upon any person,
>
> in connection with the purchase or sale of any security.

Most states have similar laws. The combined effect of these laws and the other provisions of the federal and state securities laws is to make it very risky, and potentially costly, to deal in company securities in any manner that is not honest, straightforward, and in strict compliance with the law.

The securities laws, rules, and regulations are complex, and courts have been expansive in their interpretations of the 10b5 and other antifraud provisions of the securities laws. To avoid problems, legal counsel should *always* be consulted before company securities are offered for sale. *See: Going Public, Lawyers, Private Placements, Reg D, 33 Act.*

Think Capital is a company's technology and the brainpower of key employees who supply the company with its technological edge. In high-tech companies, the protections taken to preserve this think capital are very important to prospective investors. These protections include careful documentation of the company's title to important technologies, safeguards to prevent the theft or loss of company secrets, agreements to prevent competition by employees, and incentives to keep key personnel employed with the company. *See: Confidentiality Agreements, Copyrights, Golden Handcuffs, Noncompete Agreements, Patents, Software Protection, Trade Secrets.*

33 Act refers to the federal Securities Act of 1933. Any time a company attempts to raise capital through the issuance of its securities it becomes subject to a variety of laws regulating the offering and selling of securities. The most important of these are the 33 Act and the states' securities acts. These laws make it unlawful for any person to offer, sell, or deliver any "security" unless a registration statement meeting requirements contained in the law is in effect as to the security or an exemption to the registration requirements applies.*

The securities these laws apply to have been broadly defined by the statutes and courts. They include corporate stock and debt instruments as well as similar interests issued by individuals, partnerships, and joint ventures. They also include other types of "investment contracts" that are not commonly thought of as securities.

* For jurisdictional reasons, the 33 Act applies only to securities offered, sold, or delivered using the mail or a means or instrument of transportation or communication in interstate commerce. In most circumstances it is easy to meet the requirements of this condition and find a basis to apply the 33 Act.

Detailed disclosure or ready access to information must be given to investors in connection with a securities offering. This is generally true whether the offering is registered or exempt from registration. This disclosure is usually made through the use of a registration statement and prospectus (also referred to as an offering circular) that contain pertinent information concerning the offering, the securities being offered, and the entity issuing the securities. In limited circumstances, however, such as venture capital transactions involving only certain specially qualified (or "accredited") investors, the information may be made available in other ways that do not involve the preparation of an extensive offering memorandum. *See: Going Public, Investment Reps, IPOs (Initial Public Offerings), Private Placements, Reg D, Restricted Securities, 10b5.*

Three Questions investors invariably ask entrepreneurs are: How much money do you need?; how will you spend it?; and how will I get it back? To obtain funding, entrepreneurs must be prepared to answer these questions intelligently. *See: Business Plan, Due Diligence, Exits, Summary.*

Track Record is a person's or company's operating history. The best and most relevant track record management can have is to have created a successful business before. Second best is experience working in the company's industry or in other start-ups. The better the track record management has, the easier it will be to attract capital to the company, and to attract it at a favorable price.

Track records can transcend a company or industry in special cases. For example, John Sculley's track record with PepsiCo enabled him to establish himself at Apple Computer. In this case Sculley's track record in a specific functional area was so outstanding that it could transcend an industry. *See: Entrepreneur, Five Factors, Turnarounds.*

Trademarks are words or design elements that identify a company product and distinguish it from others. Service marks identify and distinguish a service. Businesses can prevent others from using their marks on competitive products by following federal and state laws that govern trademarks and service marks.

Trademarks can become very important to a new company as it builds a reputation for its product.

In general, a mark must be used in commerce and identified as a trademark or service mark before a company can protect it. After it has been used, a company must file required registrations.

Companies can conduct searches to be sure their mark is available to them before they begin using it. Thus, they can avoid promoting a mark that cannot be protected or used. The first type of search that can be conducted is one of the records of the trademark office to determine whether anyone has already registered the mark. If no registration can be found, the company can next pay a service bureau to conduct a common-law search to see if it is already being used in commerce in an unregistered form. If the mark clears both searches, the chances are good that it can be registered and protected. Company counsel can often advise on the best and most appropriate method for conducting these searches. *See: Copyrights, Patents, Trade Secrets.*

Trade Secrets are all of a company's proprietary know-how that gives it an advantage in the marketplace. Different states define trade secrets differently, but most state laws only protect a company's trade secrets that are not generally known to its competitors and only when the company takes actions to identify and protect them.

Unlike patents, which entitle the holder to preclude others from using patented technologies, trade secrets protection prevents others from using company technologies only by keeping them secret. If others discover the company's secrets by "reverse engineering" or by developing the same secrets on their own, the company cannot stop them from using the knowledge. Trade secrets protection can prevent others from stealing the company's secrets, however, only as long as the company takes appropriate actions to prevent unauthorized disclosure of its information.

Confidentiality and secrecy agreements with company employees, owners, and consultants who have access to secrets are common methods of protecting them. Investors who put money into companies with valuable secrets usually require the companies to enter into secrecy agreements with their employees.

Some also require management members to enter into secrecy and noncompete agreements directly with the investors.

Confidentiality agreements alone will not protect company secrets. Other measures must be taken to ensure the secrecy of the information. These include limiting access to company secrets (only those persons who need to know the secrets to perform their job and who are bound by a secrecy agreement should have access), marking secrets as confidential, and distinguishing between secrets and nonsecrets. Material containing company secrets should be stored in a safe place and destroyed when it is no longer needed so that it cannot be "leaked."

Trade secrecy laws vary from state to state. Some states, for instance, distinguish between technical trade secrets and nontechnical confidential information, allowing a company to protect nontechnical information only by contract and only for a limited period of time. Some states require stricter definitions of technical trade secrets than they do of nontechnical confidential information. Others make no distinction at all. All prescribe definite limits to the availability of trade secrecy protection.

Attempts to extend protection beyond these legal limits, even if inadvertent, can jeopardize the trade secrecy protection a company relies upon. This, coupled with the fact that companies must comply with all of the conditions and requirements set out by their state's laws before they are able to claim trade secrecy protection, makes it important for companies to have an experienced professional review the precautions they take to protect their secrets and to review the form of any secrecy agreements they use. *See: Confidentiality Agreements, Lawyers, Software Protection, Think Capital.*

Turnarounds are situations in which new funds are needed to get a company out of trouble. Some turnarounds involve companies whose management buys out the controlling shareholders and tries to turn around the company and make it profitable. Certain managers excel at turnaround situations because they have the necessary skills and guts to make the hard decisions required in these cases. These managers are called turnaround specialists, and their track records are far more important than the industry or the company they corrected. Two of the most famous turnarounds in recent history are Lee Iacocca's revitalizing of Chrysler Corporation and Felix Rohatyn's restructuring of New York City's finances. In both cases, the financial health of the entities today reflects the expertise of the turnaround specialist. *See: Leveraged Buyout (LBO).*

U

Underwriters refer to stock brokerage firms and others who market and sell company securities to the public.

Most initial public offerings are sold (or underwritten) by underwriters who specialize in such transactions. The sale is typically conducted through a syndicate of firms that are selected by the company's underwriter. The managing underwriter in the syndicate (the one selected by the company) attempts to select the right combination of underwriters to achieve a distribution of the company's shares between private individuals and institutional purchasers that will assure a good price in the offering and adequate trading in the shares after it is completed. The managing underwriter usually continues to support the company in the financial community after the offering by making a market in the company's stock, providing research and analysis on the company for investors, organizing communications with investors and potential investors, and generally helping the company create a following among them.

Because of the variety of services they provide and because their ability to provide those services efficiently can affect not only the offering price of the company's shares but also their continuing strength in the public marketplace, the selection of the right underwriter is important. Among the characteristics management should consider when selecting an underwriter are:

- *Stature within the financial community*. The underwriter's professional reputation as an investment banker can determine, in large part, his ability to put together a strong syndicate to sell the company's shares. The strength of the syndicate can, in turn, influence the quality of the investors attracted to the offering.

- *Experience in the company's industry.* Underwriters develop reputations within industries. An underwriter who is experienced at taking businesses public in the company's industry can enhance the credibility of the company's offering. Experience can also help an underwriter price a company's shares properly so that the offering is sold and its share price holds steady or increases.
- *Research reputation.* The company's managing underwriter will be a primary source of information about the company to the financial community. It is helpful, therefore, to select an underwriter whose analysts are experienced and follow the company's industry closely. An underwriter's reputation for reliable research in a company's industry can help sustain investor interest in the company's stock.
- *Ability to support the market.* Once issued, the company's stock will be traded on the over-the-counter market. The ability of the underwriter as a "market-maker" to support the market is important. By purchasing and selling the company's stock in the market, the "market-maker" gives the company's stock needed liquidity, which helps stabilize trading prices.

It is a good practice to interview several underwriters before selecting one to conduct a public offering. Accountants, bankers, lawyers, and other entrepreneurs can introduce a company to underwriters. A good deal of information about underwriters and the types of deals they do also can be obtained by watching the financial press, particularly the *Wall Street Journal.* Underwriters regularly run advertisements (called "tombstones" by the trade—see Figure 2) that show public offerings that have and the syndicate members who participated. *See: Going Public, IPOs (Initial Public Offerings), Investment Bankers, Syndications.*

Unit Offerings are sales of company securities when more than one type of security is sold as a single unit, or when investors are required to purchase securities in blocks of shares. The term is usually used to refer to private placements or public offerings where investors are offered the opportunity to purchase "units" that consist of a share of stock and a warrant to purchase more stock in the future. *See: Going Public,*

Eastern Wall Street Journal

This advertisement is neither an offer to sell nor a solicitation of an offer to buy any of these securities.
The offering is made only by the Prospectus.

1,300,000 Shares

Scan-Optics, Inc.

Common Stock

Price $11.875 Per Share

Copies of the Prospectus may be obtained in any State only from such of the undersigned and the other several Underwriters as may lawfully offer the securities in such State.

Thomson McKinnon Securities Inc.

Bear, Stearns & Co.
The First Boston Corporation
A. G. Becker Paribas
Incorporated
Blyth Eastman Paine Webber
Incorporated
Alex. Brown & Sons
Dillon, Read & Co. Inc.
Donaldson, Lufkin & Jenrette
Securities Corporation
Drexel Burnham Lambert
Incorporated
Hambrecht & Quist
Incorporated
E. F. Hutton & Company Inc.
Kidder, Peabody & Co.
Incorporated
Lazard Frères & Co.
Lehman Brothers Kuhn Loeb
Incorporated
Merrill Lynch Capital Markets
L. F. Rothschild, Unterberg, Towbin
Shearson/American Express Inc.
Smith Barney, Harris Upham & Co.
Incorporated
Wertheim & Co., Inc.
Dean Witter Reynolds Inc.
Allen & Company
Incorporated
Robert W. Baird & Co.
Incorporated
A. G. Edwards & Sons, Inc.
Montgomery Securities
Oppenheimer & Co., Inc.
Robertson, Colman & Stephens
J. C. Bradford & Co.
Incorporated
Butcher & Singer Inc.
Furman Selz Mager Dietz & Birney
Incorporated
Interstate Securities Corporation
Janney Montgomery Scott Inc.
Johnson, Lane, Space, Smith & Co., Inc.
Josephthal & Co.
Incorporated
Ladenburg, Thalmann & Co. Inc.
Legg Mason Wood Walker
Incorporated
Moseley, Hallgarten, Estabrook & Weeden Inc.
Robinson Humphrey/American Express Inc
Tucker, Anthony & R. L. Day, Inc.
Wheat, First Securities, Inc.

Figure 2 Sample Tombstone

IPOs (Initial Public Offerings), Penny Stock, Private Placements.

Unlocking Provisions are mechanisms that enable investors to disengage their financial arrangements with management. One typical unlocking provision is a buy-sell agreement, which allows an investor to force management either to buy the investor's shares at a price he sets or sell its own shares to the investor for the same price. Another provision creates a mechanism through which either management or the investor can force the other to sell its interest in the company to a third party or buy the stock of the other party. Typically, this arrangement allows either management or the investor to accept a third party's offer to buy the company's assets or the stock of both shareholders in the company. The other party must then either buy the first party's shares at the per-share price contained in the third party offer or sell his interest, along with the interests of the other shareholder, to the third party. *See: Buy-Sell Agreements, Exits, Liquidity Agreements.*

Upside is the potential profit an investor hopes to receive from his investment under ideal circumstances. It is what the venture capitalist measures against the downside when evaluating a company. The greater the upside and the more likely it will be obtained, the less the investor will require in return for his investment.

When businessmen speak of the "dollar signs dancing in their eyes" they are envisioning the upside. For venture investors, the upside represents the potential for their shares to appreciate significantly. This can be achieved by company growth and success and can be supplemented by the market increasing the stock's P/E ratio. *See: Downside, P/E, Pricing, ROI (Return on Investment).*

V

Value Added refers to the knowledge, management advice and related nonmonetary input investors sometimes offer a young company. Many venture investors do provide more than money to their portfolio companies. They provide management with the benefit of their experience with emerging growth companies. They also help management by using their contacts in the company's industry and with other financial sources.

This value added by the venture capitalist can be important but is difficult to measure. In addition to the risk (or downside), it is the reason many professional venture firms try to charge a management fee to the portfolio company. Entrepreneurs often fail to see the "value added" of a venture capitalist's advice at first, but many recognize it later when the value of the advice becomes more apparent. *See: Consulting Agreements, Geography, Management Agreements.*

Venture Books treat a number of issues of interest to entrepreneurs. Several of them deal with venture financing and are worth reviewing. One of the best is *Pratt's Guide to Venture Capital Sources*, edited by Stanley E. Pratt and Jane K. Harris and published by Venture Economics, Inc. It comes in two volumes and contains a good short course on venture capital financing. It also contains a detailed listing of venture capital firms, the sizes of their funds, the type of companies they invest in, and the names and telephone numbers of their principals. The books can be obtained by calling Venture Economics at 617–431–8100. The price is approximately $100. A less expensive, one-volume version of the book without the venture capital firms listing is also available under the title *How to Raise Venture Capital*.

Other good books include the following:

- *Venture Capital Handbook* by David Gladstone (Reston Publishing Co., 1984). This is a good practical guide to the venture capital process written by a venture capitalist.
- *How to Start, Finance, and Manage Your Own Small Business* by Joseph R. Mancuso (Prentice-Hall, Inc., 1978). This volume has a good section describing the manner in which venture capitalists analyze business plans. Also by Joseph Mancuso is *How to Write a Winning Business Plan*. Both books can be ordered through the Center for Entrepreneurial Management, 29 Greene Street, New York, NY 10013, or by calling (212) 925–7304.
- *Investing in Private Companies*, by Arthur Lipper III (Dow-Jones Irwin, 1984). Available through *Venture* at (212) 682–7373. The investor's perspective on the venture process is discussed here in detail.
- *Up Front Financing*, by A. David Silver (John Wiley & Sons, 1982). This short book is written by an investment banker and identifies several methods of funding.
- *Venture's Guide to International Venture Capital*, by the editors of *Venture* (Simon & Schuster, 1985). Available through *Venture* at (212) 682–7373. Notwithstanding its title, this volume has a good listing of U.S. venture capital firms.
- *The Handbook for Raising Capital*, edited by Lawrence Chimerine, Robert F. Cushman, and Howard Ross (Dow-Jones Irwin, 1986). This is a collection of articles by investment bankers, accountants, lawyers, and others about methods of raising money.
- *Raising Venture Capital and the Entrepreneur*, by Leonard A. Batterson (Prentice-Hall, 1986). This book contains a directory of venture capital firms and some helpful checklists.
- *Business Plans That Win $$$*, by Stanley Rich and David Gumpert (Harper & Row, 1985).
- *How to Write a Business Plan*, by Edwin T. Crego, Jr., Brian Deaton, and Peter D. Schiffrin (American Management Association, 1986). It can be ordered by writing the AMA Extension Institute at 135 West 50th Street, New York, NY 10020, or by calling (212) 586–8100.

See: Business Plan, NASBIC (National Association of Small Business Investment Companies), National Venture Capital Association, Venture Capitalists.

Venture Capital is money invested in a company or individual at high risk to the investor, usually in situations in which the company is unable to secure needed funds from traditional lending sources, such as a commercial loan from a bank. Usually, the status of the company is such that the investor will be unable to withdraw his money in the near future. Venture capital can be invested through the purchase of stock (equity), by making a loan (debt), or through a combination of the two.

Venture capital investors require a very high rate of return and thus only invest in companies with good prospects for rapid growth. Often, venture capital investments come bundled with management assistance and oversight by the investor, known as value added services. Companies most likely to obtain venture capital are those for which an eventual public offering of their stock in five years or less is envisioned by the investor. Turnarounds and leveraged buyouts are also good prospects for venture capital. *See: Adventure Capitalists, Angels, BDCs (Business Development Corporations), CDCs (Community Development Corporations), Corporate Venture Capital, Emerging Growth Companies, Leveraged Buyout (LBO), P/E, Pools, Pricing, ROI (Return on Investment) SBICs (Small Business Investment Companies), Specialty Funds, Turnarounds, Value Added, Vulture Capitalists.*

Venture Capital Clubs are informal groups of venture capitalists, entrepreneurs, financial strategists, accountants, and lawyers that meet regularly to discuss matters of interest, exchange ideas, and share opportunities. They provide a common meeting ground for persons interested in entrepreneurial activity. There are many of these clubs across the United States. If one exists nearby, management should explore the opportunities it provides to become acquainted with the venture capital infrastructure of the area. *See: Networking, Venture Capital Conferences.*

Venture Capital Conferences are forums at which venture capitalists meet to exchange information and to hear presentations from companies seeking funding. Typically, the sponsor of the conference screens applicants who want to present their companies' funding needs. The applicants who pass the screening then describe their opportunities in short oral presentations to an audience of investors. Interested investors can follow up with the entrepreneurs later in the conference.

The best sources of information about upcoming venture capital conferences are local accounting or law firms, which may cosponsor them, local venture firms, which may participate as plan screeners, local colleges and universities with entrepreneurship courses, which may provide professors as speakers, or organizers like *Venture*, which publishes notices of these conferences in its monthly events calendar feature. *See: Networking, Shopping.*

MISTAKES I MADE AT A BUSINESS PLAN FORUM

The opportunity to present my entrepreneurial business idea to the New Ventures Workshop at the Harvard Business School was too great to pass up. I thought of the exposure to a roomful of investors eager to pour hundreds of thousands of dollars into my venture and the tremendous profits their dollars would initiate. I thought of the feedback I would get from the panelists—surely they would be impressed with the idea, and with me as an entrepreneur. No doubt they would be equally impressed with my wife [the company's cofounder] and her ability to handle the public relations aspects of the firm. Certainly people would be thrusting Offers To Purchase at me before the presentation was over. I made a note to have Offers To Purchase with me.

Judging by the process of getting scheduled, how bad could the experience be? Mr. Burt Alimansky, Chairman of the Workshop, was patient and thorough as he explained the ground rules of the workshop and the costs involved. I would need to submit my complete business plan to the panelists at least ten days before, and have handouts ready for the audience. To be most effective, he recommended that I accompany my talk with a slide show, highlighting certain key aspects of the business. He provided me with a suggested outline and asked for my suggestions for panelists. For $350, I would benefit from the candid business advice of four panelists, all of whom would be familiar with the industry in which I hope to operate. And one of the panelists would be a venture capitalist—so if the deal looked good, I'd make contact right there.

I began working on the presentation months in advance. For a public talk, I thought I would omit a lot of the routine financial information, and instead include more industry background. Instead of pie charts and pro formas, I decided to include color slides depicting the problems the industry is having, and how the new company expects to solve them. Instead of iffy sales projections, I listed the product benefits and hinted at possible unit sales. I wrote jokes into the script here and there to provide comic relief.

Wrong, wrong, wrong. The first comment from the first panelist was, "Mr. Cohen, when it comes to investments of this magnitude, you shouldn't be joking." The first comment from the second panelist was, "Mr. Cohen, instead of providing sales projections, you've given us conjecture. We need solid sales projections, for every product, for ten years, in order to properly analyze your chances for success."

The third panelist said, "Mr. Cohen, your slides are very nice, but you haven't shown us a single slide of your product, nor have you provided a Sources and Uses Statement. As investors, how will we know where our money is going?" And the fourth panelist said, "Mr. Cohen, you've wasted your time and ours. Without detailed financials, including projected profit and loss statements and balance sheets for each of the first ten years, the industry background you've provided is nothing but interesting reading. You've got a lot of work to do."

And so, $350 and many late nights working on the plan later, I learned to heed the advice I had been hearing from venture capitalists for many years: Don't go looking for capital until the plan is complete, and answers the questions investors are bound to ask. The Plan Forums we cover in *VCCM* [*Venture's Capital Club Monthly*] aren't places for theatrics or creativity. Just stick to the basics, and make sure all your homework is done. Don't agree to be a presenter unless you are certain your plan is complete, including all financials and the shareholder's agreement. Because, like the Emperor and his new clothes, if you're naked up there, somebody will notice.

—From an editorial by Steven M. Cohen,
editor and publisher,
Venture's Capital Club Monthly, which appeared
in the September 1985 issue of *VCCM*

Venture Capitalists are those professional money managers who provide risk capital to businesses. Venture capitalists come in many forms and specialize in different ways, but all share the common trait of making investments in high-risk situations that have the potential to provide them a very high rate of return on their investment.

Venture capitalists include over one thousand private funds, fewer than 100 companies funded by public offerings of their securities, bank and corporate subsidiaries charged with investing budgeted funds, and private individuals, often called "adventure capitalists" or "angels." Venture firms can be highly leveraged companies, such as SBIC's and MESBIC's, or completely unleveraged.

Some good sources for identifying venture capitalists interested in a given industry are:

- the National Association of Small Business Investment Companies (NASBIC), 1156 15th Street, N.W., Washington, DC 20005; (202) 833-8230
- the National Venture Capital Association, 1655 North Fort Meyer Drive, Arlington, Va. 22209; (703) 528-4370
- *Venture's Guide to International Venture Capital*, by the editors of *Venture* (Simon & Schuster, 1985)
- *Pratt's Guide to Venture Capital Sources*, edited by Stanley E. Pratt and Jane K. Morris (Venture Economics, Inc., 11th Ed. 1987)
- *Raising Venture Capital and the Entrepreneur*, by Leonard A. Batterson (Prentice-Hall, 1986)

See: Adventure Capitalists, Angels, BDCs (Business Development Corporations), CDCs (Community Development Corporations), Corporate Venture Capital, MESBICs (Minority Enterprise Small Business Investment Companies), Pools, SBICs (Small Business Investment Companies), Specialty Funds, Venture Books, Vulture Capitalists.

THE VENTURE CAPITAL 100: SOME LEAP UP THE LADDER; OTHERS HANG TIGHT

Venture capital firms took big jumps up and down the Venture Capital 100, a ranking of the 100 most active investors in 1985. The dollars put into seed and startup investments fluctuated even more wildly between 1985 and 1984. One firm invested 680% more in this category in 1985. Several other firms dropped by

100%. All in all, seed and startup investments dropped to $441.15 million in 1985 down from $471.47 [million] in 1984 and $571.38 [million] in 1983.

The firms on the Venture Capital 100 invested $2.29 billion in 1985, essentially the same as 1984's $2.28 billion. In 1983 investment by the 100 most active firms came to $2.33 billion. The total number of deals in 1985 rose disproportionately to 3,696 from 2.651 in 1984.

Later-stage investments rose to $557.64 million in 1985, up from $491.11 million in 1984 and $543.32 million in 1983. Follow-on dollars grew to $821.96 million last year from $793.7 million in 1984 and $602.92 million in 1983. LBOs declined slightly to $471.23 million in 1985 from $481.46 million.

Venture prepared the Venture Capital 100 from information provided by more than 200 venture capital firms.

—From an article by Jim Jubak
that appeared in the August 1986
issue of *Venture*. A complete
list of the *Venture* Capital 100
is reproduced in Appendix D.

Vesting Schedules refer to a method used to make a person's stock ownership contingent upon some future event, such as the passage of time or the achievement of a stated goal. They are commonly a part of an agreement pursuant to which management or certain company employees are denied full ownership rights in their shares until the future.

When a vesting schedule applies, an employee is granted the rights to a specified number of shares of the company's stock, but those shares do not really become his until certain defined events have occurred. For example, an employee may be granted ten thousand shares of the company's common stock "subject to vesting." Those shares may vest upon his remaining employed with the company for five years. Each year, for instance, two thousand of his shares may vest and become his providing he is still employed by the company. If he remains with the company for the full five years, he will receive all ten thousand shares. If he leaves after three years of employment, he will receive certificates for only six thousand shares.

Vesting schedules often tie an employee's rights to own shares to employment longevity and some other factor such as company earnings or sales. Often, they are used in conjunction with non-compete agreements and employment incentives to encourage effort and loyalty from important employees. They are commonly used by investors to encourage founding management to stay with a company.

Because of the complexity of the Internal Revenue Code and certain technicalities it contains, anyone who receives stock subject to vesting requirements should consult with an attorney or accountant to determine the tax effect of receiving it and the advisability of filing an 83(b) election. *See: 83(b) Elections, Golden Handcuffs.*

Voting Agreements are also referred to as shareholders' agreements. These are contracts, usually in writing, that are signed by two or more shareholders and govern the manner in which those shareholders will vote their shares of company stock. In most situations, if shareholders holding a majority of the shares of voting stock agree to vote their shares together, they can control a company. Voting agreements are commonly used by minority shareholders to assure themselves a seat on a company's board of directors or to restrict the issuance of additional shares of a company's stock. *See: Control, Shareholders' Agreements.*

Voting Trusts are agreements used to transfer control from management to an investor if the company does not meet its goals. They work by placing management's stock in a trust with the investor's shares. The trustee is instructed to vote the entrusted shares as the venture capitalist directs if the company fails to meet its goals. Voting trusts are the exception, not the rule, these days. *See: Benchmarks, Control, Voting Agreements.*

Vulture Capitalists is a term used by disappointed entrepreneurs to describe investors who refused their deal or whom they believe demanded too much equity in return for funding. It is sometimes used by an entrepreneur to identify an investor who has exercised a contractual right and taken an action the entrepreneur disagrees with, such as firing management or liquidating the company. The term is pejorative and reflects the attitude of a disgruntled entrepreneur.

Venture capitalists do not invest in companies to make

friends. They invest to make money. Without profits, the investors in the venture capitalist's fund or pool will not participate in later funds, and the venture capitalist will go out of business. As a result, venture capitalists are extremely picky about the companies they invest in and how well they perform. They do not want their portfolio companies to fail and will usually exercise their rights to prevent a failure they perceive, even if doing so makes them a vulture capitalist in the eyes of the entrepreneur. *See: Deal Flow, Golden Rule, Venture Capitalists.*

W

Warrants are a form of stock option that entitles an investor to purchase shares of company stock in the future at a price fixed on the warrant. Warrants are usually given in connection with a loan to a company. The lender is given the warrant as an inducement to make the loan. The lender then can "exercise the warrant" by paying cash for the share price on the warrant or by cancelling a portion of the debt equal to the warrant exercise price. When they are issued in connection with a loan, they are often called equity kickers to refer to their ability to give debt investors an opportunity to share in the company's capital appreciation. *See: Options.*

I GET AN EQUITY KICKER OUT OF YOU

Sometimes all a bank needs is a little equity kicker in the pants to spring a loan for the young company.

"We were a pretty rocky company from a financial standpoint, but we knew we had potential," says Gordon G. Nelson, president of Sielox Systems Inc., Sunnyvale, Calif. But two years ago investors and lenders weren't impressed with the company's future. Venture capitalists weren't interested in the electronic security industry. Bankers wanted to see more than two years of operating history. Annualized sales were only $1.5 million and Sielox had yet to turn a profit. Nelson began to consider selling stock, even at an enormous dilution to the original investors, or closing up shop.

But Sielox got lucky. It stumbled across one of the fewer than a dozen banks in the nation willing to do equity-kicker financing. As an incentive to take on the higher risk of lending to a young company, Silicon Valley Bank in San Jose, Calif., got a "kicker" —a 1.4% equity position in the company in the form of 5,000 warrants exercisable at $3.00 a share for the next year. Sielox got a $200,000 line of credit at about prime plus three. Later, the bank increased the line of credit by $100,000 and dropped the interest rate by a point in exchange for more favorable collateral support.

"It was a nice return to us," says David Titus, then a senior vice-president at the small two-and-a-half-year-old bank that specializes in working with fast-growth technology companies. Early this year, after Sielox's sales increased to $2 million for 1985, Checkpoint Systems Inc. of Thorofare, N.J., acquired the company for $6.50 a share. Silicon Valley reaped a $13,000 profit on the warrants, approximately 25% of the bank's total return on the loan, says Titus.

Most banks shy away from deals like this, however, because taking equity "goes against their grain," says Davis N. Pearl, manager of high-technology programs with Coopers & Lybrand's emerging business services group. And those banks willing to take on more risk in the form of equity kickers won't deal with just any company. "We're looking for companies that have been properly capitalized, that is, with venture capital or sophisticated individual investors," says Barbara Mastro, who heads up Bank of Boston's high-tech division. Such backing signals to the bank that the company has a good chance of growth, and after several years, of going public or being acquired at a good earnings multiple.

Banks that take equity kickers still use the same standards to evaluate loans. "We aren't playing this on a high-risk, high-reward angle. A ton of warrants does not make a bad deal good," says Titus. So far, of the 15 equity kicker deals done by Silicon Valley Bank, only Sielox has proved a sure winner. Titus expects three or four others will also pay off and another two or three will return nothing.

—From an article by Marie-Jeanne Juilland in the August 1986 issue of *Venture.*

We Always Do It This Way is a phrase managements sometimes hear from an investor or his lawyer, normally, at the point where management has negotiated the main deal points with the investor and the parties are in the process of putting that deal onto paper. Suddenly, the investor's lawyer presents the company with forty-five pages of representations and warranties he wants management to sign. Management remembers the investor saying that he wanted to keep the deal simple, with the minimum reps and warranties. Management protests, and the lawyer says, "But we always do it this way."

Management is supposed to roll over and gladly comply with the lawyer's request. After all, they always do it that way. This is the first venture capital financing the company has been involved in, and the investor has done dozens. So he must know what's appropriate. Right?

Wrong. There are certain conventions observed in venture capital financings, including "normal" types of representations and warranties that companies and their managements customarily make. Nonetheless, management is entitled to receive a rational explanation about anything the venture capitalist asks it to do that it does not understand (or agree with).

An explanation such as "we always do it this way" is not enough. That explanation probably means the company has been presented with the lawyer's standard form, which he always uses as a starting point in negotiations. Like all standard forms, much of what is in it will not apply to the company or its funding.

"We always do it this way" implies that the way the investor did his deals in the past is the way the current deal should be done. But this company and its needs are different from all those other deals. And, while it may be unrealistic to expect an investor to abandon the deal structure or basic deal documents that have worked well for him, it is realistic to expect him to deal openly with management and to explain why each provision of his deal documents is necessary. *See: Boilerplate, Reps and Warranties.*

We Never Exercise Our Rights under This Section is a phrase that often follows "we always do it this way," and begins with "don't worry . . ." It's designed to comfort management when the venture investor insists on a particularly onerous provision. Sometimes the phrase is different; "We don't expect to have to use this provision," or "We never use this provision, but we always require it."

Management should be careful when someone asks for something they insist they will never use. If they really will not use it, then they really do not need it. *See: Boilerplate, Reps and Warranties, We Always Do It This Way.*

Windows is a phrase used in two distinctly different contexts, but in both cases the aspect of timing is crucial.

Firstly, venture capitalists are very sensitive to the timing of the introduction of a company's new product into the market. If the technology is too revolutionary, the cost of creating a market for the product may be prohibitive. On the other hand, if the product does not have enough to distinguish it from its competition, it may be too late for the product to gain a profitable market share. That period of time when the company's technology is new enough to distinguish its products in the marketplace but not too new so that no one understands its application is sometimes called "the window of opportunity." Introducing the product "while the window is open" is critical to a company's prospects for success.

Secondly, window is used to refer to the period of time when the stock market is receptive to new issues of stock in the particular industry of a company. When one company conducts a successful initial public offering in computer software, for example, other software companies will rush to complete their offerings "while the window is open."

Unlike windows in a building, the windows of opportunity for technology or new issues are never partially open: They are open or closed, nothing in between. *See: Five Factors, Going Public, IPOs (Initial Public Offerings), Market Research.*

Z

Zeal . . . is something investors want and expect to see in entrepreneurs they fund. No one wants to invest in a lethargic entrepreneur. *See: Commitment, Entrepreneur.*

APPENDIX A

A Few Words About Tax Reform

A lot has been said about the effects the Tax Reform Act of 1986 will have on the availability of venture capital and the way venture capitalists structure their fundings. To hear some people talk, this latest round of tax reform may bring an end to venture capital and entrepreneurial incentive. Other observers believe tax reform will make it more difficult but not impossible to raise money and exit profitably from investments. Still others think there will be little negative impact on venture capital because of offsetting nontax factors (such as the increasing numbers of tax exempt organizations investing in venture funds) and lower tax rates. Some even speculate that lower tax rates and new restrictions placed on tax shelters by tax reform will actually increase the amount of funds available for venture investing.

Who's right and who's wrong? The best bet is that the 1986 Tax Reform Act will not destroy venture capital but may change some of the ways people structure their businesses and financing packages. What those changes will be, however, will depend not just on tax reform but also on how people think tax rules will change in the future. Changes in securities laws and accounting standards may also affect the practices of investors and entrepreneurs in the future.

Venture capital and entrepreneurial activity should not suffer unduly from tax reform. Certainly, tax code provisions that give tax breaks (resulting in higher after-tax yields) to long-term investors encourage venture capital investments compared to other less tax favored investments. But tax breaks are only a small part of what makes venture capital possible. The basic underpinning of venture capital is not the acquisition of specific tax benefits but the ability of investors to obtain higher than market returns for money invested. As long as there are businesses that can convert ideas into healthy profits for investors, venture capital will survive.

How will tax reform change the way investors and entrepreneurs do business? Some of the changes that promise to have the most dramatic impact are:

- An increase in long-term capital gains rates so they are no longer lower than ordinary income rates.
- Top individual tax rates become lower than top corporate tax rates for the first time in history. Beginning in 1988, the top corporate rate becomes 34 percent while the top individual rate becomes 28 percent.
- The General Utilities Doctrine preventing double taxation of capital gains on the sale and subsequent liquidation of a company's assets is repealed, increasing potential tax rates to shareholders who sell their company's assets from 20 percent to 52 percent.
- The ability to use net operating loss carryforwards to reduce taxes is restricted when a majority of stock changes hands in three years.
- The use of losses generated by passive activities are restricted so that they may only be used to offset certain types of "passive" income.
- Individual and corporate tax rates decrease.

Many observers believe the demise of preferential rate treatment for capital gains investments may have the most onerous effect on venture capital and the availability of funds for entrepreneurs. With the same tax rate now for ordinary income and capital gains, entrepreneurs may be less inclined to defer compensation and fund long term growth when their deferral is not rewarded with lower future tax rates (even though the deferral itself is a tax benefit). Investors may find long-term investments in venture funds less attractive without the reward of lower capital gains rates.

Lower individual tax rates may encourage entrepreneurs to remove funds from their companies as compensation to avoid corporate taxation and obtain lower individual tax rates on the earnings withdrawn. Removing more earnings as salary or bonuses may enable an entrepreneur to retain more money after taxes and still allow him to fund corporate growth with the after-tax remainder by lending those after-tax dollars back to the company. The interest payments on the note should create additional income to the entrepreneur and tax deductions for the firm. At the same time, more cash may be preserved for the company because of lower individual tax rates.

S corporations may become more prevalent. S corporations avoid the double taxation associated with the more common C corporation by causing the shareholders to be taxed directly on the corporation's earnings without the intervention of a separate corporate income tax. With top individual tax rates becoming lower than top corporate tax rates, companies may be able to preserve more capital by structuring themselves as S corporations and dividending out to shareholders only enough money to pay the tax liability generated by the S corporation's earnings. *See: S Corporations.*

Limited partnerships may become more popular for the same reasons. Like S corporations, they avoid double taxation and provide passive investors with the benefits of limited liability. They also provide greater flexibility than S corporations. Limited partnerships can have an unlimited number of investors (S corporations are limited to 35) and have more freedom to allocate profits, cash flow and tax losses among investors and management. This flexibility may prove attractive to a number of entrepreneurs, especially since limited partnerships are not restricted in the types of persons and entities they can take as investors.

Just how popular S corporations and limited partnerships will become remains to be seen. Most venture capitalists will be unable to invest in S corporations without causing them to lose their S corporation status because of restrictions the tax code places on the types of investors S corporations can have. The limited term and restrictions on transferability of limited partnership interests customarily imposed by organizers to insure partnership tax treatment may limit the usefulness of limited partnerships as well. Also, a venture capitalist's desire to be involved with management may restrict his ability to obtain limited liability as a limited partner. What's more, changes relating to passive losses will limit the utility of losses allocated to many S corporation investors and most limited partners by permitting them to use those losses only to offset passive income, the definition of which excludes income from wages, salary, dividends, interest, royalties and the sale of certain types of property. *See: Limited Partnerships, R&D Partnerships, S Corporations.*

The repeal of the General Utilities Doctrine may make it more difficult for investors to exit as profitably when a sale of the business is the method for removing cash from the investment. That doctrine permitted a company to sell its capital assets (as opposed to its capital stock), then liquidate the company and distribute the purchase price to its shareholders and only pay one tax on the liquidation. Under tax reform, that same sale of assets will now generate a capital gains tax on the difference between the sales price for the assets and their tax basis plus a tax on each shareholder's gain upon liquidation. The combined effect of this and the change in capital gains rates could increase a shareholder's taxes in this situation from 20% (before reform) to about 52% (after reform), reducing his after-tax return by 32%. *See: Exits.*

The double tax can be avoided if the buyer does not step-up the values of the assets he purchases to the amount of the purchase price (a common practice before tax reform because it enabled purchasers to depreciate larger values against the acquired assets which reduced future taxable income and generated cash flow). Prohibiting a mark-up of asset values for tax purposes, however, may make an acquisition less attractive by decreasing the purchaser's ability to write off large portions of the purchase price as depreciation in the ensuing years. The net result may be lower returns to sellers because of the buyer's inability to write up the value of the assets without increasing the seller's tax.

Since the repeal of the General Utilities Doctrine will affect purchasers as well as sellers, leveraged buyouts of company assets may also suffer. With management now being unable to write-up the value of the assets purchased without creating additional taxable income to the seller, management's buying from companies that do not have enough losses to offset the additional tax may be less able to convince the seller to allow them to step-up the basis of the assets being acquired. Traditionally, this step-up in basis was used to create additional depreciation for the acquired company which, by reducing taxes, increased cash available to support the debt service for the funds borrowed to make the buyout possible.

Another change that may affect LBOs and venture capitalists are new limitations on the use of net operating loss carryforwards. Now, when more than half of a company's stock changes hands during any three year period, the company's ability to use past losses to offset current and future income will be severely curtailed. For an LBO candidate with loss carryforwards, this can prevent management from using most of those loss carryforwards to reduce taxes and generate extra cash flow to pay debt service. *See: Leveraged Buyout (LBO).*

The change may also affect venture capital investors. The loss of net operating loss carryforwards whenever 50% of the stock changes hands within three years may cause the loss of those carryforwards to a fast growing company when it completes a second or third round of financing that causes more than 50% of the stock in the company to change hands in three years. This, in turn, may increase company taxes and reduce after-tax returns to investors. *See: Stage Financing.*

Will public offerings become less popular? To the extent decisions to take a company public depend upon tax consequences, there are certainly things in the tax reform package that will make going public less attractive. For example, the elimination of rate preferences for capital gains may discourage public offerings by reducing the entrepreneur's incentive to defer withdrawing value from the company in order to obtain lower capital gains tax rates in the future. At the same time, public stockholders may become more demanding for dividends and cash flow since they too will be denied lower tax rates for deferred capital gains. They may also look for higher returns to offset higher capital gains rates. But will the changes seriously reduce the number of companies that go public? Probably not. For most entrepreneurs, the decision to go public has more to do with generating large sums of cash, improving stockholder liquidity, and improving the status of their enterprise than with obtaining tax preferences. *See: Going Public, IPOs (Initial Public Offerings), Penny Stock, Public Offering.*

Methods of investing may also change—particularly if capital gains rate preferences do not reappear in the near future. Investors may rely more heavily on debt financing than equity financing to satisfy a new desire to generate current returns and to obtain preferences over management shareholders in the event of liquidation. Revenue participations may become more prevalent. Without the carrot of lower capital gains rates, investors and entrepreneurs alike may find the revenue participation approach more attractive because it generates liquid returns to the investor and leaves equity ownership in the entrepreneur. *See: Convertible Securities, Debentures, Equity, Revenue Participations.*

Some investors may become less interested in venture capital without the reward of lower capital gains rates. But will venture capital suffer as a whole? No one knows. Certainly, any ill effects will be mitigated in part by the increasing role pension funds and other tax exempt entities are playing in venture capital fund formation. These entities, which pay no federal income taxes, care little about changes in capital gains tax rates.

It may well be that while certain types of venture financings suffer or even disappear, others will become more prevalent and the amount of money available to venture capitalists may actually increase. Some of the large sums of money previously invested in tax shelters may now find its way into venture investments because tax shelter investors no longer have the high individual tax rates or the sheltered investments that made tax shelter investing so popular. This influx of capital, in turn, may make it easier for entrepreneurial companies to find money.

If the effects of tax reform on venture capital are uncertain, two things do seem relatively sure: Venture capital will not disappear as long as investors can obtain healthy returns from investing in entrepreneurial companies and more tax reform will come in the future. In fact, many venture investors privately speculate that preferential rates for capital gains will return soon and that other changes are sure to follow. And while this speculation may be nothing more than wishful thinking, it is based, in part, on a history of constant change in the tax laws and Congress's seemingly insatiable desire to tinker with taxes.

APPENDIX B

Venture's Fast-Track 100

Composition

The fifth annual *Venture* Fast-Track 100 is composed of 100 companies, ranked by revenues, that are 10 years old or younger, had at least one founder on board during the fiscal year (Apple Computer still qualifies), and posted at least $42.06 million in revenues in their 1985 fiscal year.

Explanatory Notes

The 28 private companies are marked with a P. Percent change for net income could not always be calculated, so full dollar figures are reported. An asterisk denotes losses in two consecutive years. Parentheses indicate decreases in dollars, while minus signs note declines in percentages.

The High-Tech Group

Forty-eight companies on this year's list are computer or computer-related. The group brought in $7.53 billion, or 42.89% of the total Fast-Track revenues. Three computer companies made it to the top 10: Apple Computer (No. 1), Compaq Computer Corp. (No. 8), and Convergent Technologies Inc. (No. 9). Ten showed revenue growth of 100% or more, and of those who supplies earnings data, eight were up over 100%. But some companies felt the industry slump: Six reported losses; of those, three recorded reveue drops of over 35%. And of those computer companies reporting earnings, three showed declines of nearly 100%.

Comings

Of the 32 newcomers to the Fast-Track this year, the largest group is comprised of nine computer-related companies. Medical companies come in second; the five entrants run the gamut from psychiatric hospitals to medical equipment. Membership warehouses, videotape distributors, and energy firms come in sets of two. Others deal in leasing, cable systems, construction, air travel, international freight forwarding, art supplies, electronic security, and products for nonprofit groups to resell. And the most novel entry, as well as the only food company on the *Venture* Fast-Track 100, is Delta Catfish Processors Inc.

Goings

Fourteen Fast-Trackers dropped off the list this year because they turned 11 years old. American Healthcare Management and Micro D Inc. are no longer run by their founders. At press time, Kelly-Johnston Enterprises was under Chapter XI. Activision Inc., Cordata Technologies Inc., Energy Supply Inc., and SEEQ Technology Inc. came in below the minimum revenue figures. Four firms were involved in mergers: Allnet Communications Services Inc., CompuShop Inc., Home Club Inc., and Telepictures Corp. Finally, we were unable to obtain data from Advanced Technology Inc., Hayes Microcomputer Products, Marc's, and SEIS Pros Inc.

Rank	Company	Rank Last Year	Date Founded	Founder(s)	Founder's % of Stock	FY Ended	FY '85 Revenues ($mil.); % Change From FY '84	FY '85 Earnings ($mil.); % Change From FY '84	FY '85 No. of Employees; % Change From FY '84	Type of Business
1	Apple Computer Cupertino, Calif.	1	1977	Steven Jobs[a]	7.28%	9/85	$1,918.28 26.55%	$61.22 −4.42%	4,300 −20.10%	Microcomputers
2	The Price Co. San Diego	2	1976	Sol Price Robert E. Price	11.00%† 2.94%†	8/85	1,886.61 62.09%	45.96 60.79%	2,216 36.29%	Discount buying clubs
3	People Express Inc. Newark, N.J.	3	1981	Donald C. Burr Melrose K. Dawsey	5.77% N.A.	12/85	977.86 66.64%	(27.54) '84 1.65	3,500** −11.66%**	Airlines
4	The Home Depot Inc. Atlanta	8	1978	Bernard Marcus Arthur M. Blank	7.44%† 5.21%†	2/86	700.73 61.91%	N.A. N.A.	5,800** 65.71%**	Home-improvement stores
5	Republic Health Corp. Dallas	4	1981	M. Ray Ferguson[b] Charles R. Miller[b] David Steffy	1.25% 1.36% 0.70%	12/85	679.09 41.03%	21.80 −4.08%	10,000** −5.66%**	Hospital management
6	Liz Claiborne Inc. New York	9	1976	E. C. Ortenberg Arthur Ortenberg Jerome A. Chazen Leonard Boxer	5.33%† 5.29%† 7.25%† 4.71%†	12/85	556.55 42.24%	60.58 44.45%	2,000 25.00%	Designer clothing
7	Universal Health Services Inc. King of Prussia, Pa.	6	1979	Alan B. Miller Sidney Miller	16.00%† 4.85%†	12/85	505.84 13.37%	21.75 46.03%	6,800 29.52%	Hospital management
8	Compaq Computer Corp. Houston	11	1982	Joseph R. Canion William Murto James Harris	2.14%† N.A. N.A.	12/85	503.88 53.15%	26.60 106.71%	1,838 39.45%	Microcomputers
9	Convergent Technologies Inc. San Jose, Calif.	10	1979	Allen Michels[c]	N.A.	12/85	395.17 9.23%	11.51 '84 (13.83)	1,994 19.69%	Computer work-group clusters for OEMs

[a] Jobs resigned Aug., 1985 [b] Ferguson resigned Dec. 31, 1985; Miller resigned Jan. 31, 1986. [c] Michels resigned Oct. 30, 1985.
† Proxy or prospectus used for figures. ** Estimated. N.A. Not available. — Not applicable.

Rank	Company	Rank Last Year	Date Founded	Founder(s)	Founder's % of Stock	FY Ended	FY '85 Revenues ($mil.); % Change From FY '84	FY '85 Earnings ($mil.); % Change From FY '84	FY '85 No. of Employees; % Change From FY '84	Type of Business
10	US Healthcare Inc., Blue Bell, Pa.	17	1982	Leonard Abramson	13.61%	12/85	362.92 76.47%	24.54 126.59%	764 67.18%	Health maintenance organizations
11	Apollo Computer Inc. Chelmsford, Mass.	15	1980	J. Michael Greata David L. Nelson Charles P. Spector	N.A. N.A. 0.51%†	12/85	295.58 36.89%	(1.52) '84 23.91	3,200 6.67%	Engineering workstations
12	Gemcraft Inc. Houston	16	1978	Jerome Hutchins G. Russell Hutchins Frank L. Romero	22.55%† 19.71%† 22.63%†	12/85	283.36 31.01%	7.08 493.72%	654 26.26%	Residential construction
13	PACE Membership Warehouse Inc. Aurora, Colo.	—	1982	Henry W. Haimsohn	9.95%	2/86	275.10 261.50%	(5.25) *	2,605 181.62%	Membership warehouses
14	Businessland Inc. San Jose, Calif.	22	1982	David A. Norman Enzo N. Torresi	9.49% 2.71%	6/85	267.45 198.35%	0.24 '84 (4.77)	1,359 89.80%	Business computer retailer
15	Lotus Development Cambridge, Mass.	23	1982	Mitchell Kapor	14.93%†	12/85	225.50 43.65%	38.10 5.70%	1,100 48.45%	Business software
16	Seagate Technology Scotts Valley, Calif.	12	1979	Alan F. Shugart Douglas K. Mahon David T. Mitchell	2.99%† 1.01%† 1.32%†	6/85	214.65 −37.59%	1.05 −97.35%	4,445 40.62%	Winchester disk drives
17	The Yankee Cos. Cohasset, Mass.	38	1977	Paul J. Montle	22.67%	6/85	213.08 111.40%	3.45 −49.64%	251 −9.39%	Energy and financial services
18	Softsel Computer Products Inc.[P] Inglewood, Calif.	19	1980	Robert Leff David Wagman	N.A. N.A.	12/85	206.79 28.80%	N.A. N.A.	389 −1.02%	Microcomputer and software distributor
19	FFV Realty Inc.[P] Pittsburgh	18	1978	Robert Freeman F. Lynn Foltz	50.00% 50.00%	12/85	174.65 3.96%	N.A. N.A.	273 9.20%	Real estate

20	Diasonics Inc. Milpitas, Calif.	28	1977	Albert Waxman Arthur Rock Robert Noyce	5.01%† 6.91%† 5.94%†	12/85	157.94 16.19%	7.32 '84 (45.62)	1,200 9.09%	NRI and mobile X-ray systems
21	Endevco Inc. Dallas	27	1977	James W. Bryant	16.00%	12/85	155.29 12.19%	3.68 32.19%	100 42.86%	Natural gas production
22	ISC Systems Corp. Spokane, Wash.	26	1977	Gary Norton	15.72%	6/85	150.00 17.49%	8.19 −17.99%	1,696 2.29%	Financial hardware and software
23	BRAE Corp. San Francisco	5	1977	William J. Texido	6.05%	3/85	146.40 24.54%	27.78 539.33%	970 −28.15%	Transportation leasing
24	Drug Emporium[P] Worthington, Ohio	50	1977	Philip I. Wilber Catherine K. Wilber	N.A. N.A.	2/86	144.50 79.95%	N.A. N.A.	2,150 187.43%	Discount drugstores
25	MEDIQ Inc. Pennsauken, N.J.	—	1980	Bernard B. Rotko Bernard J. Korman	38.67%† 8.13%†	9/85	143.21 48.13%	7.87 20.83%	2,300 35.29%	Medical products and services
26	LSI Logic Corp. Milpitas, Calif.	48	1981	Wilfred J. Corrigan Mitchell Bohn William O'Meara	11.43% 0.01% 0.95%	12/85	$140.01 65.72%	$10.11 −34.57%	1,380 30.07%	Custom semiconductors
27	AST Research Inc. Irvine, Calif.	—	1980	Albert Wong Safi Qureshey Thomas C.K. Yuen	16.87%† 16.87%† 16.87%†	6/85	138.58 117.16%	19.04 233.00%	532 94.87%	Workstation enhancement products
28	ComputerCraft Inc. Houston	59	1977	William E. Ladin Jr.	46.85%†	4/85	137.24 94.77%	(2.94) '84 1.12	632 83.19%	Computer retailer
29	Mentor Graphics Beaverton, Ore.	46	1981	Thomas H. Bruggere	3.74%	12/85	136.75 55.56%	7.99 −19.21%	775 46.78%	Computer-aided engineering systems
30	LTX Corp. Westwood, Mass.	29	1976	Graham C. C. Miller Roger W. Blethen	7.05%† 2.44%†	7/85	133.42 48.18%	6.85 1.81%	1,172 5.11%	Semiconductor testing equipment
31	J. P. Industries Inc. Ann Arbor, Mich.	67	1979	John Psarouthakis Marvin L. Huston Lothar Goiny Reid White	7.61% 3.30% 2.27% 1.86%	9/85	133.25 99.97%	6.41 54.19%	2,150 151.46%	Plumbing and transportation products

[P] Private † Proxy or prospectus used for figures. * Losses in two consecutive years. N.A. Not available. — Not applicable.

Rank	Company	Rank Last Year	Date Founded	Founder(s)	Founder's % of Stock	FY Ended	FY '85 Revenues ($mil.); % Change From FY '84	FY '85 Earnings ($mil.); % Change From FY '84	FY '85 No. of Employees; % Change From FY '84	Type of Business
32	First Software Corp.[P] Lawrence, Mass.	69	1982	Rick Faulk Ken Carpenter Michael G. Hajjar	15.00% 15.00% 15.00%	12/85	130.00 113.12%	N.A. N.A.	275 14.58%	Software and peripherals
33	Altos Computer Systems, San Jose	36	1977	David Jackson	38.96%†	6/85	124.45 21.13%	10.40 6.67%	664 26.72%	Microcomputers and software
34	Daisy Systems Mountain View, Calif.	63	1980	Aryeh Finegold David A. Stamm Harvey C. Jones Jr.	2.20% 4.78% 0.11%	9/85	122.55 77.23%	21.16 91.82%	923 63.36%	Computer-aided engineering systems
35	Quantum Corp. Milpitas, Calif.	33	1980	James L. Patterson	0.74%	3/85	120.35 79.44%	20.97 96.51%	688 9.55%	Disk drives
36	Iomega Corp. Stamford, Conn.	88	1980	Roderick J. Linton David G. Norton	0.58% 1.42%	12/85	115.52 123.68%	14.89 490.80%	1,154 44.25%	Disk drives
37	Sun Microsystems Mountain View, Calif.	60	1982	Scott McNealy A. Bechtolsheim William N. Joy	4.94%[d] 6.76%[d] 3.80%[d]	6/85	115.25 196.58%	8.53 221.03%	1,100 175.00%	Technical workstations
38	Cincinnati Microwave Cincinnati	51	1976	James L. Jaeger	66.53%	12/85	112.61 46.35%	24.47 53.74%	440 39.68%	Radar-warning devices
39	Corinthian Communications[P] New York	52	1976	Larry Miller Mike Kubin Bob Ingram John Miller	50.00% 16.66% 16.66% 16.66%	12/85[e]	112.00 43.59%	N.A. N.A.	22 22.22%	Media buying
40	Forever Living Products,[P] Phoenix	44	1978	Rex Maughan	100.00%	12/85	109.00 14.98%	N.A. N.A.	500 5.26%	Health, beauty and nutritional products
41	Computer Memories Inc. Chatsworth, Calif.	45	1979	Irwin Rubin Marshall Butler Laurence Hootnick	4.82%† 3.97%† 0.00%†	3/85	108.71 129.21%	(3.81) '84 1.40	1,273 198.83%	Winchester disk drives

42	The Ultimate Corp. E. Hanover, N.J.	24	1978	Ted M. Sabarese Ted C. Sabarese Ernest J. Sabato John W. Keogh	8.83% 6.27% 2.92% 3.94%	4/85	107.31 51.69%	12.34 21.17%	265 143.12%	Minicomputer systems
43	PRIAM Corp. San Jose, Calif.	49	1978	William J. Schroeder Alonzo A. Wilson Joe T. Booker	0.86% 0.89% 1.46%	6/85	105.03 2.92%	(20.93) '84 4.63	1,000 −4.76%	Rigid high-capacity disk drives
44	Emulex Corp. Costa Mesa, Calif.	41	1979	Fred B. Cox	9.04%†	6/85	103.17 28.69%	7.84 −33.51%	862 6.03%	Computer storage and communications
45	TeleVideo Systems Sunnyvale, Calif.	20	1976	K. Philip Hwang	67.28%	10/85	103.09 −36.76%	(19.18) '84 4.52	751 −39.09%	Video display terminals
46	The Sharper Image[P] San Francisco	39	1977	Richard Thalheimer	N.A.	4/85	100.00 3.09%	N.A. N.A.	415 48.21%	Catalog sales and retail stores
47	Micropolis Corp. Chatsworth, Calif.	70	1977	Stuart P. Mabon Ericson M. Dunstan	7.61%† 2.24%†	12/85	94.90 57.77%	2.78 238.95%	1,050 61.54%	Disk drives
48	Lee Data Corp. Eden Prairie, Minn.	37	1979	John M. Lee	2.62%	3/85	91.05 −7.77%	0.46 −97.41%	994 −14.01%	On-line computer terminals
49	Genentech Inc. S. San Francisco	62	1976	Herbert W. Boyer Robert A. Swanson	2.80%† 3.51%†	12/85	89.60 28.39%	5.61 106.18%	893 32.49%	Biotechnology
50	Warehouse Club Niles, Ill.	—	1982	Walter H. Teninga	12.44%†	9/85	88.95 242.14%	(0.52%) *	550** 69.23%**	Membership warehouses
51	Zond Systems Inc.[P] Tehachapi, Calif.	—	1980	James G. P. Dehlsen	64.00%	12/85	\$88.80 77.20%	\$12.20 38.59%	227 92.37%	Wind-generated energy systems
52	American Cablesystems[P] Beverly, Mass.	—	1978	Steven B. Dodge	N.A.	12/85	82.94 50.86%	N.A. N.A.	841 15.36%	Owns and operates cable tv systems
53	Stratus Computer Marlboro, Mass.	100	1980	William Foster R. Freiburghouse	1.84% 1.57%	12/85	80.16 90.23%	8.62 59.12%	775 79.40%	Fault-tolerant computer systems

[d] Fiscal-year figures not available; calendar-year figures used. [e] Fiscal-year changed from Sept. to Dec. in 1985.
[P] Private. † Proxy or prospectus used for figures. * Losses in two consecutive years. ** Estimated. N.A. Not available. — Not applicable.

Rank	Company	Rank Last Year	Date Founded	Founder(s)	Founder's % of Stock	FY Ended	FY '85 Revenues ($mil.); % Change From FY '84	FY '85 Earnings ($mil.); % Change From FY '84	FY '85 No. of Employees; % Change From FY '84	Type of Business
54	Wyse Technology San Jose, Calif.	—	1981	Bernard Tse Grace Tse Larry Lummis	6.12%† 6.12%† 2.19%†	3/85	77.59 331.99%	7.46 365.50%	855 156.76%	Microprocessor-based display products
55	Mark III Industries[P] Ocala, Fla.	58	1978	Roy T. Boyd	100.00%	12/85	77.00 71.11%	N.A. N.A.	265 8.16%	Van conversions
56	Micron Technology Inc. Boise, Idaho	47	1978	Ward D. Parkinson Joseph L. Parkinson Douglas R. Pitman	4.19% 1.06% 1.55%	8/85	75.88 −13.13%	(6.57) '84 36.51	722 −24.64%	DRAM components for microcomputers
57	Pacesetter Steel Service[P] Marietta, Ga.	55	1977	Steven B. Leebow	N.A.	8/85	75.20 2.17%	N.A. N.A.	90 0.00%	Distributes flat-rolled steel
58	Information Resources Inc. Chicago	—	1980	John Malec Gerry Eskin	19.12% 8.30%	12/85	75.10 22.91%	8.70 47.46%	954 55.12%	Marketing information and services
59	SAS Institute Inc.[P] Cary, N.C.	81	1976	James Goodnight John P. Sall	N.A. N.A.	11/85	75.10 41.70%	N.A. N.A.	700 40.00%	Software
60	Maxtor Corp. San Jose, Calif.	98	1982	James M. McCoy Jack Swartz	5.49% N.A.	3/86[1]	75.05 91.89%	8.46 '84 2.74	1,000 111.86%	Winchester disk drives
61	Ungermann-Bass Santa Clara, Calif.	85	1979	Ralph K. Ungermann Charlie C. Bass	7.90% 6.70%	12/85	72.17 37.98%	3.72 −40.78%	719 43.80%	Local-area networks
62	Sigal Construction Corp.[P] Washington	—	1977	Gerald Sigal Ellen Sigal	N.A. N.A.	9/85	72.00 94.60%	N.A. N.A.	100** N.A.	Commercial and institutional construction
63	Caremark Inc. Newport Beach, Calif.	75	1979	James M. Sweeney Dick Allen	3.50% N.A.	6/85	70.45 51.03%	7.42 430.47%	900 125.00%	Health-care services and products

64	Dupey Management Corp.[P] Irving, Tex.	—	1977	Mike Dupey Pat Dupey	50.00% 50.00%	12/85	70.43 28.79%	1.80 57.07%	800 6.67%	Retail and wholesale art supplies
65	Sytek Inc.[P] Mountain View, Calif.	—	1979	Michael Pliner Kenneth Biba	N.A. N.A.	5/85	70.40 130.07%	N.A. N.A.	490 19.51%	Local-area networks
66	Symbolics Inc. Cambridge, Mass.	—	1980	Russell Noftsker	3.15%	6/85	69.01 69.58%	4.38 316.37%	610 45.24%	LISP-based computers
67	Western Health Plans Inc. San Diego, Calif.	—	1979	Allan H. Goodman	0.61%†	6/85	68.11 34.22%	8.10 52.50%	213 50.00%	Regional health-plan operator
68	Sunrise Medical Inc. Torrance, Calif.	—	1983	Richard H. Chandler	27.54%	6/85	67.58 29.44%	1.86 34.76%	1,004 12.18%	Medical equipment
69	Healthcare Services of America Inc. Birmingham, Ala.	—	1983	Charles Speir Kerry G. Teel Thomas Rodgers Jr. Carl M. Holden Jr.	13.64% 1.36% 2.29% 0.63%	12/85	67.00** 135.65%**	3.30** 961.27%**	1,525 62.58%	Psychiatric hospitals
70	Solectron[P] San Jose, Calif.	71	1977	Roy Kusumoto	21.78%	8/85	66.99 23.94%	1.08 –1.28%	1,280 –34.06%	Printed circuit boards
71	Video Products Distributors[P] Sacramento, Calif.	—	1977	Ben Saia	100.00%	6/85	66.44 17.06%	1.60 416.77%	142 16.39%	Video software distributor
72	Horizon Air Industries Inc. Seattle	—	1981	Milton G. Kuolt II Frank Bryant Joe Clark	39.87% 0.91% 1.08%	9/85	66.10 35.54%	(5.36) '84 3.38	981 6.98%	Regional airlines
73	Expeditors Intl. of Washington, Seattle	90	1979	John M. Kaiser	20.47%	12/85	66.05 29.47%	2.86 35.57%	217 34.78%	International freight forwarding
74	Sage Energy Co. San Antonio	57	1977	K. K. Amini	64.73%	6/85	65.14 –12.30%	(10.27) '84 12.39	160 –5.88%	Energy production

[1] Fiscal-year figures not available; calendar-year figures used.

[P] Private. † Proxy or prospectus used for figures. * Losses in two consecutive years. ** Estimated. N.A. Not available. — Not applicable.

Rank	Company	Rank Last Year	Date Founded	Founder(s)	Founder's % of Stock	FY Ended	FY '85 Revenues ($mil.); % Change From FY '84	FY '85 Earnings ($mil.); % Change From FY '84	FY '85 No. of Employees; % Change From FY '84	Type of Business
75	The National Guardian Corp. Greenwich, Conn.	—	1981	William R. Berkley Frank C. Cole	11.68% 2.44%	12/85	64.39 145.92%	4.66 115.94%	2,700 63.64%	Sells electronic security systems
76	Star Video Entertainment Inc.[P] Jersey City, N.J.	—	1979	Bernard Herman Arthur Bach	50.00% 50.00%	10/85	$63.74 49.49%	N.A. N.A.	180** 50.00%**	Prerecorded videocassette distributor
77	ERC International Vienna, Va.	—	1976	Jack Aalseth	4.18%	12/85	62.79 62.56%	$2.17 47.45%	900 18.42%	Technological services
78	ICO Inc. Fort Worth	64	1978	Bobby L. Payne Alan H. Bush C. O. Ted Collins Richard L. Lowe	19.82% 4.53% 9.47% 4.89%	9/85	60.07 −10.80%	(5.00) '84 2.89	950 −20.83%	Oil-field services
79	Tallgrass Technologies[P] Overland Park, Kan.	72	1981	David M. Allen Steven Volk	N.A. N.A.	6/85	60.00 0.00%	N.A. N.A.	400 14.29%	Disk and tape drives
80	Archive Corp. Costa Mesa, Calif.	—	1980	D. Howard Lewis J. V. Howell	4.35% 2.52%	9/85	57.85 51.58%	1.03 −43.00%	607 29.15%	¼-in. tape drives and controllers
81	Intertrans Corp. Irving, Tex.	—	1980	Sam N. Wilson M. K. McKinney Jr.	19.11% 24.41%	10/85	56.59 51.74%	1.43 48.61%	325 62.50%	International freight forwarding
82	International Game Technology, Reno	56	1979	William S. Redd	55.56%	12/85	56.56 −22.79%	1.48 −86.77%	675 −12.90%	Video games and gambling machines
83	Valid Logic Systems Inc. San Jose, Calif.	93	1981	Jared A. Anderson Thomas McWilliams Curtis Widdoes	0.00% 0.92% 3.70%	12/85	56.06 16.09%	1.84 −70.52%	418 11.47%	Computer-aided engineering hardware and software
84	Microscience International Corp.[P] Mountain View, Calif.	—	1982	Geffrey Liu Hower Tong	N.A. N.A.	12/85	56.00 100.00%	N.A. N.A.	485 90.20%	Winchester disk drives

85	Syntrex Inc. Eatontown, N.J.	89	1979	Daniel Sinnott James Bruno James R. Folts	5.08% 3.89% 1.68%	10/85	55.73 5.99%	(0.81) '84 3.24	627 −3.54%	Office automation equipment
86	Diceon Electronics Inc. Irvine, Calif.	84	1980	Roland G. Matthews Peter S. Jonas Dennis A. Repp	14.61%† 11.22%† 12.84%†	9/85	55.00 5.15%	6.87 13.86%	665 −3.34%	Multilayered circuit products
87	Delta Catfish Processors Inc.[P] Indianola, Miss.	—	1981	Sam Hinote Turner Arant	N.A. N.A.	4/85	54.50 35.57%	N.A. N.A.	785 42.73%	Processes and markets farm-raised catfish
88	Corvus Systems San Jose, Calif.	87	1979	Michael L. D'Addio Mark Hahn	4.27% N.A.	5/85	53.22 5.30%	(6.64) *	372 −0.80%**	Local-area networks
89	Alpha Microsystems Santa Ana, Calif.	78	1977	Richard C. Wilcox Robert B. Hitchcock	13.54%† 13.12%†	2/85	51.74 −0.52%	2.11 −51.65%	427 50.88%	Computer products
90	Sky Courier Network[P] Reston, Va.	91	1978	Gilbert Cartel Joseph Wolinsky	N.A. N.A.	12/85	51.00 21.43%	N.A. N.A.	300 7.14%	Air courier
91	Bay Pacific Health Corp. San Bruno, Calif.	—	1984	Stephen C. Schwartz Bruce Carp Denise Hanson	3.63% 1.59% 0.34%	12/85	50.19 39.01%	1.03 10.01%	120 42.86%	Health maintenance organizations
92	Institutional Financing Servs.[P] Benicia, Calif.	—	1981	Mike Rippey Dennis Snyder Steve Savage	35.00% 7.50% 7.50%	5/85	49.10 g	5.60 g	609 g	Products for non-profit organizations to sell
93	Buffton Corp. Fort Worth	—	1980	Robert M. McLean Hampton Hodges	3.15%† 6.28%†	9/85	48.22 11.41%	0.89 −69.11%	750 −6.25%	Diversified: oil, gas, and plastics
94	ZBS Industries Inc.[P] Mayfield Village, Ohio	—	1979	Larry Beyer Jay Schulpz	N.A. N.A.	2/86	46.23 20.88%	N.A. N.A.	126 27.27%	Videotape distributor

[g] Fiscal year changed from Oct. to May in 1985; percent change cannot be calculated.
[P] Private. † Proxy or prospectus used for figures. * Losses in two consecutive years. ** Estimated. N.A. Not available. — Not applicable.

Rank	Company	Rank Last Year	Date Founded	Founder(s)	Founder's % of Stock	FY Ended	FY '85 Revenues ($mil.); % Change From FY '84	FY '85 Earnings ($mil.); % Change From FY '84	FY '85 No. of Employees; % Change From FY '84	Type of Business
95	Western Micro Technology Inc. Cupertino, Calif.	92	1977	Marshall G. Cox Bernard T. Marren	12.44% 15.90%	3/85	46.23 25.17%	2.12 39.89%	156 0.65%	Electronics distributor
96	Amplicon Inc.[P] Santa Ana, Calif.	—	1977	Patrick E. Paddon	N.A.	6/85	45.93 29.14%	3.03 59.07%	45 28.57%	Leasing company
97	MASSCOMP[P] Westford, Mass.	—	1981	C. Forbes Dewey Jr. Lorrin G. Gale	1.88%† N.A.	6/85	45.20 106.02%	0.98 '84 (1.00)	540 51.26%	Computer systems
98	Data Technology[P] Santa Clara, Calif.	—	1979	David Tsang	N.A.	2/86	44.70** 9.83%**	N.A. N.A.	126 −41.12%	Controllers and disk drives
99	MicroPro International Corp. San Rafael, Calif.	66	1978	Seymour I. Rubenstein	30.23%	8/85	42.65 −36.29%	0.21 −96.43%	300 −24.05%	Business software
100	Zycon Corp.[P] Santa Clara, Calif.	—	1976	Ronald H. Donati John Dunning	N.A. N.A.	3/85	42.06 54.38%	N.A. N.A.	547 19.96%	Circuit boards and laminates

[P] Private. † Proxy or prospectus used for figures. ** Estimated. N.A. Not available. — Not applicable.

APPENDIX C

The Venture Capital 100

The Venture Capital 100 — 1985 Investments

This Year's Rank	Last Year's Rank	Total 1985 Investments		Firm Location	Paid-In Capital	Seed/Startup Investments		Later-Stage Investments		Follow-On Investments		Buyouts	
		$ In Mil	No. of Deals		$ In Mil	$ In Mil	No. of Deals	$ In Mil	No. of Deals	$ In Mil	No. of Deals	$ In Mil	No. of Deals
1	1	$119.23	59	First Chicago Venture Capital/ First Capital Corp. of Chicago (SBIC)‡ Chicago	$264.00	$ 1.50	1	$13.77	8	$31.13	38	$72.83	12
2	4	109.51	53	TA Associates Boston	403.54	14.22	6	25.48	10	15.94	27	53.87	10
3	8	101.31	67	Citicorp Capital Investors Ltd./ Citicorp Venture Capital Ltd. (SBIC) New York	210.00	6.21	10	13.20	7	13.40	40	68.50	10
4	5	96.58	128	Hambrecht & Quist Venture Partners San Francisco	N.A.	10.49	16	29.84	23	56.25	89	0.00	0
5	2	92.06	20	Warburg, Pincus Ventures New York	440.00	24.10	4	3.88	4	24.96	11	12.12	1
6	7	67.24	44	Security Pacific Capital Corp./ First SBIC of California‡ Costa Mesa, Calif.	N.A.	7.05	8	11.55	11	4.24	9	44.40	16
7	12	55.66	41	Brentwood Associates/ Brentwood Capital Corp. (SBIC) Los Angeles	210.71	6.75	4	6.87	2	37.11	32	4.93	3
8	3	51.26	51	Hillman Ventures Inc. Pittsburgh	N.A.	1.53	4	6.65	6	43.08	41	0.00	0
9	36	45.50	13	Narragansett Capital Corp. Providence	N.A.	0.00	0	0.00	0	0.85	4	44.65	9
10	—	44.50	34	Harvard Management Co. Inc./ Aeneas Venture Corp.[1] Boston	396.00	1.50	2	21.00	23	4.00	6	18.00	3

11	9	44.05	45	Welsh, Carson, Anderson & Stowe New York	330.00	7.25	5	2.00	1	30.00	36	4.80	3
12	89	43.91	72	Investors in Industry[2] Boston	60.00	12.66	29	17.75	18	4.40	16	9.10	9
13	—	39.16	279	Clinton Capital Corp. (SBIC) New York	11.15	4.67	29	31.64	243	2.85	7	0.00	0
14	—	36.98	10	Palms & Co. Inc. Seattle	N.A.	21.33	5	2.85	3	2.80	1	10.00	1
15	11	35.87	73	New Enterprise Associates Baltimore	124.77	14.35	19	3.45	4	18.07	50	0.00	0
16	14	33.48	40	Rothschild Ventures Inc. New York	N.A.	5.70	9	7.74	6	20.04	25	0.00	0
17	21	33.41	49	Oak Investment Partners Westport, Conn.	160.54	5.67	6	8.14	5	19.60	38	0.00	0
18	16	31.18	34	General Electric Venture Capital Corp. Fairfield, Conn.	200.00	8.36	13	4.00	3	18.82	18	0.00	0
19	—	30.70	10	Summit Ventures L.P. Boston	159.70	1.30	1	29.40	9	0.00	0	0.00	0
20	18	28.85	43	Kleiner Perkins Caufield & Byers San Francisco	238.00	2.72	3	8.75	5	17.38	35	0.00	0
21	31	28.68	49	Norwest Venture Capital Management Inc.‡ Minneapolis	98.76	6.86	6	5.15	4	12.71	36	3.96	3
22	25	28.22	12	BT Capital Corp. (SBIC) New York	35.01	0.00	0	2.60	3	1.95	4	23.67	5
23	17	27.43	39	J. H. Whitney & Co. New York	N.A.	3.97	3	0.00	0	23.46	36	0.00	0

‡ Bank-affiliated. N.A. Not Available/Not Applicable.

Reported by Marion Arkin, Michele H. Fleischer, and Webster Williams.

[1] Subsidiary of Harvard University.

[2] Figures represent fiscal year ended March 31, 1986.

The Venture Capital 100 — 1985 Investments

This Year's Rank	Last Year's Rank	Total 1985 Investments $ In Mil	Total 1985 Investments No. of Deals	Firm Location	Paid-In Capital $ In Mil	Seed/Startup Investments $ In Mil	Seed/Startup Investments No. of Deals	Later-Stage Investments $ In Mil	Later-Stage Investments No. of Deals	Follow-On Investments $ In Mil	Follow-On Investments No. of Deals	Buyouts $ In Mil	Buyouts No. of Deals
24	15	24.71	22	Adler & Co. New York	236.00	13.07	7	3.34	7	8.30	8	0.00	0
25	49	24.53	24	Regional Financial Enterprises/ Regional Financial Enterprises/ L.P. (SBIC) New Canaan, Conn.	142.00	0.60	1	8.00	5	8.02	16	7.91	2
26	30	$24.06	66	Alan Patricof Associates Inc. New York	$114.15	$11.26	13	$ 1.94	4	$10.86	49	$ 0.00	0
27	52	23.80	26	T. Rowe Price Threshold Fund, L.P. Baltimore	74.00	0.00	0	20.90	18	2.90	8	0.00	0
28	38	23.70	11	Lubrizol Enterprises Inc.[3] Wickliffe, Ohio	75.91	8.03	3	5.25	1	10.42	7	0.00	0
29	—	23.20	62	RIHT Capital Corp. (SBIC)‡ Providence	5.50	1.52	3	11.30	29	5.82	20	4.56	10
30	19	23.13	39	Allstate Insurance Co. Northbrook, Ill.	N.A.	9.93	16	2.85	3	10.35	20	0.00	0
31	34	21.08	35	Montgomery Securities San Francisco	88.63	4.69	9	8.75	11	7.64	15	0.00	0
32	40	20.52	31	U.S. Venture Partners Menlo Park, Calif.	109.80	4.25	5	4.15	6	12.12	20	0.00	0
33	24	20.20	49	Robertson, Colman & Stephens San Francisco	117.00	5.00	8	3.40	3	11.80	38	0.00	0
34	96	19.83	20	Institutional Venture Partners Menlo Park, Calif.	77.60	1.97	1	7.83	5	10.03	14	0.00	0
35	—	19.31	21	Michigan Venture Capital Fund Lansing, Mich.	55.00	1.05	2	5.31	6	10.80	12	2.15	1
36	98	19.20	2	Founders Equity Inc. New York	N.A.	1.20	1	0.00	0	18.00	1	0.00	0

37	50	19.00	12	Bridge Capital Advisors Inc. New York	50.00	0.00	0	15.50	8	3.50	4	0.00	0
38	53	18.87	22	Golder, Thoma & Cressey Chicago	113.66	0.17	2	3.00	1	10.15	16	5.55	3
39	47	18.67	8	Prudential Venture Capital New York	N.A.	0.00	0	18.67	8	0.00	0	0.00	0
40	35	18.15	21	Sprout Group New York	N.A.	5.29	8	0.00	0	3.86	10	9.00	3
41	—	17.75	363	Edwards Capital Co. (SBIC) New York	4.20	13.29	271	0.00	0	4.46	92	0.00	0
42	33	17.60	38	John Hancock Venture Capital Management Inc. Boston	283.00	2.75	3	5.25	5	9.60	30	0.00	0
43	56	17.32	89	Allied Capital Corp.[4] Washington	14.21	8.92	54	6.35	27	0.68	5	1.37	3
44	58	17.18	23	Greylock Management Corp. Boston	73.67	2.21	2	6.85	6	8.12	15	0.00	0
45	23	17.07	35	Cable, Howse & Cozadd, Inc. Seattle	125.72	0.82	2	3.88	4	12.37	29	0.00	0
46	71	17.05	21	Crosspoint Venture Partners Mountain View, Calif.	65.00	9.65	12	0.00	0	7.40	9	0.00	0
47	—	16.52	132	Pierre Funding Corp. (MESBIC) New York	1.77	16.52	132	0.00	0	0.00	0	0.00	0
48	29	16.23	35	Burr, Egan, Deleage & Co. Boston	N.A.	4.63	4	2.00	2	5.14	28	4.46	1
49	—	15.60	186	Transportation Capital Corp. (MESBIC) New York	7.86	10.60	106	1.65	36	3.35	44	0.00	0
50	6	15.57	16	Manufacturers Hanover Venture Capital Corp.‡ New York	N.A.	0.00	0	0.00	0	0.04	1	15.53	15

[3] Includes SBIC. [4] Includes SBIC and MESBIC.
‡ Bank-affiliated. N.A. Not Available/Not Applicable.

The Venture Capital 100 — 1985 Investments

This Year's Rank	Last Year's Rank	Total 1985 Investments		Firm Location	Paid-In Capital	Seed/Startup Investments		Later-Stage Investments		Follow-On Investments		Buyouts	
		$ In Mil	No. of Deals		$ In Mil	$ In Mil	No. of Deals	$ In Mil	No. of Deals	$ In Mil	No. of Deals	$ In Mil	No. of Deals
51	45	$15.11	7	Mesirow Venture Capital[3] Chicago	$ 43.77	$0.00	0	$ 4.01	2	$ 3.45	2	$ 7.65	3
52	—	15.00	15	Hutton Venture Investment Partners Inc. New York	N.A.	3.87	5	2.31	4	2.82	5	6.00	1
53	37	14.83	24	BancBoston Capital Inc./ BancBoston Ventures Inc. (SBIC)‡ Boston	N.A.	0.48	1	3.54	7	2.16	12	8.65	4
54	28	14.78	52	ABS Ventures Limited Partnerships Baltimore	80.41	2.65	3	1.48	2	10.65	47	0.00	0
55	—	14.74	164	Medallion Funding Corp. (MESBIC) New York	5.27	8.65	93	1.72	19	4.37	52	0.00	0
56	—	14.42	5	Wheat First Securities[2] Richmond, Va.	N.A.	1.75	1	1.32	1	11.35	3	0.00	0
57	22	14.37	33	Mayfield Fund Menlo Park, Calif.	136.25	3.84	6	1.50	2	9.03	25	0.00	0
58	13	13.99	3	Bradford Associates Princeton, N.J.	70.45	0.00	0	12.70	1	1.29	2	0.00	0
59	—	13.71	24	Sequoia Capital Menlo Park, Calif.	104.00	3.48	4	3.30	4	6.93	16	0.00	0
60	—	13.65	19	Rainier Venture Partners Mercer Island, Wash.	19.24	7.36	8	3.17	5	3.12	6	0.00	0
61	80	13.51	17	Concord Partners New York	114.55	3.25	2	1.70	1	6.56	13	2.00	1

62	57	13.49	23	Menlo Ventures Menlo Park, Calif.	90.70	3.00	3	5.10	7	5.39	13	0.00	0
63	65	13.00	21	Merrill, Pickard, Anderson & Eyre Palo Alto, Calif.	85.00	7.80	9	0.00	0	5.20	12	0.00	0
64	10	12.90	16	R. H. Chappell Co.[5] San Francisco	N.A.	0.00	0	0.25	1	12.65	15	0.00	0
65	95	12.64	18	Fairfield Venture Partners Stamford, Conn.	65.25	4.90	6	3.50	3	4.24	9	0.00	0
66	44	12.50	12	Eberstadt Fleming Inc.[6] New York	55.00	5.50	4	1.00	1	6.00	7	0.00	0
67	—	12.47	16	Sevin Rosen Management Co. Dallas	85.00	3.00	3	0.00	0	9.47	13	0.00	0
68	41	12.37	28	Charles River Ventures Boston	108.10	0.00	0	2.24	3	10.13	25	0.00	0
69	32	12.10	25	MVenture Corp (SBIC) Dallas	16.25	1.51	4	1.52	4	2.84	9	6.23	8
70	88	12.00	25	The Southwest Venture Partnerships San Antonio, Tex.	58.41	1.25	2	3.70	4	4.05	17	3.00	2
71	—	11.80	16	Chemical Equity Inc./Chemical Venture Capital Corp. (SBIC)‡ New York	100.00	2.40	4	0.00	0	2.30	9	7.10	3
72	43	11.74	31	InterWest Partners Menlo Park, Calif.	103.07	2.43	2	2.29	4	7.02	25	0.00	0
73	—	11.45	6	Interscope Investments Inc. Los Angeles	N.A.	1.45	3	0.00	0	10.00	3	0.00	0
74	—	11.05	28	Enterprise Capital Corp. (SBIC)‡ Houston	5.00	1.85	5	5.05	13	1.14	4	3.01	6
75	—	11.00	2	Philadelphia Industries Inc. Philadelphia	29.95	0.00	0	0.00	0	0.00	0	11.00	2

‡ Bank-affiliated. N.A. Not Available/Not Applicable. [2] Figures represent fiscal year ended March 31, 1986. [3] Includes SBIC.
[5] Figures cover May, 1985, through Dec., 1985. [6] F. Eberstadt & Co. Inc. merged with Robert Fleming Inc.

The Venture Capital 100

1985 Investments

This Year's Rank	Last Year's Rank	Total 1985 Investments		Firm Location	Paid-In Capital	Seed/Startup Investments		Later-Stage Investments		Follow-On Investments		Buyouts	
		$ In Mil	No. of Deals		$ In Mil	$ In Mil	No. of Deals	$ In Mil	No. of Deals	$ In Mil	No. of Deals	$ In Mil	No. of Deals
76	69	$10.70	26	Vista Ventures New Canaan, Conn.	$104.68	$6.45	7	$1.00	1	$3.25	18	$0.00	0
77	—	10.52	23	DSV Partners Princeton, N.J.	57.00	2.43	4	2.50	2	5.59	17	0.00	0
78	68	10.35	19	Oxford Partners Stamford, Conn.	67.17	1.25	2	4.95	5	4.12	12	0.00	0
79	72	10.25	13	Analog Devices Enterprises[7] Norwood, Mass.	36.85	0.43	1	0.98	3	8.84	9	0.00	0
80	—	10.20	15	Edelson Technology Partners Saddle Brook, N.J.	36.00	2.00	3	6.60	10	1.60	2	0.00	0
81	—	10.00	10	The Pittsford Group Inc. Pittsford, N.Y.	74.50	2.10	5	7.90	5	0.00	0	0.00	0
82	—	9.90	7	Revere AE Capital Fund Inc. New York	47.70	0.00	0	3.00	2	1.25	2	5.65	3
83	—	9.52	10	MarketCorp Ventures Westport, Conn.	32.83	1.92	4	1.75	1	5.85	5	0.00	0
84	59	9.29	21	Larimer & Co.[8] Denver	80.89	2.14	5	0.00	0	7.15	16	0.00	0
85	75	9.25	12	Sierra Ventures/Wood River Capital (SBIC) Menlo Park, Calif.	80.00	5.20	5	2.00	1	2.05	6	0.00	0
36	60	9.18	15	ML Venture Partners I L.P. New York	60.60	0.00	0	7.06	9	2.12	6	0.00	0
87	—	9.17	13	Euclid Partners Corp. New York	22.80	4.10	6	2.56	3	2.51	4	0.00	0

88	73	9.16	15	InterFirst Venture Corp. (SBIC)‡ Dallas	24.99	4.35	6	1.75	2	3.06	7	0.00	0
89	92	8.80	16	Matrix Partners Boston	114.00	2.60	3	2.90	4	3.30	9	0.00	0
90	—	8.80	4	McGowan Leckinger Berg Braintree, Mass.	N.A.	0.10	1	4.20	2	0.00	0	4.50	1
91	70	8.69	25	Venrock Associates[7] New York	90.00	2.78	4	0.80	1	5.11	20	0.00	0
92	—	8.57	23	InnoVen Group Saddle Brook, N.J.	70.00	0.75	1	0.00	0	7.82	22	0.00	0
93	—	8.50	4	Caterpillar Venture Capital Inc. Peoria, Ill.	N.A.	6.50	3	2.00	1	0.00	0	0.00	0
94	—	8.22	30	Inco Venture Capital Management[2] New York	66.34	4.35	7	0.00	0	3.87	23	0.00	0
95	79	8.10	30	Venture Founders Corp. Lexington, Mass.	55.70	4.11	11	0.00	0	3.99	19	0.00	0
96	83	8.10	14	Dougery, Jones & Wilder Mountain View, Calif.	100.00	1.50	3	4.90	5	1.70	6	0.00	0
97	55	8.09	11	Bessemer Venture Partners New York	65.00	0.65	1	5.08	5	2.36	5	0.00	0
98	90	8.05	20	Asset Management Co. Palo Alto, Calif.	N.A.	2.30	3	2.28	4	3.47	13	0.00	0
99	62	8.00	19	Harvest Ventures Inc. New York	63.75	0.77	3	3.15	4	3.08	10	1.00	2
100	—	8.00	7	Julian, Cole & Stein Los Angeles	15.31	8.00	7	0.00	0	0.00	0	0.00	0

‡ Bank-affiliated. N.A. Not Available/Not Applicable. [2] Figures represent fiscal year ended March 31, 1986.
[7] Figures represent fiscal year ended Oct. 31, 1985. [8] Formerly The Centennial Funds.

SUBJECT MATTER INDEX

I. The Venture Capital Arena and Its Players

II. Attracting the Right Investors

III. The Deal and Its Structure

IV. The Company's Securities

V. Keeping Employees and Protecting the Future

VI. Other Important Terms

PLUME

EXECUTIVE'S CHOICE

(0452)

☐ **ROBERT HALF ON HIRING by Robert Half.** The most important management function of all is hiring the best employees. As head of one of the largest personnel recruiting firms in the world, Robert Half shows you how to hire smart in this book filled with wit, wisdom, and solid experience. (258111—$8.95)

☐ **CREATING EXCELLENCE: Managing Corporate Culture, Strategy, And Change In The New Age by Craig R. Hickman and Michael A. Silva.** The indispensible guide to the new era of business competition, for executives who must operate in a world where being "pretty good" is no longer good enough. (258103—$8.95)

☐ **THE WORKBOOK FOR CREATING EXCELLENCE: The Essential Guide For Thoroughly Analyzing Your Company And Making It Work For You by Craig R. Hickman and Michael A. Silva.** Creating excellence is every executive's job—and this unique "hands-on" workbook is the best way ever devised to help you do it. (257492—$12.95)

☐ **THE WALL STREET JOURNAL ON MANAGEMENT: The Best Of "Manager's Journal", David Asman and Adam Meyerson, eds.** "Whether you manage the world's premier city, a Fortune 500 corporation or a mom and pop business, this book will help you get more from your staff and more from yourself."—Edward Koch, Mayor of the City of New York. (258626—$8.95)

☐ **THE BEST U.S. CITIES FOR WORKING WOMEN by Jill Andresky.** As a working woman, your choice of city may be the most important job-related decision you will ever make. Whether you're an up and comer just starting out, relocating, changing jobs, or a well-established career woman, this ground-breaking city-by-city guide analyzes 70 of the best places for professional women to live and work. (258138—$9.95)

Prices slightly higher in Canada.

To order use coupon on next page.